A Faraway, Familiar Place

A Faraway, Familiar Place

An Anthropologist Returns
to Papua New Guinea

Michael French Smith

University of Hawai'i Press
Honolulu

Printed in the United States of America

18   17   16   15   14   13   1   2   3   4   5   6

Library of Congress Cataloging-in-Publication Data
Smith, Michael French, author.
A faraway, familiar place : an anthropologist returns to Papua New Guinea /
Michael French Smith.
pages   cm
Includes bibliographical references and index.
ISBN 978-0-8248-3686-3 (cloth : alk. paper)
1. Kairiru (Papua New Guinean people)—Social life and customs—21st century.
2. Kairiru (Papua New Guinean people)—Economic conditions—21st century.
3. Kragur (Papua New Guinea)—Social life and customs—21st century.
4. Kragur (Papua New Guinea)—Economic conditions—21st century.
5. Smith, Michael French—Travel—Papua New Guinea—Kragur.
I. Title.
DU744.35.K33S65 2013
305.899'5—dc23   2012044805

University of Hawai'i Press books are printed on acid-free
paper and meet the guidelines for permanence and
durability of the Council on Library Resources.

Designed by Integrated Composition Systems, Spokane, Washington

Printed by Sheridan Books, Inc.

To Theodore Schwartz,

who told me to write books

*Think of the long trip home. Should we have
stayed at home and thought of here?*
—Elizabeth Bishop, "Questions of Travel"

*Scientists in New Guinea discovered a new genus
of mice, which they described as "very beautiful."*
—"Findings," *Harper's Magazine*, December 2010

Contents

Acknowledgments

No words can fully express my appreciation for the hospitality and generosity Kragur people have shown me, whenever and wherever we have met. My wife, Jana Goldman, has provided inestimable encouragement and wise counsel, helping not only to make this book possible, but also to make it much better than I could have made it on my own. She is beginning to make this a habit. Margaret French Smith has done more to make this book possible than I think she realizes. Once again, it has been a pleasure to work with everyone at University of Hawai'i Press; special thanks are due to Masako Ikeda. I also thank Lee Motteler for his copyediting expertise and Diane Buric for her map-making skills.

Chapter 1
An Eccentric Longing

And the traveler hopes: "Let me be far from any Physician."
—W. H. Auden, "Journey to Iceland"

My first mother-in-law never forgave me for taking her daughter to an island in Papua New Guinea. She would find other reasons to dislike me in years to come, such as my uneasy relationship with stable employment, but I think the trip to Papua New Guinea got her started. It was 1975, the year Papua New Guinea—or PNG as many call it—gained its independence from Australia, and I was going there for at least a year to do research for a PhD in cultural anthropology. I'd been to PNG in 1973 for three months on Manus Island and nearby Baluan Island as an assistant to Ted Schwartz, my professor at the University of California–San Diego (fig. 1). But this was going to be my first solo effort, and I was just as scared of setting off alone as I was excited about it.

My stage fright helped me convince myself that going with me was a rare opportunity for Sarah (not her real name) that she would greatly enjoy. It was an honest mistake, but a bad one. Sarah had a BA in anthropology, she loved the ocean and was a good bodysurfer, and she'd gone backpacking in California's Sierra Nevada wilderness with me several times. She hadn't told me yet, however, that she didn't really care for backpacking but was trying to learn to like it for my sake. Still, it might have crossed my mind that without a strong purpose or a real love of rugged outdoor living for its own sake, one could find life in a PNG village rather trying. The natural beauty of many villages comes with a number of discomforts, such as constant high heat and humidity; rather elementary cooking, bathing, and toilet facilities; many forms of itching; and travel only via muddy treks on foot, bumpy journeys in small boats, or both.

I'm not fond of itching, but the physical challenges that still keep much of PNG relatively secluded were part of its original attraction for me. Looking back, I think I found the physical challenges not just exhilarating but also comforting, because they gave me something I knew I could handle. I was not

Figure 1. Theodore Schwartz filming from the bed of an outrigger canoe near Pere
Village, Manus Island, in 1973, on my first trip to Papua New Guinea. I'm in the background, adjusting my snorkeling mask. Photo by Geoffrey White.

sure I could do good research, finding the unspoken patterns beneath the
surface of everyday life and reaching some understanding of people's beliefs,
values, hopes, and fears. If at the end of a day of observing, questioning, and
listening all I had to show was a few clichés and some contradictory scraps of
information, I could at least give myself credit for matching the steady pace
villagers set over the bush trails and not complaining about the Spartan
accommodations.

All this, of course, had nothing to do with Sarah, and I probably shouldn't
have dragged her into it. She and I did talk about research projects she could
pursue on her own. With a little time and a larger object than being with me
(I was rather preoccupied), she might have come to enjoy village life. Unfortunately, she met with a string of mishaps that sent her home in sorry condition
within about three months of her arrival.

Sarah waited to join me in PNG until I had found a site for my research and
arranged for work to begin on a small house for us; it was built, like other village houses, of timbers from the forest and palm-leaf thatch. The place that
accepted me as its anthropologist, an identity that in those days meant nothing
to many of its residents, was a village of just over two hundred people called
Kragur. Kragur looks out over an apparently endless expanse of ocean from

Map 1. Kairiru Island and Mushu Island. Kairiru lies at approximately 3.35 degrees south latitude and 143.57 degrees east longitude. The "statue" (of the Virgin Mary) stands alongside the main trail across the island at an altitude of about 600 meters (1,970 feet). It is impossible to show here the trail's myriad twists and turns. (Neither does the map show the several island villages other than Kragur.) Map by Diane Buric and Michael French Smith.

the top of a cliff on the seaward side of an island called Kairiru (map 1), which lies about twenty miles by sea from Wewak, the main town in the East Sepik Province, on the north coast of PNG (map 2), which lies north of Australia (map 3). Kairiru is made up largely of volcanic rock, but this is mixed with sedimentary rock, the whole mass of which, some thirty million years old, was molded by seismic activity and erosion into its present shape, a vaguely conical mountain.[1] Kairiru is easily visible from Wewak on a clear day. During the monsoon season, however, dark banks of cloud hide it from view from the mainland much of the time.

Sarah arrived at Wewak's tiny airport in January 1976, about two months after we said good-bye in San Diego. I'd arranged for us to stay just outside town with a Papua New Guinean family I met soon after I first arrived in Wewak through a chance connection with a young Australian plumber and surfer, Bruce McGorkle (not his real name), who worked at the PNG Defense

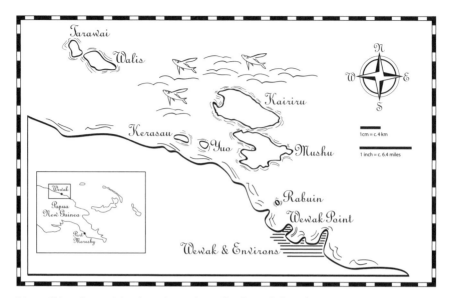

Map 2. Wewak-area islands and coastline. The flying fish in these waters are not actually this big, but they are much more plentiful. A more detailed map would show the coastal road west of Wewak—much of which is unpaved and fords several rivers—and the roads from the coast to interior towns. Map by Diane Buric and Michael French Smith.

Force base near Wewak. By the time Sarah arrived, Bruce had gone back to Australia, having lost his job at the military base due in part to suspicion—completely justified, I knew—that he was cultivating a patch of marijuana in the dense bush (what Americans would call jungle) along the road to the base. My association with McGorkle led to the Defense Force military police picking me up for questioning too, but on the whole meeting him was a stroke of luck. Not only had I never before ridden in the detainee cage of a military police vehicle, Bruce was good company, he knew his way around Wewak, he had the use of a truck, and before he left he bequeathed to me his coworker Leo Titus. Leo and his wife Elizabeth lived in government housing for public employees along the dirt road to the villages of Brandi and Mandi, not far from the provincial prison.

I had hoped we could travel to Kragur within a couple of days, but it was the heart of the monsoon season, with rain and wind so heavy and seas so rough that few boats were traveling to Kairiru and the other islands off Wewak. For about a week, on every day that was even slightly dry, Sarah and I walked from Leo and Elizabeth's to the main coastal road and took one of the infrequent minibuses to Wewak to see if any boats were going out to Kairiru. We carried

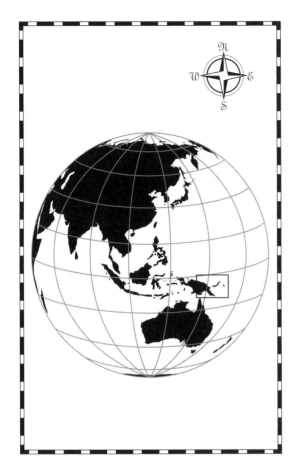

Map 3. Papua New Guinea on the globe. Papua New Guinea shares the island of New Guinea with the Indonesian province of Papua (the western half of the island) and lies only about 150 kilometers (93 miles) from the northern tip of Australia, across the Torres Strait. Map by Diane Buric.

our full rucksacks, ready to travel. We were looking in particular for the *Tau-K*, the venerable flat-bottom landing craft that, weather permitting, came and went a couple of times a week from St. Xavier's, the Catholic boarding high school for young men on the near side of Kairiru.

The *Tau-K* finally made it in and returned to Kairiru the same day, tightly packed with cargo and passengers. We reached Kairiru after about two hours of pitching and rolling, soaked and chilled by rain squalls and the sloppy waves washing over the *Tau-K*'s sides. It is amazing how shivering cold you can get in the deep tropics when the sun disappears and you're wet to the skin. The Catholic brothers who ran St. Xavier's, mostly Australians, put us up for the night in their austere two-story residence, much in need of paint on almost every surface and, in places, its interior only rather casually separated from its exterior. It rained heavily most of the next day, so we stayed on another night. It rained heavily most of the next day, too, and the next. While we waited for better weather, we learned a lot about Kairiru from chatting with the brothers, some of whom had lived there for many years. During occasional short breaks in the rain, we took walks to villages along the coast near the school.

When there was nothing else to do, Brother William was always looking for people to taste the liqueurs he concocted in the school's chemistry lab, trying out local plants as flavorings. There was also a large stock of musty paperbacks in the open-walled, second-floor common room. I remember particularly enjoying Leonard Gardner's *Fat City,* described by one reviewer as a "sordid saga of cheap hotels, cheap women, cheap dreams, and little or no fulfillment." Sitting and sipping liqueurs, reading, and looking out at the steady, dead-vertical flow of rain gradually drowning the school grounds was diverting at first, but by day three Sarah and I were getting very restless.

Kragur lies on the opposite side of the island from St. Xavier's, less than four miles distant as the crow flies but reached overland by a trail that climbs about half a mile through dense forest to a pass just below the island's highest point and drops sharply down the other side. The Japanese military forces that occupied Kairiru during World War II improved some sections of the route for their own use, broadening it and cutting switchbacks in the mountainside. But lots of rain had hammered the improved sections since the war, and other parts of the trail went almost straight up and down through red clay and twisting tree roots. I was already familiar with the trail, and on my own I would have made the trip rain or no. I was hoping, however, that Sarah could have a more pleasant and safer trip. There were some grand vistas, crystalline streams, and cool forest glades along the way that she would enjoy much more if she weren't cold and wet. And if the trail were dry, she would be less likely to slip and fall on her face on the way up, on her behind on the way down, or—God help her—the other way around.

Finally, Stephen Umari and Agnes Munbos, a Kragur couple who had taken me under their wings shortly after I arrived, showed up at St. Xavier's to escort us to the village, come what may.[2] This was a rather dramatic gesture of hospitality. Umari and Munbos had lots of other things to do and plenty of good reasons to avoid monsoon travel. I already knew something about the complexities of friendship and hospitality in Kragur. Generosity there walked hand in hand with dark fears of the potentially lethal consequences of angering others by either being too selfish or flaunting one's prosperity. You might also simply shame people by giving more than they could reciprocate. I knew that by Kragur standards, I was rich and might look to some villagers like a potentially powerful friend, not for any political clout I had or even for my present comparative wealth, but for what they assumed was my esoteric knowledge of how to obtain wealth. For his part, I later learned, Umari strongly suspected

I was a reincarnation of his deceased brother and thus in touch with a host of mystical secrets.

Yet even as I came to understand this subtle terrain better, I still found much of what my American countrymen would recognize as simple kindness in the way Umari, Munbos, and many other villagers treated me. Reading people's motives is always tricky and frequently impossible, especially across cultures, and people's motives are seldom one-dimensional. Even so, I often felt from villagers a basic sympathy with another human being far from home, not just in striking gestures like Umari's and Munbos' escort over the mountain but also in a quiet sign to come sit beside someone in a village gathering, a tone of voice, or the quality of a smile. A very practical sign of human sympathy was the sudden smack of someone's hand on some exposed part of my skin, sending a mosquito to its death. I'll also never forget esteemed elder Benedict Manwau's habit of coming to get me whenever he was on his way to one of the rare village events at which beer brought from Wewak was served. A very thoughtful man was Manwau—and a keen judge of character.

Villagers of Umari's and Munbos' generation generally did not know in what year they were born. Umari knew only that he was a young boy during the Japanese occupation. Munbos had been born around the time of the Japanese invasion of New Guinea. So, Umari was in his forties and Munbos in her thirties. At six feet tall, I towered over them, especially Munbos, but their physically demanding lives had made them strong in a way most large, well-fed North Americans, even those who "work out," would find difficult to imagine. Umari looked tough, an effect enhanced by the rough blue-black "UMARi" unevenly emblazoned across his bare chest (fig. 2). This was a souvenir of his days as a laborer on a coconut plantation, where young men passed some of their free time tattooing each other with makeshift tools. Munbos did not look tough, but her soft face and thin body belied her ability to work for hours in the pounding tropical sun and carry heavy loads on her back, leaning into the taut line around her forehead that balanced dense dead weights of firewood, taro, or coconuts (fig. 3). She did all this in the wake of bearing five children without, I believe, any modern medical assistance.

The rain had thinned to a light drizzle the morning we set out from St. Xavier's for Kragur, but the monsoon torrents had already eroded sections of the trail to narrow, crumbling ledges and turned the red clay into a soup of miracle organic lubricant. Nevertheless, we kept our feet and arrived in Kragur muddy but uninjured. Within a few days, however, Sarah's serious problems began. A group of women took her with them to one of the steep mountainside gardens where Kragur people grow taro, yams, sweet potatoes, and a variety of other crops. I stayed in the village talking to some of the older men, trying to figure out who was who and what was what in Kragur. Sarah

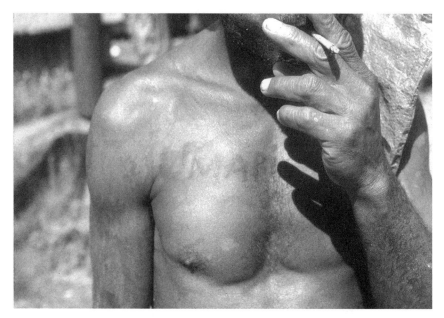

Figure 2. Stephen Umari the elder's name tattoo, 1976. Photo by the author.

returned late in the afternoon, complaining that the backs of her legs were itching furiously.

The women said Sarah must have brushed against a noxious forest plant, but they didn't recommend a remedy and I foolishly neglected to ask them what they would do if this happened to them. This must have been a very potent and crafty plant, because Sarah wasn't exposing much leg. Women in Kragur, even little girls, didn't wear trousers or shorts in those days and, both for modesty and comfort, Sarah was wearing what Kragur women usually wore: a broad length of colorful cotton wound around the waist, reaching to below the knees, called a *laplap* in PNG. The women may have assumed we had some powerful American medicine on hand, but they were wrong. We tried the two or three salves and lotions we did have with us, but the angry red welts kept getting bigger and spreading farther up her legs.

Sarah spent a night of misery, and the next day we packed our rucksacks and walked back over the mountain to St. Xavier's. We were able to take the *Tau-K* back to Wewak the day after that and get a minibus to Wewak General Hospital, a cluster of low wooden buildings at Cape Boram, just east of town. An Australian doctor gave Sarah a strong antihistamine and advised us to stay close by until it was certain the welts were responding, so we checked into one of the inexpensive rooms at the Windjammer Motel, one of Wewak's few commercial lodging places. The Windjammer's economy quarters didn't have air-

Figure 3. Agnes Munbos weeding the village grounds with a bush knife, 1976. Photo by the author.

conditioning or private bathrooms, but we had a ceiling fan, our door opened onto a view of Wewak's long curving beach, and cold beer was available in the beachfront bar. The bush bumps, as Sarah christened them, cleared up within a couple of days, and within the week we made the trip back to Kragur via the *Tau-K* and the mountain trail.

Not many days later Sarah came back from bathing in the stream, walking as if in pain. Kairiru is blessed with many fast-flowing streams, dropping from high on the mountain, through the forest, and down to the sea. At its western end, Kragur is adjacent to one of the largest and perhaps the most constant of these. Where it flows near the village, it is a composition of shallow rapids and slower-moving pools beneath a high forest canopy, framed by porous volcanic boulders sprouting green ferns glistening with spray. The water is cool enough to deliver a slight shock if you submerge quickly and, in my experience so far, clean enough to drink without concern. I doubt Eden offered anything better. Kragur people are careful to bathe and wash clothes and dishes below where they take water for drinking and cooking. The main men's bathing place is some distance upstream from the women's. In the 1970s, men feared—and many still do—even the hint of contact with female effluvia, which they believed could cause life-threatening illness, often marked by chronic shortness of breath. Fear of what anthropologists David Lipset and Jolene Stritecky call the "mystical impurities left by the residue or odor of sexuality" is common in PNG. Both men and women may be subject to such pollution, but male precautions are frequently more obvious.[3] The men's bathing place was not only free of sexual pollution, it also boasted higher cascades, deeper pools, and greater privacy than the women's bathing place. Questions of pollution aside, men generally take precedence over women in PNG.[4] Sarah probably could have lived with this denigration of women and lack of convenience, but on this day she slipped as she walked across a broad, wet rock as she approached the women's bathing area, and she sat down hard. The pain was sharp and immediate.

We had to go to Wewak again, but because of Sarah's injury we couldn't hike over the mountain. Fortunately, the *Tau-K* was to make one of its rare appearances on the Kragur side of the island that week. A group of villagers had chartered it to take them and many bulky burlap bags of taro to the mainland for a feast and exchange of food, part of the extended observations of a death some years before in a village not far from Wewak. Although the sea was calm and smooth that day, even the occasional light smack of the hull against a swell made Sarah grimace. At the hospital, an X-ray showed hairline cracks in her coccyx. The doctor prescribed a week of rest and a follow-up X-ray before we thought about going back to Kragur. So we checked into the Windjammer again.

Here I can either cut Sarah's story short, or it goes on and on. The short version is this: Sarah recovered quickly from her injury, and we went back to Kragur. Then she came down with hepatitis. This took us to Wewak for several weeks, during which she improved only a little. While in the hospital she got a tropical ulcer on her foot that, in her weakened condition, resisted efforts to cure it. She also had a few bouts of high fever, which didn't appear to be malaria but might have been dengue, then flourishing in the East Sepik. It became obvious that waiting in PNG for her to recover was pointless, probably dangerous, and that she had to go home. Her parents in Connecticut finally solicited the help of the U.S. State Department, which coordinated with the American consulates in Port Moresby (PNG's capital, usually called simply Moresby) and Australia to arrange for someone to meet her with a wheelchair at each juncture of her trip. By this time her foot was so badly swollen—in a scary purple way—she couldn't walk without a stick. She stayed with her parents in Connecticut until I got back, many months later. By then her foot had long since healed and the fevers hadn't returned, but she still didn't have all her strength back—and her mother had developed very, very serious doubts about my judgment.

My health suffered from that trip, too. I had had some gastrointestinal complaints during my 1973 trip to PNG with my professor and mentor Ted Schwartz, followed by a couple of bad bouts of two kinds of malaria working in tandem—*Plasmodium vivax* and *Plasmodium falciparum*—a few months after returning, even though I had taken my antimalarial medication faithfully. But, being young and still believing myself indestructible, I regarded the vomiting and diarrhea as very unpleasant but fundamentally trivial and the malaria as an anomaly.

One of the first things I noticed about Kragur was the comparative lack of mosquitoes. The Kragur side of Kairiru is so steep that there is almost no standing water, whereas the flatter St. Xavier's side is home to swarms of mosquitoes as well as greater numbers of venomous snakes. In Kragur I slept comfortably without a mosquito net, as did most villagers. I also seldom bothered with insect repellent, except on my ankles on particularly buggy afternoons and when I went into the forest. In 2007 I met a medical researcher from the United States who was studying malaria in the East Sepik. He told me that his team had a hard time getting an adequate sample of mosquitoes from the seaward side of Kairiru, there were so few. But it only takes one.

I avoided malaria in 1975–1976, but I contracted dengue, which is also insect borne and that brought me low more and more frequently as the months wore on, with shuddering cold that seemed to emanate from my very bone marrow, followed by soaring fever, which on one occasion rendered me unconscious for about thirty-six hours. It took a couple of days to get up and around after each bout of fever subsided. I passed a lot of my recuperation days reading. A favorite volume was selections from the diaries of the Russian scientist and explorer Nikolai Miklouho-Maclay, who spent some twelve years in the 1870s and 1880s on the north coast of what Europeans then called simply New Guinea. It was morbidly enjoyable to read of his many attacks of fever, how he thought his Swedish assistant's mind was becoming "disordered" by loneliness, and—in an editor's epilogue—of Miklouho-Maclay's ruined health, rapid decline, and early death on his return to Russia.[5] My attacks of fever recurred at long intervals for several years more. I knew that my grandfather Harry French had contracted dengue and nearly died of it when he was a carpenter on a sugar plantation in Fiji around 1905, but I didn't appreciate his story of this experience until I joined the dengue club myself.

I also got an infection in my knee that turned it overnight into a bloated, throbbing, red-streaked mass. Fortunately I had antibiotics with me that beat back the infection after a few days of lying on my foam mattress—badly gnawed by rats while I was in Wewak with Sarah—taking pain pills and smoking cigars to keep the flies at bay and cultivate a low buzz of my own. A few years later when I suffered from chronic exhaustion, my doctor finally discovered that I was entertaining a population of hookworms. This was, however, undoubtedly another anomaly. I still have some resident amoebas, but I'm told they are doing me no harm and that killing them would be harder on me than continuing to live with them amicably.

Ted Schwartz started doing research in Papua New Guinea in the early 1950s. He worked closely with Margaret Mead for many years and said once that Mead had told him that anthropologists got sick while doing field research because they didn't really want to be wherever they were. I'm sure that unhappiness is not good for your immune system, but I doubt my dread that I would make a hash of my work in Kragur, fail to get my degree, and become a derelict sleeping in a cardboard box (my backup career plan) can account for all the invasions of microorganisms I suffered. I only met Mead once, but by all accounts she was extraordinarily sure of herself. In contrast, I have always lived with ambivalence. If Mead was right that wanting to be somewhere else makes you sick, I would have been sick a large part of my life.

The danger of disease in PNG, however, is real. Added to this, violent crime in towns and political violence, particularly in the highlands provinces, have been bad enough to dampen the country's tourist trade for many years. When I stayed at the Windjammer again in 1981—before heading out to Kragur on my second trip there, a stay of only a few weeks—the front doors still stood open and there was no visible security. After that I didn't pass through Wewak again until 1995. By then, things at the Windjammer had changed. Newer, heavier front doors had been installed and were kept closed, attended by security guards. Another guard patrolled the beachfront.

I spent about two months in PNG in 1998, thanks in part to an opportunity to serve as a lecturer on an American Museum of Natural History tour of the country, a rather posh affair that brought everyone back to cool, comfortable, modern lodgings at the end of each day and often for lunch as well. My wife Jana Goldman (her real name) went with me for the tour and then flew home. That was enough to give her some feeling for the place I talk about so much, without risking her health. She is an adventurous traveler, but I would never live it down if I nearly lost another wife.

After the tour, I stayed on in PNG to visit Kragur again. The few weeks I spent in the village that year went well. I stayed healthy, avoided questioning by the authorities, and found people for the most part pleased to see me and ready to recount at length what had been happening since my previous visit. As soon as I got home and went back to work at the social research firm that employed me, I started wanting to go back to Kragur again. Life, however, can get very full. During the next few years my mother was hospitalized several times; Jana and I bought our first house and I rediscovered my ancestral love of moving dirt, making compost, and planting and pruning things; and it never seemed to be the right time to take a leave of absence from my job. But by 2008 ten years had passed, and I realized that only a few more ten-year intervals would run out my clock. Stephen Umari's clock ran out in 1996, just a few months after I'd visited Kragur for a weekend sandwiched between travels to several parts of PNG on a consulting assignment for the World Bank. Agnes Munbos was still alive, and I was pretty sure she was still working in the gardens, even though I knew from occasional letters from her children that her knees were giving out and her back was sore; grandmothers in Kragur don't retire. But if I wanted to be sure to see her and the other Kragurs who had been so extraordinarily kind to me again, I knew I'd be foolish to put it off.

I also had started to feel the press of time in my own life. I was healthier than I had been in years, but friends both here and in Kragur had been distressing me by showing signs of age and, even more inconsiderate, dying. Many men and women of Umari's generation were dead. My oldest friend in the United States, acquired in the sixth grade, had had a heart attack; another dear old friend had died of cancer; and Ted Schwartz was over eighty and suffering from several seriously debilitating ailments. It was also getting harder to think of myself as in the bloom of youth, in light of my softening belly, badly sun-damaged skin, and the many painful reminders of old injuries in my spine and joints.

Theodore Roosevelt spoke of his 1914 journey down Brazil's River of Doubt, when he was fifty-four, as his "last chance to be a boy." The harrowing trip nearly killed him and certainly shortened his life; he died at sixty.[6] This was hardly my last chance to travel to distant places, and for hazard it wasn't even in the same universe as Roosevelt's journey, but I understand the sentiment. On my last two trips to Kragur prior to 2008, I had sometimes felt I was in touch with a past time in my own life, a time when the whole world seemed as young as I was.

This was partly a trick of memory. When I did research in Kragur in the 1970s, I'd already started to lose the youthful feeling of endless possibilities, and I would never want to relive the anxious fear of failure that drove me to stay on in PNG even as my health deteriorated. But that wasn't all there was to it, and I say let memory work its magic on the worst of the unpleasantness. On my first night in Kragur in 1998, I woke up while it was still dark, realized where I was, and felt I had stepped out of time into a place that I thought was lost to me. Planning for my 2008 trip, I sometimes feared I might find that what I thought was a living concern for Kragur was only nostalgia and the trip would turn out to be a bad idea. Nostalgia can be delicious, but it is a snack, not a meal. Well, if it turned out that there was no meal for me in Kragur, I didn't have to go again. The next time I took a long leave, Jana and I could go somewhere cool and sanitary, where the sea breeze has a brisk northern tang, and they make good scotch and serve it with sharp cheese in cozy pubs where fluffy puppies doze on the warm hearth.

I also had occasional doubts about the possible physical toll of the trip. I was in "pretty good nick" for my age, an Australian acquaintance had told me. Even if he was just being nice, I could probably claim at least average nick. But parasitic diseases make better stories than recreations, so I planned to take more precautions than I had in the past. I wouldn't tempt hookworms again by going barefoot and I would sleep under a mosquito net (a resolution I broke after a few days, the night air being so sweet). There are few other serious physical dangers in the village and the forest, as long as you don't walk too close to the edge of the cliff, linger under a heavily laden coconut tree, fail to watch your step where the trail is slippery, or walk in the dark without watching for snakes. Kairiru's snakes include death adders, but villagers say they are shy. And there are sharks in Kragur waters. Standing on the top of the cliff, I've seen sharks, including a smallish hammerhead, in the bay below Kragur more than once. But the beach is too rocky for casual swimming for people with tender feet, I don't surf anymore, and in any case, no one can remember the last time a shark bothered anyone, including the children and young men who ride the waves in the bay on homemade wooden boards.

Disease aside, the greatest physical challenge is simply being able to put up with low-grade irritations, like working up a sweat before you even get back to your house after a delicious soak in the cool bathing pool, doing without furniture, occasionally having to go out in thunderous downpours if you can't put off going to the outhouse, or going to the outhouse in a pouring rain and finding that a falling coconut has neatly holed the thatch roof directly above the squatting spot. (Inside Kragur outhouses are deep pits, covered with logs, except for the necessary apertures.) The danger of violent crime in towns is real enough, but I wasn't planning to spend much time in towns, and I knew the rules for staying safe. These had always served me well, except for one quick, profane, but ultimately harmless scuffle over the contents of my pockets at a dusty outdoor bus terminal in Boroko, a suburb of Moresby.

Such cautionary memories were usually quickly followed by thoughts of how nice it can be to return somewhere after a long absence and see familiar, friendly faces. Walking along the sidewalk on Wewak's main street the day after I arrived in 1998, Kragur people in from the island whom I hadn't seen in years greeted me with smiles and handshakes. It's also nice to still know how to get around and to get the smile of recognition that you're not a naïve newcomer. *"Ah, yu man bilong longtaim!"* a cab driver in Moresby said to me in Tok Pisin in 1998 when I used my own Tok Pisin to negotiate the fare. (His taxi had a meter, but it was spinning out of control.)

Tok Pisin is the principal lingua franca for the speakers of PNG's hundreds of indigenous languages, and a *man bilong longtaim* is roughly an "old-timer." Tok Pisin grammar mirrors many of the features of some types of indigenous PNG languages, but it has incorporated vocabulary not only from numerous indigenous languages but also from the languages of all the foreign explorers, traders, and governing powers that have stopped on the islands and beaches of what is now PNG. I start dreaming and talking in my sleep in Tok Pisin as soon as I've been in PNG a few days, or even a few hours. But Tok Pisin is changing rapidly, and it seems as if people generate new idioms almost every day. You can register every word someone is saying, but if you're out of touch with recent usage, you may not know what the particular combination of words means. Tok Pisin is also incorporating more and more English words, especially in the towns. This can make it easier to understand, except when people use the English words to form distinctively Papua New Guinean idioms or when they use unfamiliar pronunciations. I lose the thread of conversations most often when people mix their Tok Pisin liberally with English words and phrases rendered PNG-style. When I quote Kragur people in this book, I'm translating from Tok Pisin, unless I indicate otherwise. (See the appendix for more on written and spoken Tok Pisin, including a guide to pronunciation.)

Many Kragur people mix their Tok Pisin with English, and virtually all villagers mix Tok Pisin liberally into their indigenous language. Linguists call Kairiru people's indigenous language simply Kairiru, although the people of the nearby islands of Kerasau and Yuo, parts of Mushu Island (also sometimes spelled Muschu), and a few small coastal areas on the mainland also speak it. Kragur people call their native tongue *leiny* Kairiru—Kairiru language—or sometimes *leiny* Tau. Tau, they say, is the original name for the island, while Kairiru is originally the name of the lake at the top of the mountain and of the supernatural being, with the head of a man and the body of a snake, who created it.[7] When and how the confusion came about no one is exactly sure, but apparently early European visitors and mapmakers are at fault.

I blame my crumbling health and my declining spirit for my failure during my first stay in Kragur to learn to speak and understand more than very rudimentary Kairiru, although the prevalence of Tok Pisin in the village made it easy for me to give in to those weaknesses. By mixing the little Kairiru I knew into my Tok Pisin and occasionally responding appropriately to a remark made in Kairiru, I sometimes managed to leave the impression that I spoke Kairiru. On my return visits, then, some villagers commented on how I'd lost my former fluency in their language in the intervening years.

I never went to Kragur thinking I could help the people of the village much in any immediate way. I went into cultural anthropology, however, not only because it is fascinating but also because I thought, if the people of the world would pay attention, anthropology could help them understand each other better. I have even hoped that economists and international development planners somewhere might read what I'd written and think a little more carefully about how their policies affected people who had their own distinctive visions of the good life and the future. Like any field of endeavor, anthropology generates its fair share of bosh and flapdoodle. Nevertheless, its larger effect, I think, is to make us wiser. I never, of course, expected Kragur people to accept my presence among them because it might benefit humanity in general. My basic ethical obligations to Kragur people are to answer honestly their questions about my own life and my intentions in Kragur and to strive to be fair and discreet when writing about their lives.

When I wrote my previous books about Kragur, I judged that discretion included concealing Kragur people's real names, so I devised a system for assigning pseudonyms that still allowed me to use authentic Kairiru personal names. This was as much to protect villagers' privacy within Kragur as to protect it from outsiders. Although very few resident villagers were literate in English when my first book came out, the number increases with each generation, and I have sent many copies of both my earlier books to Kragur people in the village and in towns. Most Kragur people familiar with the events I described in those books could probably discern people's real identities whatever names I used, but the pseudonyms at least avoided overt finger pointing. More important for discretion than using pseudonyms, I provided only minimum identifying information, excluding even pseudonyms, when I wrote of people doing or saying things that I thought might possibly anger other Kragurs.

So far, the only complaint I've had about this from Kragur people is that some of the stories in the books would have been more interesting if I'd used real names. So I decided that in this book I would dispense with pseudonyms, while continuing to draw a veil over individual identities when a topic is too hot. To be certain this would be alright, I asked individual villagers if they'd mind if I put their names in my next book, explaining when I did so that I intended to keep people's names out of stories that might stir up any feelings against them. Everyone I asked said to go ahead and some seemed quite pleased at the prospect. (A few may even now be wondering who they would like to portray them in the movie, but maybe I'm alone in that.)

I felt satisfied with this, until I explained my intentions to a couple of older

men of refined political sensitivity. People might say it's okay to use their
names, they said, but some who did were naïve about the possible consequences; not everyone might understand that there were malicious people
who would take even the slightest excuse to cause trouble. Using people's real
names, one of these elders said, could even result in people dying. What he
meant was that, as many Kragur people believe, anything that stirs up anger
can cause people to die, either by inspiring someone to use death-dealing
magic—that is, sorcery—or by dragging the powerful spirits of the dead into
a quarrel. The latter happens when someone's anger festers and the spirits of
their ancestors finally decide to take revenge for the wrong, real or imagined,
done to their living kin. I don't believe that sorcery or spirits of the dead can
kill, but I understand very well that for those who do believe, the suspicion that
you have angered someone who has knowledge of sorcery or is inclined to hold
a grudge can be powerfully unsettling, especially if you happen to fall seriously
ill. It might even hasten your demise. I considered what these learned elders
had said to me, and I decided that I didn't want to risk anyone even speculating that something I had written was implicated in an illness or a death.

Then I began writing, and I changed my mind. One reason I did so is that
some of the Kragur people I write about in this book are public figures well
beyond Kragur; for example, some hold regional or national public offices or
have been candidates for such offices. Their names and pictures have already
been spread around Kairiru, other islands, and on political campaign posters
throughout the Wewak area. I considered allowing the identities of the public
figures to stay public while changing the names of other Kragur people. But
it is hard to know where to draw such a line in times when national, regional,
and village events spill over each other in ways they never did in the past. And
to conceal the identities of those at the margins of wider events, I would have
to conceal not only their names but also their relationships with more widely
known figures—as supporters, opponents, friends, and family members. This
would make for some very awkward writing and it would obscure large parts
of Kragur's story, because much of Kragur's story is about relationships among
people. In addition, I also want to give Kragur people unconcealed credit for
their intelligence, humor, generosity, and the other qualities that make it a
pleasure for me to recall them by name (even though in a single short book I
can't mention everyone who deserves my applause). I started out in Kragur
depending on the kindness of strangers, but Kragur people are no longer
strangers to me, and it is hard to write about them as if they were.

Will this choice lead to people dying? I think not, of course. In this book I
use an extra measure of my usual discretion in deciding when to identify
people by name and how much to reveal about people whose names I with-
hold. Given the events I write about, Kragur people would find it easy to guess

from context the identities of most of the people involved, named or not. But even the most malicious will have to work hard to find reasons for anger in what I write that were not already available. Anyone who speculates that something I've written has caused an eruption of dangerous anger will be, I think, on extremely shaky ground.

In addition to practicing discretion, Kragur people also expect me to return the favor of their help and hospitality in more concrete ways. This is how things are done in PNG. When one receives a gift, one is expected sooner or later to return a commensurate gift. The kind of sharing Kragur people practiced when I first met them and that many still practice today isn't as clear-cut as barter, in which people exchange things they explicitly agree are of equal value. In fact, in Kragur, as in nonmoney exchange in much of PNG, the parties prefer to leave things a little out of balance, so there is a reason to get together to give or receive generosity again. That builds long-term relationships, perhaps more valuable than a one-time heap of taro or smoked fish. This can sound rather cozy, but in PNG giving can also be competitive, part of elaborate and never-ending contests for prestige and political dominance.[8]

I've never had to cope with such a contest, but the fact that I've never used money in transactions with Kragur villagers has made it trickier for me—familiar from birth with a world in which a host of disparate things can be expressed and compared in terms of money—to handle my obligations to villagers. I know how to calculate and negotiate money prices for things. But when I first went to Kragur, most villagers were adamant that there should be no buying and selling within the village. Based on their observations of white people, they equated using money with selfishness, and they were trying hard to maintain what they said was their ancestral custom of sharing food freely among kin and helping each other in gardening, house building, and other labor-intensive work instead of paying each other for labor in cash or kind. Many villagers in those days also held that being true Catholics, which most villagers professed to be, meant keeping commerce out of the village. This made a virtue of a necessity, given how little money most people in the village had at their disposal. But it accorded not only with an indigenous ideal of generosity but also with what villagers had heard some foreign priests preach: people should put care for others and concern for their own souls ahead of the pursuit of money.[9]

In any event, rather than pay for the help I relied on to live decently and to do my research, I gave away my stocks of rice, canned mackerel, flashlight batteries, and other store-bought goods—replenished in Wewak periodically—to those who became my teachers of local ways and who provided me with food that they had grown, caught, and hunted. My efforts to help in things like house building or gathering firewood were clumsy and of little real use, but they did, I hope, show my goodwill. In the years since, I've helped a number of my closest collaborators pay their children's school fees or the costs of marriages or funerals, and I've contributed to a number of village-wide improvement efforts, such as starting a village business development fund, erecting medical clinic buildings, and buying tools to repair earthquake damage. Even so, I wouldn't be surprised if some villagers think that I've exploited them. But I do what I think is right, within the limits of what is possible and knowing that I'll sometimes get it wrong. When I get it really badly wrong, I expect I'll hear about it.

I like to think that my most important contribution has been to put a part of Kragur's story down on paper for future generations. It looks like this is beginning to work out. I sent copies of my first two books about Kragur to numbers of individual Kragur villagers and to schools in the area, and I know that at least a few of the literate Kragur people have read them. In 1998, younger villagers who had read the first book, which portrays a period in Kragur's life they hadn't seen for themselves, were eager to talk with me about it.

As I prepared to leave for Kragur in 2008, I realized that there was always the possibility that this time I wouldn't be as welcome as I hoped; that few people might care anymore if I come again or not. Some of my Kragur friends had written and asked me when I planned to visit again, so I didn't really have a reason to worry about total rejection. I was probably more worried that *I* might not care anymore. In the end, I knew I'd just have to make the trip and see how it went.

Chapter 2

Thoroughly Modern Kragur

To be modern is to find ourselves in an environment that
promises us adventure, power, joy, growth, transformation
of ourselves and the world—and, at the same time, that
threatens to destroy everything we have, everything we know.
—Marshall Berman, *All That Is Solid Melts into Air*

I left for Kragur in early May of 2008 with a muddle of feelings, including lurking fear that I would find some things in Kragur had changed in ways I would find unsettling. I used to dream occasionally that heavy equipment had leveled Kragur's irregular stone-walled terraces, bulldozed the shade trees, and silenced the rattling of the coconut palms. This was extremely unlikely. For several years, however, some Kragur residents and Kragur people living in towns had been trying to get a small hydroelectric generator installed in one of the island's streams to supply Kragur with electricity for the first time. Electricity could power lighting in people's houses, refrigeration, laptop computers, and satellite telephones. Electric light could make it easier for schoolchildren to study and for literate adults to read in the evenings, and telephone or Internet service could be life-saving in medical emergencies. Better communication could also help villagers stay in touch with their families, now spread across the country and even the world; and it could help villagers market garden crops more efficiently to buyers in Wewak or run small tourist businesses by working with hotels in Wewak to give foreign visitors a taste of rural life on day trips or overnight stays in rustic guesthouses. It was hard not to appreciate villagers' excitement about these possibilities.

Electricity, however, wouldn't be an unmixed blessing. I had to wonder, if Kragur installed a hydroelectric generator, could the village afford to maintain an electrical system? A 1997 engineering report on the feasibility of installing a generator recommended thinking carefully about the costs of safe wiring, regulation, and maintenance of a power system.[1] In all the talk I'd heard of the promise of electricity in Kragur, almost no one had spoken of such issues. When people talked of, for instance, electric light for schoolchildren to study by, I often found myself picturing a tangled mess of patched wiring strung among the trees and through thatch roofs and aging wooden rafters. Such practical considerations aside, I feared electricity would bring blaring radios at all hours, uninterrupted by dead batteries, and the glaring fluorescent tubes that light yards and draw insects in some urban PNG neighborhoods. Villagers might well find ways to avoid such problems, and it's none of my business anyway if they want noisier and more brightly lit nights. As for me, however, among the things I like about Kragur are the night sounds of the forest, the sea, the wind, the rain, and the gradual monthly alternation of brightly moonlit nights with thick darkness relieved only by the glow of wood fires and kerosene lamps.

Electricity would, of course, make some things easier for me in Kragur, like using a laptop computer. But I am still content with using paper notebooks rather than going to the trouble of rigging up solar panels or arrays of car batteries. Also, while notebooks can get lost, burned, or sunk in the sea, leaving you with no copies of your work, they don't break down. And I like paper notebooks for the musty tropical aroma they acquire, along with rain and perspiration smudges and flakes of homegrown Kairiru tobacco caught between the pages. No matter how thorough your notes, you always leave something out, but paper notebooks contain a lot more information than is written in them. I could, for example, chart the increase in the quantity of betel nut I was chewing over the course of my 1975–1976 stay in Kragur by measuring the amount of bright pink saliva stain on the pages of my notes and journals from that year.

I freely admit that many things I like about Kragur are things many villagers would be glad to be rid of. I like the unlit and unamplified night. I also like Kragur's isolation. I know a lot of villagers would like to be able to get to the mainland or even just to the other side of the island more easily, and in the 1970s I would have predicted that by 2008 they could. There was talk in those earlier days of building a coastal road that would at least take people quickly and easily to the landward side of Kairiru, and there was talk of providing more regular and affordable sea transportation to and from Wewak. But none of this has happened. There is still no road around the island, and if you walk from Kragur to St. Xavier's on the same rugged trail you won't even find the *Tau-K* making its twice-weekly runs. It was retired years ago and replaced with a much smaller boat that carries very few passengers and very little cargo.

Since schooling in English first became available in Kragur in 1959, most villagers have taken as much of it as they could get. But the country's economy hasn't produced enough jobs for those who can read, write, and juggle numbers to absorb all of Kragur's bright young people; so, many literate villagers stay at home. A few are highly literate. In 1998, one young husband and father who had attended a Catholic seminary school would have been happy to dis-

cuss St. Thomas Aquinas with me, in excellent English, if I had known anything about Aquinas. He had also drafted an outline for an autobiography.
But he still couldn't make telephone calls, afford to go to Wewak except when
absolutely necessary, or even regularly send and receive mail. He must have
found this a very frustrating state of affairs.

Still, when I'm in Kragur I enjoy knowing that no one in the United States
can reach me. When I get back, I'm glad to be home again. But when I'm gone,
I enjoy being completely gone. True, I was sometimes morbidly homesick
in the 1970s, but being able to call home would only have made it worse. The
best remedy was work and opening myself more to the company of the two
hundred–plus human beings packed close around me. My visits to Kragur
since then have not only been shorter, they also have been untroubled by the
fear that my career would implode before it could really begin. This lets me
enjoy the sheer novelty of being unreachable and appreciate its instructive
aspects. What you can't get in the village or don't bring with you, you have to
do without. With limited outside communication and no electronic diversions,
you have to pay attention to where you are and what's going on around you.

During days of unrelenting rain or in the baking stillness of a dry-season
afternoon, many young people may dream of escaping to the relative bustle
and variety of Wewak or some other town. When we met again in Moresby in
2008, a Kragur man living and working there whom I have known for many
years recalled that he was in high school in 1975 when he heard that an anthropologist had settled in Kragur to study the village. He wondered then, he said
with a laugh, "What is there to study? Village life is so boring!" But Kragur not
only offers much of interest to an anthropologist, it offers any visitor a golden
opportunity to heed Ram Dass and *Be Here Now,* as the title of his famous
book advises. This entails, of course, not only tuning in to the beauties of the
evanescent present but also accepting its irritations.

I selfishly enjoy Kragur's lack of electricity and distance from the beaten
path, however much villagers may deplore these conditions. There is one preference, however, I'm quite sure I share with many villagers. This is a deep distaste for working under orders and by the clock. Kragur people felt strongly about
this in the 1970s, and I know many still do. A young Kragur man with whom
I became friends for the first time in 2008 had left Kairiru several times to
work for wages on the mainland, pressed by needs for money he couldn't fill
on the island. Yet although he occasionally had to give up the independence of
his life in the village for awhile, it didn't change his sense of who he really was.
As hard as he had to work for his livelihood in Kragur, he was proprietor of his
own house and land and master of his own time: he was proud to say to me,
"I'm no laborer!"

Even if my new friend had been able to get white-collar work in a PNG town, he probably still would not have escaped some of the fundamental indignities of being a "laborer." I have more than enough experience with unemployment to properly appreciate a regular paycheck, and I'm a borderline workaholic. But I truly hate the unremitting climate of urgency that has permeated most of the professional jobs I've held, mostly as a social researcher in consulting firms. I have special animus toward the daily time sheets I've often had to keep, showing how much of my time should be billed to which project or client account. Such jobs didn't require punching a clock or sticking tight to your welding station, drill press, or mop bucket until official break time, like the jobs that put me through college. But I still had to manage my workdays with industrial vigilance, labeling every activity, marking every change from one to another, and sometimes—despite my coat, tie, and college degrees—enduring the unsubtle surveillance of an employer. I've often had more fun wielding a pitchfork or a shovel all day, as long as no one was hanging over my shoulder pushing me to fork the horse manure more neatly or shovel the dirt faster.

I admired Stephen Umari for many reasons. For one thing, if he wasn't one of the greatest hunters and deep-sea fishermen who ever lived, he was at least one of the greatest tellers of stories of hunting and fishing prowess. If I thought I could bring it off, I would steal some of his stories for myself. I would be the hero in the story of how, after tracking a wild boar deep into the rain forest near the top of the island, he heard ahead of him the sound of his dogs cornering the huge animal. Rushing through the forest, his venerable shotgun in hand, he soon came upon the boar, wrapped around by a huge python that was slowly squeezing the life out of it, the boar and the python circled by Umari's frantic hunting pack. Umari bagged the pig, but only after hacking the snake to death with his bush knife. He also once hooked a fish so large that it pulled him in his small outrigger canoe so far from Kairiru that the island became no more than a dark line on the horizon, before the fish pulled him back again. His life, it seemed, had been filled with such perilous encounters. But Umari really endeared himself to me forever when I once saw him lose his temper with an officious village leader who tried to boss the other men the way colonial plantation foremen had pushed their "native" workers to work faster and harder. "We're not pigs! We're not dogs! We know how to work!" Umari shouted back; and, in sight of the assembled village, he stalked off to work as he saw fit.

There is some irony here, because I have explained to more than one Kragur villager trying to make a little money selling food crops in Wewak the absolute necessity of keeping track of every single kina and toea (PNG's dollars and cents) spent producing and transporting goods to market, just as employers have kept careful track of my time on the job. I dropped out of business school after less than a year, but I understand at least that much. Some villagers who make market sales do keep good records of income and expenditures. This often leads to painful but accurate awareness of how small their profit margins are. Many don't, which often leads to surprise that they are either earning nothing at all or losing their shirts.

I've never, however, recommended that villagers keep track of the time they spend on these endeavors. As long as they still have time to produce their own food, build and repair their houses, and do all the other work that is necessary but earns them no money, this isn't a serious accounting failure. Kragur villagers have been complaining about increasing demands on their time for years, but they don't generally behave as though they were on tight schedules, and I feel safe saying that most villagers don't equate time with money as is so common in the industrialized world.[2] Even if they did, their time has very little money value. No matter how low the cash returns on market gardening or cultivating cacao trees, Kragur villagers have few if any alternative ways to trade their time for money unless they leave the island, so it's hard for them to waste time in a financial sense.

In the Kairiru language, there isn't even an equivalent for the English word "time," and the present day of the week is always "now" or "today" and nothing more. In the 1970s, Kragur men who had worked for what they usually called in Tok Pisin Yuropian (that is, European, generally used for white people of all national origins) foreigners on plantations, in mines, or as "houseboys" laughed at the Yuropian custom of working, eating, and sleeping at set times. They would describe in careful detail the unvarying daily routines of a job they had held or of a Yuropian employer, shaking their heads in wonder, amusement, and dismay.

Time has become a much more familiar concept to villagers since the 1970s, when the oldest villagers still remembered the coming of early Catholic missionaries and islanders' very first encounters with bells calling them to worship at set intervals. They also remembered well their pioneering experiences with wage labor, with its own regulating bells and strict schedules. Yet even today, many if not most villagers still organize their days more by the broad stages of the passage of the sun than by the narrow demarcations of the few watches and clocks in Kragur. This doesn't mean that they never worry about the passage of time, but worrying about time in the village is worrying about things like setting out on a boat trip before the wind rises, finishing a task before dark, or having gardens ready to harvest when you need the food. Villagers don't try to beat the clock and they don't worry about the ticking off of the minutes and seconds the way people in much of the so-called developed world do. They are not obsessed with doing everything, including enjoying themselves, faster; and they never talk on cell phones or send text messages while driving, drinking coffee, and adjusting the car's sound system.

Nonetheless, in spite of isolation; lack of electricity, telephones, plumbing, and Internet access; no need to curry favor with employers; and a rather causal attitude toward time, Kragur villagers are modern people in a very important sense, and it would be hard to understand them without recognizing this. Most of what one hears about PNG in the news or reads in travel literature discourages such recognition. Papua New Guinea has had a tough time shedding the "Stone Age" label. A 1973 article in *Time* magazine on PNG's move to self-government in that year was entitled "Papua New Guinea: Out of the Stone Age."[3] Even today if you search Web sites pertaining to PNG, you can easily find tour operators promising to take you into a prehistoric past. Papua trekking.com offers travel to "New Guinea Island . . . where it is still possible to meet the primitive people of the Stone Age . . . where most people live like it was still the Neolithic Era." PNGTRAVEL.com allows that although PNG has "one foot in the Stone Age," it does have the other "in the Jet Age." Asia Transpacific Journeys, however, promises visions of "barely Stone Age agricultural practices." One of my favorites, although it does not speak specifically of the Stone Age, is an online advertisement, replete with references to the dangers of cannibalism, for a surfing film released in 2010 called *Isolated: Papua New Guinea,* in which "world-class surfers" travel to "a forbidden land on the most secluded corner of the globe . . . a world left behind."

To be accurate, the Stone Age began to draw to a close more than two thousand years ago among the islands that would eventually become PNG, as bronze objects arrived via trade with Asia. As long ago as the early seventeenth century, some people of the region were forging their own iron implements, probably having learned the technology from Malay traders. The Stone Age made a rapid finish in the late nineteenth century, as trade with Asians and Europeans escalated and metal items moved farther and farther into the hinterlands through generations-old indigenous trading networks. I've been told that the grandfather of a man of about my own age was the first Kragur villager to obtain a metal axe head.

The name "New Guinea" is still used as the geographic (as opposed to the political) designation for the entire large island and adjacent smaller islands, currently occupied by the Indonesian province of Papua on the west and the country of Papua New Guinea on the east. Human habitation of Sahul, the ancient landmass from which New Guinea and Australia were born, dates— by a conservative estimate—from some forty thousand years ago. The name New Guinea comes down only from the mid-sixteenth century, when Spanish explorer Yñigo Ortiz de Retes claimed the islands for Spain and dubbed the whole Nueva Guinea, because to Europeans of the day the inhabitants resembled West Africans.[4]

Trade with Europe and Asia over hundreds of years brought not only material things but also ideas. Anthropologist Donald Tuzin made a fascinating study of a myth of great importance to a mountain people of the East Sepik Province, the Ilahita Arapesh, which led him to conclude that the story's major motif made its way to New Guinea from the Malay Archipelago. The motif is the transformation of a wild creature into a human woman who produces children with a human man, leading to events that dramatically alter human society. The motif may have originated in India thousands of years ago, Tuzin writes, and spread from there to many parts of the globe. The type of animal invoked varies with the fauna of the places where the story has taken root. In many European versions of the story, a swan becomes a woman; in the Ilahita version, the "swan maiden" is a cassowary woman.[5] On Kairiru, there is a story of a dolphin woman, tricked into remaining on land in her human form by a Kairiru man named Mutabau. The dolphin woman eventually escapes back to the sea, but on her death she leaves to her descendants magic for fishing and gardening and a stone in the shape of a dolphin, found within her dead body. I was privileged to hear this story from Valentine Wamuk, a descendant of Mutabau. He is the current proprietor of the dolphin stone, which I was allowed to examine. The polished stone easily fit in the palm of my hand, and its elegant shape does resemble the head of a dolphin (fig. 4).

The dolphin and cassowary women of PNG suggest that while New Guinea was long at the very edge of the world known to Europeans, it has been part of a global flow of things and ideas for a very long time. From the perspective not only of the antiquity of the peopling of New Guinea but also its people's relationships with a wider world, even the earliest European claims to various parts of the island date from scarcely yesterday. Nineteenth-century encounters with Europeans, however, led to more rapid and dramatic changes than did the passage of beads and metal tools through trading networks or the drift of mythic motifs over continents and oceans. The Netherlands claimed the western half of the island in 1828 and Germany the northeast quadrant in 1884. To thwart Germany, which it feared had larger designs in the Pacific, Great Britain claimed the southeast quadrant of the island in the same year.[6]

Australia took control of German New Guinea at the outbreak of World War I, governed the area under a League of Nations mandate until World War II, and returned after the war with a United Nations mandate to govern while preparing what were then the separate "territories" of Papua (the area claimed by Great Britain in 1884 and handed over to Australia in 1906) and New Guinea (the former German colony to the north) for national indepen-

Figure 4. The stone found inside the body of the Dolphin
Woman, many generations ago, 2008. Photo by the author.

dence. Independence was granted, following relatively mild local agitation for
speeding up the process, in 1975.[7] The administrative districts of the Territory
of Papua and New Guinea (as my passport was stamped on my first visit there
in 1973) then became the provinces of the new country of Papua New Guinea.

News of the condition of Papua New Guinea as a young nation can be pretty
discouraging. Here's what Mike Manning, director of the Institute of National
Affairs, a Papua New Guinea nonprofit policy research organization, said in a
2006 issue of *Islands Business* magazine: "Law and order [problems] and corruption are deep-seated and pervasive, infrastructure has virtually collapsed,
human development indicators are bad and getting worse, and services barely
reach most of the population." But Manning was fundamentally optimistic
about the country. He saw PNG leaders struggling to find "homegrown Papua
New Guinea solutions . . . which are achievable and lasting." He also found
hope in the fact that in its short life, the country had never had a coup. "The

glass is half full, not half empty," he wrote. I'm inclined to say half full, too, although this may be as much the result of my fondness for the PNG people I know best as it is of cold-eyed analysis.

Yet whether the country's glass is half full, half empty, or has a thick, creamy head like a glass of Guinness—and no matter how bad its infrastructure or how fragile law and order—one can still speak of the people of PNG as modern. I don't mean by this that they all take a scientific view of the world. That standard would exclude from the modern world many citizens of Western industrial countries, such as the nearly half of Americans and nearly a quarter of Canadians who don't believe in biological evolution.[8] And I don't mean that Papua New Guineans lead daily lives like those of the people of economically and technologically highly developed countries or have social institutions like those found in the United States or Western Europe. They don't. And in conversation, you'll seldom mistake the average Papua New Guinean for a resident of Los Angeles, Stockholm, or Tokyo.

When I say that the people of PNG are modern people, I mean that they face the same great challenge that most other people of the contemporary world do. This is the challenge, in the words of scholar Marshall Berman, of how to "make [themselves] at home in a constantly changing world."[9] Toward the end of the nineteenth century, when European nations began trying to incorporate what is now PNG into their political spheres, Europe was already deep into the modern era and about to enter the twentieth century, in which all currents of what Berman calls the modern "maelstrom"—such as scientific discovery, industrialization, mass communication, competition among political philosophies, economic and military competition among nation-states, and the expansion of capitalism—would accelerate ever more rapidly.

New Guinea at that time was no stranger to major change. The people of the mountainous interior of New Guinea developed agriculture independent of— and as early as or earlier than—the people of Mesopotamia, Indochina, and Central America. The introduction of the sweet potato (*Ipomoea batatas*) to New Guinea long before sustained European contact—perhaps through Indonesia and the Philippines or via Eastern Polynesia—resulted in social changes so substantial that some scholars have called the episode the "Ipomoean Revolution."[10] But New Guineans developed agriculture and adapted the sweet potato to their own uses over considerable periods of time. The modernity that had been developing and gaining speed in the West over hundreds of years came to New Guinea, by comparison, in one fell swoop. Within a few years, the people of New Guinea became heirs to all the historical upheavals that had been transforming the European world for centuries: the demise of feudalism, the rise of the industrial system, the Protestant Reformation, the French Revolution, and the numerous European revolutions of 1848, to name but a few. It is only a slight exaggeration to say that to completely understand the contemporary PNG political system, you need to be familiar with the Magna Carta and the English Civil War (including everyone's favorite part of that latter episode, the Rump Parliament), as well as with how precolonial New Guineans sought leadership through gift exchange, trade, and warfare.

On becoming part of the modern world, New Guineans became part of a world in which change is an end in itself.[11] This aspect of being modern is both promise and threat; change may bring good things or bad things, and it may bring something new and attractive only at the price of something comfortably familiar and still serviceable. For many, this is a world that offers more options than ever before, but there is no assurance that the choices people make among these options will get them the results they seek. Writing in the mid-nineteenth century, Nathaniel Hawthorne observed that "People never do get just the good they seek. If it come at all, it is something else, which they never dreamed of, and did not particularly want." Hawthorne was describing, very pessimistically, what he saw as the human condition. The novel in which he made this observation, however, *The Blithedale Romance*, is a story of a profoundly modern experiment in transforming human society in a utopian community.[12]

The modern world is also one in which the speed of everything constantly increases, including the speed of change. In the words of Jimmy van Heusen and Sammy Cahn, "Everything today is thoroughly modern. . . . Everything today makes yesterday slow."[13] True, lots of modern people would like to ease the pace of change or even bring it to an end. Many Americans today support political and religious movements dedicated to returning life in America to a state of stability and predictability that its people never, in fact, enjoyed. Many New Guineans reacted to the European encounter by hoping and praying for utopian transformations that would end the turmoil of change thrust upon them, leaving them richer, like Europeans, but also more secure and in control of their world. Yet whether people are comfortable with constantly accelerating change or not, having to live with it is an inescapable part of being modern.

It is probably in the economic sphere that Kragur is most obviously part of the modern world. Even for a relatively isolated and self-sufficient place such as Kragur, there is no hiding from the complications of global markets. People in Kragur were just starting to plant vanilla in 1998. Before I left Wewak, I traveled inland by truck with a government agricultural agent and several area village leaders, including some from Kragur, to a small vanilla plantation for a demonstration of vanilla cultivation methods. In 1998, world vanilla prices were rising, and they rose even more sharply in the early 2000s due to—

among other factors—two hurricanes and a civil war in Madagascar, the world's major vanilla producer at the time, and to the introduction of Vanilla Coke.[14] People in a number of tropical countries responded to rising vanilla prices by expanding production. Rural Papua New Guineans responded with exceptional enthusiasm, and within PNG the East Sepik Province led the way.[15] Growing conditions for vanilla were good in the province, vanilla growing was easy to integrate with the existing agricultural system, and vanilla is a good crop to grow where transportation is expensive because, compared with crops such as copra or even cacao beans, a valuable load of vanilla beans doesn't weigh very much or take up much room.[16]

Many Kragur people joined the rush, but by 2004 prices for PNG vanilla were starting to drop, in part because production throughout the world was expanding so fast and in part because of problems within the PNG industry.[17] As prices continued to drop, many PNG growers left the market. By 2008, virtually all the Kragur growers had given up on vanilla and the forest had overrun the plantings they had nurtured so carefully just a few years before.

Living with the complexities of a global economy is rough. But being modern also means coping with a fluid and confusing moral world. Kragur people and other Papua New Guineans have now been grappling for several generations with the question of what it means to be good people in a world that constantly upsets old moral certainties and aggravates familiar moral dilemmas. A critical moral issue for many modern Papua New Guineas is how to balance obligations to their communities and extended families with the pull of loyalty to a more restricted family circle or the temptation of an even narrower individual autonomy.

This dilemma is familiar to people struggling with being modern throughout the world, but it has its own distinctive face in PNG. The importance of wide sharing of every kind of material plenty, both informally and in ritual feasting and gift exchange, has deep roots in what is now PNG. Such sharing has long maintained the social order within and among communities; some would say that it continually creates and recreates the social order. It also has shaped people's identities—that is, their understandings of who they are in relationship to other people. Some anthropologists go so far as to say that Papua New Guineans tend to experience themselves as beings defined to the core by relationships with other people—in particular, relationships involving giving and receiving food—rather than as entirely self-contained individuals.[18] For people who experience themselves in that way, the necessity of sharing would be beyond question. At the very least, however, it is common for Papua New Guineans to believe that both collective and personal material well-being depend on keeping on good terms with the spirit world and that this requires generosity and cooperation within one's community.

Kragur people certainly still assume there is a strong association between getting along well with each other and maintaining or improving their material well-being. When villagers say, however, that they are better off when they work collectively rather than as individuals or in restricted family groups, I'm not always sure if they're recommending collective work because they think it's more technically efficient, because they assume it's morally superior, or a little of each. For many years, Kragur villagers' major cash crop was copra—the sun-dried or smoked meat of coconuts, the source of coconut oil. When Kragur people produced copra in the 1970s, virtually all able-bodied villagers coordinated their work in the final phases—harvesting the dry nuts, cracking the nuts with sharp blows from bush knives, extracting the meat, drying the meat over smoky fires, and packing it in burlap sacks to transport to Wewak. I understand, however, that villagers don't engage in anything like this coordinated collective effort when producing garden crops or vanilla or cacao beans for market. From a purely technical standpoint, such crops don't require the same kind of large-group cooperation that copra does. I can't recall, however, any villagers saying simply that it's easier to produce vanilla or cacao in small groups than it was to produce copra; I *have* heard quite a few say, rather sadly, that it's too bad people don't work together anymore the way they did in the days of copra.

I don't think sharing and working together and all the good things they could bring were ever taken for granted in Kragur, and getting sharing and cooperation right was undoubtedly a delicate issue long before Europeans showed up. If the PNG I know provides any insight into an older New Guinea world, it must have been very easy in the past to get sharing wrong by giving too little, giving too much, or miscalculating what to give to whom on what occasions. Kragur people generally admire those who can create and accumulate wealth, but they are likely to criticize or become downright hostile to prosperous people who don't eventually send their wealth flowing out through the community. If getting it right was a constant bother in the old world, the example of westerners and their new kinds of social institutions really cast a fog around moral guideposts.

Europeans brought with them a society that emphasized individual effort and accomplishment and saw little wrong with some people getting rich and staying rich at the expense of others. Even missionaries preaching Christian compassion and the evil of putting material before spiritual things contributed to the greater influence of a more individualistic ethic. The Catholic Church in the East Sepik Province now encourages people to value and strengthen their community ties, but it began by encouraging people to reject the indigenous religious practices and forms of leadership that helped bind their communities together. In many areas, it was also Christian missions that introduced New

Guineans to the idea of individual work for individual pay and the competition among individuals inherent in Western formal education. After World War II, as Western powers prepared to allow the people of Papua and New Guinea to govern themselves once again, they encouraged them to put aside kin, village, and ethnic loyalties and use individual judgment to choose their leaders in Western-style elections. I'm in favor of electing leaders, but it doesn't necessarily mesh easily with the kind of reciprocal obligations still important in other spheres of PNG village life.

All this hasn't destroyed forms of morality and identity based on reciprocal obligations with myriad others or led people en masse to shed extended families, but it has made it virtually impossible to avoid choices more poignant than those the ancestors of today's Papua New Guineans faced. An impulse to loosen social ties probably goes back to before the modern era among PNG villagers and among people in similar small-scale societies, where close living can pinch as well as cradle you. It doesn't take an anthropologist to notice the kinds of social pressure to which life in a PNG village subjects people. In his memoir of many years living in PNG studying the country's insects, Czech biologist Vojtech Novotny writes that in rural PNG, "everyone is bound by a thousand bonds to dozens of more or less closely related kinsmen and dozens of neighbors near and far" and that such a way of life would make him "go berserk from the excess of attentive neighbors" long before he missed the material comforts of Western civilization.[19]

Novotny goes on to speculate, tongue only somewhat in cheek, that the desire for "headlong flight from kith and kin" may be what has driven "great migrations, conquests, voyages of discovery, urbanization, and various developments in technology" that have made it possible for people to live independent of tight-knit village worlds.[20] There is no doubt that in PNG, and elsewhere, there are now more ways than ever before to leave such worlds behind, but that's not all there is to it. Many PNG villagers may, as anthropologist Stephen Leavitt puts it, "yearn to act on [their] own" without having to consider "for each action . . . myriad . . . factors relating to [their] relatives and associates." But, he continues, they also maintain "a deep sense that one's social relations define who one is."[21] Hence they live with a painful contradiction. Putting yourself and your immediate family first opens up new vistas for success in PNG's emerging national economic and political worlds, but it doesn't cauterize broken relationships, settle moral quandaries, or resolve questions about who you fundamentally are for either those who succeed in the larger world or those they leave behind.[22]

The idea of a person as a relatively detached individual has a long way to go to take over in Kragur, but it is definitely on the scene. During the 2008 elections in Kragur, for instance, while some villagers were furious with those who ignored family ties in their voting, there were just as many if not more who declared loudly that their votes were—as close as I can translate from their Tok Pisin—their own, personal, private votes, to do with as they and they alone wished. Even some villagers who worried aloud about what they spoke of in English as creeping "individualism" also favored personal choice in voting. Anthropologists Vered Amit and Nigel Rapport suggest that democracy in political life—as individual choice—doesn't stay put but tends to foster greater consciousness of oneself as a distinct individual in life in general.[23] What is certain is that in these times, Kragur people have to think about who and what they are in relation to others; it can't be taken for granted. Whatever more stable and unquestioned way of being they may have enjoyed in the past, it has now been well and truly shaken.

Despite the advent of cash crops that don't require large-group cooperation, the increasing popularity of exercising personal choice in voting, and the general speed of change in contemporary PNG, a lot of Kragur people still don't look very "modern." They would still stand out on city streets in New York or London, including in their hipper quarters; and villagers in from the islands or the rural interior on the streets of Wewak stand out from the town dwellers in both dress and manner. Some Kragur people are even still short of metal tools. One day in 2008 I was chatting with a Kragur man while he repaired the wooden handle of his bush knife with a slightly bent nail. Falling into my home-handyman mode, I suggested a screw would work better than a nail. He looked at me as though I were mentally deficient and said, "I don't *have* a screw." He had a point—maybe two. Even if he'd had money to buy screws, the nearest hardware store was in Wewak, and it would have cost him much more simply to get there and back than it would have to purchase several boxes of screws.

The man rolling his eyes at my stupidity not only lacked a screw, he was using a rock for a hammer. But as he went about his tasks that day, he probably had a lot more on his mind than a yearning for more metal tools. Maybe he wondered if the world price for cacao beans was going to go up or down. Maybe he was contemplating taking his family to live in a town where they had relatives, finding wage work, evading requests for money from the village, and saving enough money to send all his children to high school. And maybe in town he might go to some different churches and see what some non-Catholic religions were like. Maybe he even wondered in passing if there was, in fact, a God like that which all the Christian religions advocated. But, his thoughts drifting again, he might have worried that if he left the village for long or sent back too little money, he might not be able to count on his siblings to look after their elderly mother. And then, maybe for a moment, he may have grown wistful about the old way of life, before the Europeans came, that his grandfather had told him about, sometimes with nostalgia and sometimes with relief at its passing. And perhaps in the back of his mind there was the recognition that, unlike his grandfather, he had to choose between making his future in the village and taking a chance on urban life, he could choose among several ways of seeking religious satisfaction, and his children might have even more paths in life from which to choose. Perhaps these prospects intrigued and excited him, although at other times he may have wished that they wouldn't disturb his thoughts. In short, don't be fooled by stone tools, because the people using them may be very modern and face choices you might find very familiar.

Chapter 3

Hot Times on Kairiru Island

Crikey, it's hot!
—Frank Clune, *Prowling through Papua with Frank Clune*

I took a leave of absence without pay from my job to spend May and June of 2008 in Kragur. It went well. I'm glad I went. There were moments when, if a snap of my fingers would have transported me home instantly, I would have snapped. I blame a few such moments early in the trip on the crushing jet lag caused by crossing the fourteen-hour time difference between the eastern United States and PNG, pausing only to change planes in Los Angeles and Brisbane. Later, I occasionally felt like slipping quietly away and getting on the first plane out of Wewak for more complicated reasons. But if I had crept away, the feeling of relief would have been short lived, soon giving way to regret, and I probably would have been too embarrassed ever to show my face in Kragur again.

Although not to be missed, the trip was emotionally and physically demanding. One physical demand in particular sometimes made me fantasize escape. I speak, of course, of the dripping heat. According to a 1989 volume on Kairiru's flora by Brother William Borell—teacher, naturalist, and maker of fine liqueurs—who lived and worked at St. Xavier's for many years, the island gets from 120 to 150 inches (3,048 to 3,810 millimeters) of rain a year. This is a bit more rain than falls on Wewak, which gets an average of about 95 inches (2,400 millimeters) a year, and a lot more than falls on such nontropical cities nevertheless known for their moisture as London, at about 30 inches a year, and Seattle, at about 33 inches a year. According to Brother William, temperatures on Kairiru range between 75 and 95 degrees Fahrenheit (25 and 35 degrees Celsius).[1] I've lived where summer temperatures of 100 degrees Fahrenheit and above are not uncommon, but Kairiru is also fewer than five degrees south of the equator, which means that by quite early in the morning the sun doesn't just shine or even blaze, it presses down. That the climate was equatorial was certainly no surprise to me. It did surprise me that I couldn't shrug this off as easily as I had even ten years before.

Kragur people seldom linger in the sun if they don't have to, but for the most part they carry on their strenuous daily lives apparently taking for granted that they are sweating bullets. Younger people even go out of their way to tempt the heat, playing rugby on a muddy square along the path to the stream and competing with furious energy and great skill in intervillage volleyball tournaments, always played in the full sun. It's less than a half-hour walk from Kragur to the Catholic church that stands at the top of a steep, grassy slope above the neighboring village of Bou. The rocky and rambling trail from Kragur to Bou follows the ins and outs of the island's coastline, shifting closer or farther from the beach as the comparatively gently inclined strip of land between beach and mountainside narrows and widens. In a few places, the trail dips and then climbs sharply to cross deep ravines where streams cut their courses to the sea. Overall, however, the path ascends and descends little enough to count as flat by Kairiru standards. Palms, the occasional mango, and other spreading trees form a column of shade over the trail most of the way. Even so, when I walked to Bou for the Sunday service the day after landing in Kragur in 2008, I arrived at the church almost sick with heat, feeling like my internal body temperature had risen by several degrees.

The Bou church was built in the early 1970s to serve several area villages. It has a bare cement floor and a corrugated metal roof, high and peaked to let the heat rise. The plasterboard walls are open from waist height to where the supporting timbers—by 2008, deeply furrowed and mined by ants—meet the roof. A broad central aisle runs the length of the church from the wide entrance to three concrete steps mounting to the rectangular apse. On either side of the aisle, rows of squared timbers form tiers of hard, narrow seats. On this day I squatted on my timber seat, weak and speechless, fanning myself with my hat, for about fifteen minutes before I felt well enough to pay attention to what was going on around me, a spirited Pentecost Sunday service that under other circumstances would have riveted my attention from the first moment.

For several months before leaving for PNG, I had worked at strengthening my legs and wind to make sure I could roam at will up and down Kairiru's mountain trails. I was especially eager to hike to the top of the main trail that links the landward and the seaward sides of the island. The top of this trail is not the highest point on the island. Reaching the highest point, about 2,490 feet (about 760 meters), requires a final stiff climb on smaller, rougher trails. The main cross-island trail crests below that height at a level area called Iupulpul. Kragur villagers also call this place Maria Kem (Maria Camp) because they erected a statue of the Virgin Mary here in 1976. In front of the statue, they cut back the bush to create a wide clearing where people can rest before plunging down the other side of the mountain, perhaps after saying a prayer and placing some flowers or red *tanget* leaves, gathered at the edge of the clearing, at the Virgin's feet.

When I was in Kragur in 1998, I suffered from such sharp pains in my right hip that I didn't even try to hike to Iupulpul, a historic place for Kragur people and a deeply nostalgic one for me. Now, ten years and some brilliant physical therapy later, I was determined to have this pleasure. Also, I have heard Kragur people making fun of visitors to the island who couldn't make it up the mountain, and I didn't want to be lumped forever with these softies. I started with a few trial runs to lower-altitude areas crossed by the main trail with such names—some that pop and others that flow—as Sumolau, Kafow, Shikiaupulpul, Utabru, Ribeiyet, Bokashel, Siliau Vanu, Wup, Nar, and Komaru. Most of the trail is heavily shaded, but at Komaru it heads up the narrow crest of a ridge in the full sun at a disconcertingly precipitous angle. Once you get past Komaru, you move back into green shade, provided by the thick canopies of sago palms, and amble up a comparatively gentle slope to Iupulpul. Once I had mastered what villagers call the "road" (in Tok Pisin, *rot*) to Iupulpul, I was able to manage most other trails with aplomb, if not speed. Many trails I traveled were not as long or steep as the road to Iupulpul, but they balanced that in part by providing footholds only inches wide, spaced ridiculously far apart.

Still, the heat bothered me more than I'd anticipated. In the 1970s, I'd often climbed briskly to Iupulpul and back late in the afternoon just to get the kinks out of my back if I'd been sitting in the village all day. I'd also frequently run the trail to Bou and the next village along the coast, Shagur, and back just for fun. I even played a little basketball (good rebounder, bad shooter) with the Kragur team in the intervillage games held at St. Xavier's during the dry season. I had to conclude that the thirty-some intervening years had eroded more than just my innocence. I was a month into my stay in Kragur, however, before it finally dawned on me to read closely the list of side effects of the antimalarial medication, Malarone, I was taking every day. The list began, "Side effects may include nausea." That, I realized, might help account for my Pentecost sickness, the queasiness that was afflicting me during the hottest part of almost every day, and an unpleasant incident in which I had to excuse myself in the middle of consuming a heaping plate of hot taro and smoked fish to step outside and vomit over the railing of a veranda. I began to feel a lot better when I started taking my daily dose of Malarone in the evening, as the sun's heat waned, rather than in the morning, when it waxed at high speed. But I never felt as completely acclimated as I once had.

Some North American friends of my generation who have worked and lived in the equatorial Pacific Islands tell me that they, too, feel the heat more these days. One friend prefers to blame global warming rather than his advancing age. There isn't any reliable information available on temperature trends in the Wewak area over recent decades, so I can't make a case that higher temperatures contributed to my discomfort. Many Kragur people, however, had heard of global warming, and they were concerned about it.

News articles about the effects of global warming in the Pacific Islands tend to focus on the danger that rising sea levels, caused by ocean waters expanding as they warm and the melting of glaciers, pose to the people of low-lying islands. Kragur people told me that nearby low-lying islands were visibly losing ground to the sea; this even though an undersea earthquake in 2002 had elevated the shorelines of some, including Kairiru itself.[2] Villagers had noted other oddities as well in recent years. For instance, mangos seemed to ripen almost randomly rather than in predictable season. This was largely a curiosity, but villagers were truly concerned about peculiarities in the timing of the rainy and dry seasons. Some blamed the earthquake for what they said were increasingly unreliable seasonal changes. Many, however, attributed what they saw to "global warming," calling it by its English name. And many blamed global warming on "pollution" (here, too, they used the English word), and one friend was happy to remind me that America is a world leader in pumping pollutants into the air.

I arrived in Kragur in early May, and by June there should have been many dry days and even some strings of dry days. During my entire stay in Kragur, however, on only two occasions did twenty-four hours go by without the sky opening up and letting loose something denser than sheets of rain but not quite as dense as solid blocks of water. Anyone who has spent time in the less-developed parts of the tropics knows what a thundering din a monsoon rain makes on a corrugated metal roof; but the sound of the rains even on the springy palm-leaf thatch of Kragur houses during my stay was loud enough to halt conversation.

Rougher seas than expected in the dry season accompanied the rain. For people who get their livelihood directly from local land and waters, this is serious. Rough seas mean it's hard to fish. What I've been calling the dry season, Kragur people usually call *makatalal*. *Makat* (or *makyat*) is the Kairiru word for fish, so the local name for the season is roughly "fishing season." When it doesn't arrive as expected, when *yavaralal*, the season of northwest monsoon wind (*yavar*) and rain, persists, villagers miss some of the months of a more protein-rich diet that *makatalal* affords. They also may have to put off major events—such as feasts associated with funerals or dispute settlements—that can only be mounted in proper style with lots of fish. People also find it hard to start new gardens. When clearing land for a garden—either virgin forest or, more often, old gardens left to lie fallow for several years—villagers lay the trunks of the felled trees in horizontal rows across the abruptly angled garden plots to reduce erosion. But they burn the piles of smaller limbs and brush, and this is nearly impossible when it rains every day.

Rain during the day in Kragur tends to cool things off, as long as it lasts, but once it blows over the sun burns as powerfully as ever, and I always imagine that from a distance you can see a cloud of steam rising from the island. Rain at night cools things off more. My bed in 2008—a foam mattress over plywood on a metal frame, the only bed in the house—was pushed up against the wide single window in my room. On rainy nights, the damp air and the blowing spray sometimes were so chilly that I had to put on a sweatshirt, pull my thin blanket over me (actually, an old blue tablecloth I'd brought from home that's about the right weight for a tropical blanket), and even take the stick out of the window shutter, which pivoted on large nails, and let it fall closed. During one especially torrential night, I even covered myself with my rubber yoga mat.

From the day I arrived in Papua New Guinea, however, I faced no physical hardships from which Kragur people could spare me. Their hospitality started in Moresby, where many Kragur people live who were born and raised in the village but who have obtained advanced educations and entered urban professions. If they can't be said to have vaulted from the Stone Age, they do live in a world very different from that of the village, and they are not only modern people, they look like urban people almost anywhere, down to high heels for the women and shoes and socks for the men. A man of the Kragur community in Moresby—John Samar, a journalist and public relations specialist—picked me up at Jackson Airport in mid-afternoon and drove me to the air-conditioned Hideaway Hotel. My room in the hotel was actually too cold, and I couldn't find a way to adjust the temperature. I tried opening the windows, but the power went off occasionally, something not uncommon in Moresby. Then the hotel's backup generator, located rather close to my window, would switch on, roaring like a jet engine. So, I finally left the window closed and put on my sweatshirt.

I had a reservation at the Hideaway, but the desk clerk told me that Ralph Saulep had instructed him to put my room on Ralph's corporate account. Like John, Ralph, an attorney, is a scion of Kragur who started his formal education at the tiny primary school in Bou Village and went on to complete high school and university and live the life of an urban professional. He and John are what I've heard village Papua New Guineans call, in Tok Pisin, *susokman*—that is, urban men who wear shoes and socks. In fact, Ralph wore leather sandals with his dark slacks and white shirt when we got together in 2008, but the two cell phones he carried tended to distract from his casual footwear.

Ralph and John picked me up that evening to take me to dinner with several more Kragur people living in Moresby. We met them at the Gateway Hotel, a more posh establishment than the Hideaway. The Hideaway describes its restaurant as "well appointed," but the Gateway promises "some of the finest international cuisine in Port Moresby." In addition, while both restaurants provide white cloth napkins, those at the Gateway were folded in the shape of what I would call swans anywhere but in PNG, where they are undoubtedly Birds of Paradise. Most of the members of this dinner group were among the first generation of Kragur people to start out at Bou Community School and eventually earn professional degrees and make successful careers in the country's towns. I had heard most of their names from villagers, but this was the first time some of us had met. The average level of formal education among Kragur people, including both those in the village and those scattered among PNG's towns, is higher than the average for PNG as a whole. For example, in 1998, with the help of village resident Simon Kirar Waibai (whom I call Kirar in this book), I determined that about 60 percent of Kragur people, both resident in the village and living elsewhere, had at least six years of schooling, which compared very favorably with the figure of 42 percent for all Papua New Guineans determined by a World Bank study published that same year.[3]

The group gathered on this evening stood out even among Kragurs. Many had not only obtained all the formal education PNG had to give but had also worked and studied abroad. I have mingled with many highly educated and cosmopolitan Papua New Guineans, but I think I am impressed in particular by the accomplishments of this group, and other Kragur professionals of their generation, because I know firsthand the out-of-the-way village where they started out and how radically different their lives have been from those of their parents. The highest level of formal education Ralph's parents could have aspired to, for example, was literacy in Tok Pisin; and while many of his parents' generation left the village at least temporarily to work for money, it was usually manual labor for low wages. But on this evening, in air-conditioned comfort, these Kragur people chatted easily of their professions and their travels abroad, we sipped wine from stemware and refilled our glasses to exchange toasts, and Ralph periodically picked up one of his two cell phones, placed within easy reach on the crisp, white tablecloth, to take a late call from a legal client.

The following afternoon, Ralph and John drove me to the airport to catch my short flight from Moresby, at the edge of the Coral Sea on the country's south coast, northwest to Wewak, perched on the edge of the Bismarck Sea on PNG's north coast, where I arrived at dusk. Mention of Wewak tends to stump most of the travel agents I've dealt with in the United States, but the name is well known to Australians and Americans who served in the Pacific in World War II. When I gave a short talk on contemporary Papua New Guinea to the residents of the retirement apartment complex where my mother lives, elderly military veterans in the audience found Wewak a very familiar name. A couple of them had been in New Guinea during the war, and they all knew that Wewak had been the site of a heavily fortified Japanese military base, finally taken by Australian and American forces after fierce aerial and ground fighting.[4]

There is a memorial park and monument marking the 1945 surrender of the Japanese forces at Cape Wom, just a few miles northwest of what is now Wewak town. But, while Wewak was at its center, the Japanese occupation spread up and down the coast and throughout the islands, including Kairiru and Mushu. Japanese forces established a base on the flatter, landward side of Kairiru and stationed troops in many of the larger villages, including Kragur. Few Kragur villagers are alive today who remember that time, but in the 1970s middle-aged villagers remembered well the approximately three years of occupation. In particular, they remembered having to flee the village to hide in the bush from aerial attacks on the Japanese encampment, attacks that devastated the village as well as the Japanese camp.

European settlement where Wewak now stands began in 1911. German Catholic missionaries established a station at Wirui (still the center of the Catholic Church in the East Sepik Province), not far from the center of today's town. German coconut planters followed close behind. The name "Wewak" is apparently a transformation of the name of the village of Viaq, which once stood where one of Wewak's better residential areas is now situated.[5] According to the 2000 national census, Wewak had a population of 25,143 in that year, although many observers think that number is substantially low, and the population of the town and its environs had certainly increased a good deal by 2008. In any case, Wewak probably remains among the largest half dozen of PNG's urban areas, although considerably smaller than Moresby, to which the PNG census of 2000 attributed a population of about 254,000.[6]

In 2008, I had arranged to stay at the Wewak Point Guest House, whose proprietor, Martarina Wai, met me at the airport in a car just large enough for the two of us and my two duffel bags. Wewak Point, once the site of the village of Viaq, is a high, rocky headland, almost entirely occupied by quiet residential streets. In general, the nearer the flat top of the point, the nicer the houses. Wewak's main commercial street cuts across the low neck of the headland, between Wewak's eastern and western harbors. Martarina's place is a single-story house along the bumpy, unpaved road that runs around the periphery of the point. The guesthouse is unmarked and unmentioned in guidebooks, but anthropologist Nancy Sullivan had recommended it to me. Martarina, I learned, had worked for several nonprofit organizations in PNG, and her only other guest at the moment was a young PNG woman recently arrived in Wewak to work with Save the Children, training rural community health workers.

I had arrived too late to get into town to buy food, so Martarina brought me a plate of taro, sweet potatoes, rice, and greens. My quarters—two small, sparsely furnished bedrooms, a kitchen, and a bathroom—were a bit hot and stuffy. I was quite content not to wrestle with a noisy, overachieving air conditioner, but my rooms were also too low to allow for ceiling fans. There were, however, small fans affixed to the walls and a comfortable chair on the narrow but much breezier concrete veranda, from which the view was outstanding. Unless it is hidden by storm clouds, you can see Kairiru clearly from this side of the point, and that evening I could watch the island's silhouette fade slowly with the light. Seen from Wewak, Kairiru is a mass of deep green, sometimes mottled by the moving shadows of the tall, white cumulus billows such high islands attract, and betraying no signs of human habitation. Satellite views of Kairiru on the Internet also show almost nothing but dense forest cover. Approaching Kairiru by sea, you eventually distinguish stands of coconut palms among the general greenery, marking the locations of villages and their cultivated lands. You have to get quite close, however, to see low, thatched houses along the shore, and villages farther inland are invisible except for the telltale palms.

I hadn't made specific arrangements for anyone from Kragur to meet me in Wewak. Many months earlier I had broached the idea that I might come to Kragur in 2008 in letters to a few close friends in the village. I wanted to give them ample notice of my developing plans, and I hoped that their replies would give me a sense of how welcome I would be. The replies were reassuring, and in late 2007 I wrote again to say that I would come in May and June of 2008. As the time approached, I e-mailed Ralph to let him know when I would arrive in Moresby and mailed word of my arrival time in Wewak to the village. This was enough to ensure that someone would meet me at the airport in Moresby and that someone from the village would bring a boat in to Wewak to take me back to Kragur. So, on my first morning in Wewak I set out for a walk to see how ten years had changed the town's aspect and to look for familiar human faces. I knew that if I strolled up and down the main street, through the outdoor market at its western end, and along the beach at its eastern end, where Kairiru and other island boats put in when they come to town, I would eventually run into any Kragur people waiting to meet me. And if I didn't pick them out of the crowd, they would surely see me, because an unfamiliar Yuropian on foot stands out in Wewak.

Arriving at the market, just a short downhill walk from the guesthouse, I found it a lot bigger than it had been in 1998. Even then, vendors of taro, smoked fish and game, betel nut, bunches of tobacco leaves, and other local products had set out their wares on the ground in a widening circle outside the two rows of covered concrete stalls but within the market area's chain-link fence. By 2008, vendors had spread far beyond the fence. Both Kragur villagers and town dwellers say that the market is an excellent place to have your pocket picked or a bag or backpack ripped from your grasp, so I carried only small change in my pockets and kept my shoulder bag strapped across my chest. But the market is also irresistible, with its colorful displays of local products and, I have to say, local trash.

Most market vendors and patrons seem to do their best to use the oil drums set here and there as trash receptacles, but the drums are too few and too small, so trash piles up around them in drifts. Brightly colored cellophane snack packet wrappers lying among deep green betel nut stalks make up a lot of the trash, and everything in the drums and heaped around them is splattered with scarlet betel nut spit, giving the whole a rich artistic unity worthy, I think, of being encased in blocks of Lucite and transported to a New York City art gallery. I had my camera in my bag and scouted several angles from which to photograph this raw beauty, but I decided to forgo the opportunity. My close examination of the trash piles quickly began to attract attention, and I realized that onlookers might think I was seeking out and documenting Wewak's squalid side, which is a bad way for a visitor to make a first impression.

Strolling through the market, I noted the prices of stalks of betel nut and bunches of tobacco leaves because I wanted to take some of each with me to hold up my end in the sharing of betel and tobacco that is part of most social encounters in Kragur. Then I visited the displays of local beadwork. I'm a fool for PNG necklaces, strung with beads, shells, seeds, and dog, pig, and bat teeth, and I spent some time considering the offerings before choosing several to bring home as gifts and for my own collection. Minutes after leaving the bead display, I ran into Godfried Sareo, a high school teacher from Kragur, and his wife Mary. They told me they had seen a tall white man enter the market, judged by his demeanor that he was not a tourist, and, before they could see my face clearly, decided that it must be me. They also told me that there were Kragur boats down at the beach, so I left the market and headed down the main street.

I visited Wewak briefly in 1973 on my way home from Manus, and I've been there several times since then. Situated as it is, Wewak has always been picturesque. This time, however, it felt a little edgier than in the past. It was impossible not to notice that there had been a boom in the private security business, already thriving ten years before. Uniformed private guards, usually in pairs, were posted at the doors of virtually every establishment, from the air-conditioned oases of the banks and the Air Niugini office to the hot and crowded general stores that sell everything from inexpensive clothing to fishing hooks, surgical tubing for making spear guns, kerosene lanterns, Chinese-made aluminum cookware, and—of course—a wide variety of metal tools.

It was also impossible not to notice that long sections of the sidewalk were disintegrating. Ten years ago the sidewalks were cracking and tree roots had uplifted some of their concrete sections. Now, however, long stretches of the sidewalk had been ground underfoot—and these feet largely bare—into gravel and mud, and I'd never seen the streets so littered with trash. I knew that roads, bridges, and other infrastructure in PNG in general had been deteriorating for many years, an aspect of the country's struggle to stand on its own since independence, so I couldn't be surprised.[7] Nevertheless, Wewak as I now found it had a slightly postapocalyptic feel, enhanced by the fervent shouts of a sidewalk evangelist preaching the urgency of accepting Christ's redemption. This made me more eager than usual to leave Wewak for Kairiru.

Just as I reached the end of the main street and was about to cross the intersecting road to the beach, a grizzled man in much-mended shirt and shorts and a fraying baseball cap accosted me by name: "Smith!" (Some Kragur people call me Michael, but a larger number call me Smith.) For an awkward moment I didn't recognize him, but then he took off the cap that shaded his face and I realized it was Kilibop, oldest son of Stephen Umari and Agnes Munbos, now a man of about forty. It was an embarrassing start for me, and despite the many hours we'd spent together in the past, I managed only a firm handshake and profuse apologies for not recognizing him.

I tend to err on the reserved side on occasions like this. When visiting friends in Peru in the 1980s, I amused them by proffering handshakes to people I hadn't seen for many months, while all around me people who had seen each other only days before were embracing enthusiastically. I needed, they said, to *latinizarme*—that is, to "latinize" myself. My uninhibited Peruvian hosts knew from experience how to loosen up their cool northern neighbors, but my relationship with Kragur villagers is a little trickier. While a long one, it has been sporadic, and we approach each other under the shadow of generations of Yuropian dominance of PNG and across what is still not only cultural distance but also a broad gap in wealth and opportunities for mobility in the wider world. (My Peruvian friends, by contrast, were all middle-class *susok* people.) When I show up at long intervals, I'm probably not the only one who isn't completely sure what to do. In the weeks to come, however, I found that both I and the times had changed, and I loosened up considerably, to the point where Kilibop's wife Kanis laughingly paid me the compliment of calling me what—given the context—translates loosely from the Tok Pisin as a "bullshit artist" (*mauswara man*). There is plenty of such artistry in Kragur, so I felt in good company.

Whatever my momentary confusion on the streets of Wewak, I was truly glad to see Kilibop. I had just started to look for some lunch when we met, so he guided me across the street to the ramshackle Rong Song Restaurant, where a woman behind the counter served us in Styrofoam containers through a pass-through in a wire security screen. Kilibop had the chicken stew over rice, but the counter woman insisted that, because I was an American (not just white but American; it's that obvious, I guess), I have the chicken legs. This left me wondering what was in the stew, but it seemed to sit well with Kilibop.

After eating, we headed for the beach. What little promotion there is for tourism in Wewak usually touts the long, palm-lined beach that curves away southeast from the base of Wewak Point. But when people from the islands offshore speak of the beach, they usually mean the sheltered cove at the foot of the point, just opposite the eastern end of the main street, where they pull their boats up on the sand when they arrive. Here they also sit, on their boats and on the heavy driftwood logs at the edge of the water, in the shade of the causuarina trees, waiting for their parties to assemble to go home again. When Kilibop and I got there, we found several other Kragur people and a couple of Kragur boats.

Some of the Kragur men we found there had their own business in town and weren't sure when they would be going back to the island. I recognized old friends Andrew Klarok Marir (Klarok) and Melchior Munuo Marir (Munuo) immediately. They had come to Wewak to assist Dr. Moses Manwau, a close relative born and raised in Kragur, in his efforts to win a seat in PNG's national parliament. Moses had come close to winning a seat representing the Wewak Open Electorate in parliament in the 2007 election, and since the election he had been seeking a court review of what he and his supporters charged were irregularities in the voting, including ballot box tampering. He was in Wewak now, where he had a small medical practice and a house on Wewak Point, but he was waiting for news of his case that might require him to travel to Moresby, maybe taking some of his principal village supporters with him.

Joe Bokarum of Kragur, known to all as Joe Boko, whom I was meeting for the first time, was also there, and we agreed that he would take me to Kragur in his open, sixteen-foot boat two days hence. Kilibop had spent the previous night at Moses' house, but we agreed that he should come and stay with me at the guesthouse. I could use his help in assembling my supplies, and everyone agreed I also needed someone to help keep me and my goods from falling afoul of Wewak's miscreants. I knew that I, a pale newcomer who might have money in his pockets or a camera or cell phone on his person, had to stay alert on Wewak's streets, but these leathery men in their rough traveling clothes and battered hats told me that they didn't feel safe in town either. Later, other villagers told me of two Kragur men who had been beaten and robbed in broad daylight in or near town. It's one thing when a travel guidebook or a tourism Web site warns you of the danger of a country or city, but you have to take it very seriously when the local people warn you.

Kilibop and I bumped into several other Kragur men and women at the beach and as we walked back through town. I usually remembered their faces, even some that had changed considerably over ten years from loss of teeth and weathering of skin. Some of the younger people whom I'd never really known also looked uncannily like their parents. A lot of people's names, however, escaped me. When I failed to greet them by name immediately, they almost invariably asked me, grinning, "What's my name?" I was usually afraid to guess. Being wildly wrong—that is, not even placing them in the correct family—seemed worse than giving up completely. But once they stopped torturing me and identified themselves, I sometimes redeemed myself a little by being able to ask after other family members by name or mentioning some shared experience from the past.

Kilibop traveled with only a knife and materials for rolling smokes and chewing betel nut, all of which he carried in a small canvas shoulder bag, so moving him into the guesthouse required only a brief conference with Martarina. He chose to sleep on the relatively cool tiled floor, his head resting on his bag, rather than in the second bed, so he didn't even need the sheets and pillow Martarina offered. Kilibop and I discussed what supplies I would need to bring to Kragur, and we spent that afternoon and the next day comparing prices and buying things. We did our bulk shopping at Garamut Cash and Carry, a long-established bulk grocery warehouse just across the road from the beach where the Kragur boats were pulled up, and we left our purchases there to pick up the day of our departure.

The selection of stores along the main street hadn't changed much in ten years. I didn't recognize the name of the Jade Island Trading Company, but the store itself resembled all the other general stores on the block, with the exception of the R. A. Seto store, which had acquired air-conditioning since 1998. There had been a Seto general store in Wewak since I could remember, and I knew that the familiar Tang Mow store had been part of Wewak since the 1930s.[8] The only semblance of a bookstore in town, if you favored books on how to achieve salvation and avoid damnation, was still the Wewak Christian Bookshop, established around 1970. I ducked in hoping to buy a few postcards to send home and found that the shop also seemed to be purveying the same small selection of cards as in the 1970s. It looked as if the main-street tourist trade wasn't very brisk. This made me feel sorry for the beadwork vendors in the market, who probably could have beguiled tourists with their wares—if there had been any tourists and if the tourists hadn't been wary of plunging into the market crowd.

Making our way around town, we thought we were negotiating the foot traffic pretty well, but on one crowded section of sidewalk we encountered a classic urban pincer movement as three or four young men bumped into us, penned us in, and freed us just as quickly. They left my pockets and bag untouched but relieved Kilibop's pocket of my tin of small Dutch cigars, a luxury we'd planned on sharing in the evenings ahead. This proved us both real bumpkins. Just minutes before, a young woman passing us on the sidewalk in the other direction had paused to warn Kilibop that it looked like a group of young men was following us. So they had been, and so we failed this test of urban savvy miserably.

Continuing our shopping, I knew more or less what I wanted to buy, but Kilibop knew where to get the best prices and had definite ideas on what were the best brands. There were also a few brands he thought I should try because, he said, "They recommend it on television." Kilibop had watched very little television, and certainly none in Kragur, but it doesn't take much to make an impression.

Wewak is the kind of place where sometimes things go out of stock all over town—I've searched in vain for both paper clips and sugar on occasion—but this time we found everything I needed. This included such things as an extra towel, a kerosene lamp, disposable lighters, and shallow boxes of about four-inch-long, unfiltered, Spear "coarse cut tobacco sticks," for dispensing hospitality. I also bought a box of D batteries, but these were for the flashlights of friends in Kragur; I carried a very efficient crank-up flashlight for myself. Most of what we bought was food. For those perhaps planning a similar trip, here is a list of my major purchases:

- Two cases (twenty-four cans each) of Ocean Blue mackerel in "natural oil";
- Three twenty-kilogram (about forty-four-pound) bags of Roots rice;
- Two five-kilogram (about eleven-pound) bags of Flame flour;
- One case (forty-eight two-ounce packets) of thick, durable Paradise Hi-Way Hardman biscuits, each packet bearing the image of a muscular truck driver;
- One package (forty-eight bars) of yellow Klina laundry soap, with which to wash everything from dishes to my clothes to my flaxen hair (it does not, however, leave one's hair silky);
- About forty ounces of Nescafe instant coffee (the only brand available), which proved far too little;
- Modest amounts of cooking oil (Mama's Choice), salt (Crystal), dry milk (Sunshine), and sugar (Ramu);
- One "bale" (forty-eight rather skimpy rolls, in a large plastic bag) of Nature-Soft two-ply toilet tissue; and,
- Several bright red, yellow, and green packages of Zap mosquito coils.

Avoid these latter like the plague. I'm sure they work on mosquitoes, but a breath of their smoke can almost take the lining out of your lungs.

The morning of my departure for Kragur, Kilibop went out early to help Joe Boko fetch his boat's outboard engine and its petrol tank from Moses' house, where he had left them for the night for safekeeping, while I waited at Martarina's and finished packing. Kilibop soon came back with a truck and driver he'd hired for 20 kina (equivalent then to about US $8) to carry us and my gear down to the beach. There we engaged another truck to pick up the supplies we'd left at Garamut Cash and Carry and bring them to the boat. Meanwhile, Kilibop went off in the first truck to fill the boat's petrol tank and spare containers (for about 160 kina, or US $65) and get a container of kerosene for my lamp. When everything was finally heaped on the sand, Kilibop and Joe Boko carefully loaded it in the boat and secured it under a sheet of blue plastic.

Klarok and Munuo were at the beach again. They were trying to decide whether to stay in Wewak with Moses and wait for news from Moresby or to head back to Kragur. In any case, our boat couldn't accommodate them. My cargo—Kilibop, Joe Boko, the petrol tank, the spare petrol cans, and I—left no space for other passengers, and Joe had only a fifteen-horsepower motor. Kilibop explained that it took about an hour to travel from Wewak to Kragur with a full load and a forty-horsepower motor, about an hour and a half with a twenty-five-horsepower motor, and about two hours with a fifteen-horsepower. I usually seem to draw a fifteen-horse engine.

When all was ready, I got in the boat and found a comfortable seat on a corner of the cargo heap, and Kilibop and Joe Boko pushed the boat out into water deep enough to drop the propeller. Circling the point on a smooth and shining sea, cooled by the spray thrown off by the boat's prow, and seeing Kairiru rising ahead of us, just beyond Mushu, I quit worrying about the purpose of my venture, at least for the moment, and noticed the sheer beauty of the day. I took pictures of Joe at the tiller and Kilibop, relaxing with a smoke, his back against the gunwales, and then I fell asleep (fig. 5). Dozing, I missed the view of Mushu's white beaches as we passed to the east side of that island and even the usually bumpy passage around the rocks at Kairiru's Point Urur. I woke up only as we were running alongside the steep north coast of the island, nearing Kragur.

We passed the rocky beach at the base of the cliffs, near the center of the village, proceeding to where the shore slopes sharply down to the water at the place called Minamisil, at Kragur's western end. Here, we turned toward shore and a tiny sandy beach. Later, villagers told me that the earthquake of 2002 had created this pleasant spot where before there had been only the usual rocks, although elsewhere it had tumbled great chunks of earth and trees to the shore, which I would have seen had I stayed awake. We reached this patch of sand by catching a gentle swell and slipping over and through a cluster of coral heads. I knew a burial was taking place that day, so I didn't expect a

Figure 5. Stephen Kilibop Umari relaxing on the trip
from Wewak to Kragur, 2008 (Wewak Point is in the
background). Photo by the author.

formal community greeting. (I say burial rather than funeral, because the full
observation of a death in Kragur goes on for several days.) But Munbos and
her daughters and grandchildren had organized a greeting party, and as we
approached I could see them waiting, with an arch of split palm fronds for me
to walk under and wreaths of local orchids. As I stepped ashore, Munbos' oldest daughter Kaiwop led a group of women and children in performing a
welcome song she had composed, and Munbos draped the orchids around my
neck and presented me with a green coconut to drink and a plate of papaya
slices. This refreshment was very welcome. It feels cool on the water, but only
because, at outboard motor speeds, your sweat is drying as fast as it pours out.
Fortunately, it was not an occasion for speeches, and after I honored the proceedings with a few photos, members of the greeting party unloaded the boat
and we made our way to the opposite end of village on secondary paths that
avoided the burial service.

Many weeks before leaving the United States, I'd received a letter from Klarok, one of those with whom I'd corresponded about my plans, saying that a place for me to stay in Kargur had been arranged. Closer to my departure, Kirar had telephoned me from, as he said, "on the mountain." The connection was bad and I wasn't sure that I'd heard him correctly, but I learned from Ralph during my stopover in Moresby that a number of people in Kragur now used mobile phones with prepaid minutes purchased in town. Ralph explained that you can't get a signal on the seaward side of the island, and sometimes it's even difficult from sea level on the side facing Wewak. Making a call from Kairiru often required hiking to the top of the mountain and, sometimes, casting around in the forest for a hot spot. (At least the Kairiru mountain hot spots were free. I've heard of places in rural PNG where people have to pay as much as 5 kina to the landowners just to attempt calls from favorable locations.) Kirar, calling from somewhere on the mountain, had assured me that I was expected and a place for me to stay had been arranged.

I had my own house when I did my dissertation research in Kragur, and I used the same house again in 1981. Since then, however, that house had lived out its natural life and been torn down and I'd lodged in various places when I visited. In 1995 I stayed in a house belonging to Brother Herman Boyek. Herman, a Marist Brother, keeps a house in Kragur, looked after by his family there, but he has spent most of his adult life teaching in Catholic schools in PNG and both teaching and studying abroad. In 1998 I stayed in a small house belonging to Klarok, built to accommodate his younger brother, a teacher, when he was at home. In 2008 I stayed in the home of Kilibop's brother, Patrick Rokerai Umari (Rokerai), and Kilibop's and Rokerai's mother, Munbos (fig. 6). Rokerai had cleared the land between his house and the cliff for gardening in recent years. Now, it was thickly overgrown again, but without mature trees, so there was an unimpaired view of the ocean from the narrow veranda that stretched across most of the front of the house. Multitudes of flowers bloomed in the top layer of the tangle of foliage between the house and the cliff, attracting such a variety of butterflies that I immediately wished I'd brought a guidebook with me. Large ones with stark black-and-white-patterned wings stood out, but the real stars were the iridescent blues, which glowed electrically, whether in sun or shade. These amazing floating creatures aren't novelties to villagers, but I attracted attention at more than one open-air public gathering by swiveling my head this way and that trying to follow the bobbing flight of a particularly fine specimen over and around the heads of the assembled women and men.

Rokerai's house was relatively close to the men's bathing place, so I could easily saunter there wearing my beach towel and return without working up

Figure 6. Patrick Rokerai Umari pounding taro in the
main room of his house, 2008. Photo by the author.

much of a sweat again. The house also stood at a corner of the village, so there
was room to build a pristine new outhouse for me at the edge of the bush,
only some thirty yards away. Kragur outhouses that many people have used
for very long can get rather rank, so I was pleased to see this shiny new structure (fig. 7).

Like nearly all other Kragur houses, Rokerai's was set several feet above the
ground atop thick posts. This keeps houses above the water that rushes down
the slope and over the village terraces during rains, and it aids in ventilation.
Kairiru houses never have the musty smell of fully enclosed, Western-style
buildings in the tropics. Setting houses up on posts also allows people to build
level structures on uneven ground. While this aspect of Kragur building has
remained the same in the years I've been visiting there, villagers have been
gradually changing some other features of their houses. The walls of a lot of
houses in the 1970s were made of slabs of bark fitted in overlapping horizontal

Figure 7. My own private outhouse, 2008. Photo by
the author.

rows, like shingles. But by 2008 villagers were fashioning the walls of new
houses from the light but strong stalks of sago palm fronds. The horseshoe
curve along the length of these allows builders to fit them together like spoons,
in snug vertical rows. Also, as the years pass, the newer the house the more
the more likely it is to be divided into more than one room inside and the more
windows it's likely to have. The general trend seems to be toward more privacy
within and more openness to the outside.

Widely spaced log stairs ran from the ground up the front of Rokerai's
house to the veranda, amended on the outer edge by a rather rickety banister
of thin poles. At the top of the stairs, a door on the right led into the large main
room, where Munbos cooked over an open fire on a raised, rectangular clay
hearth. Metal pots and pans, carved wooden plates, and other cooking gear
were stored on a shelf along the back wall, and clothes, tools, and two finely
carved hourglass drums (in Tok Pisin, *kundu*) with heads made from the skins
of Kairiru monitor lizards hung from the walls and rafters. The main room

also boasted an unusual feature: an electric light. This was the fruit of Kilibop's inventiveness. He had discovered that the flashlight batteries people discarded still had a little juice in them, and if you combined enough of them you could light a flashlight bulb. He had built a narrow wooden box that held two long rows of discarded batteries wired to a bulb and affixed the bulb to the wall in front of an angled sheet of white paper, which combination produced a soft, white glow until the batteries finally gave their last gasp.

There was room for several people to sleep on the floor in the main room. A couple of aging foam mattresses and some worn sheets and blankets were rolled up and stored during the day along the front wall, although many Kragur people sleep only on a woven mat or a sheet of cardboard or old linoleum that smoothes out the bumps in the bamboo flooring. Munbos preferred to sleep on a pile of old clothes beside the hearth, to warm at the embers her work-sore limbs and the ache of a badly mended broken leg and to be ready to tend the fire. Two or three steps down the veranda from the main room, a second door led into what was usually Rokerai's room, which he had given up to me. This was bare except for the bed—a thin foam mattress over plywood on a metal frame—a small wooden table, and some items stored in the rafters.

A sago leafstalk wall separated the two rooms of Rokerai's house, but it didn't reach beyond the point where the peaked roof met the walls. The triangular opening this left occasioned the only serious discomfort of living there: the drifting smoke from the open fire. Breathing smoke from open fires night and day contributes to respiratory problems everywhere in the world that it is part of daily life. In Kragur, however, open fires probably contribute less to chronic health problems than the fact that large numbers of adult villagers smoke strong, homegrown tobacco (called *brus* in Tok Pisin) almost constantly.[9] The amount of smoke they sometimes inhale from the long cigarettes (also called *brus* in Tok Pisin) that they roll in newspaper—which long ago replaced banana leaves as a tobacco wrapper—has always astounded me. On one occasion, when I was sitting with a sturdy middle-aged friend while he explained to me a fine point of village politics, he paused to take a deep drag from his cigarette. As he took up his story again, for close to thirty seconds (I timed it on my wristwatch), clouds of smoke, which he seemed not to notice, gushed from his nose and mouth. If you are a smoker, try this and you will see it isn't easy.

I smoked as much as a pack of cigarettes a week during some anxious periods in my life in the 1970s and 1980s. These included my first and longest stay in Kragur, when at times I worried so much about failing as an anthropologist that I would have smoked, swallowed, or rubbed in my hair almost anything that would have taken the edge off my anxiety for a little while. Curiosity as well as the desire to alter my consciousness also got me started chewing betel nut, leaving bright red stains on my teeth that badly startled the first dental hygienist I saw when I returned to the United States. I kept away from betel nut on most of my subsequent, shorter visits to Kragur, and I don't smoke anymore at home. However, except for the fact that it is poisonous, I like tobacco, and in 2008 I decided to allow myself one local cigarette a day to make up for the absence of beer and Scotch whiskey.

Sharing, rolling, and smoking the local tobacco also makes me feel more part of the group in Kragur, and I admit I am proud of my facility in drying the tobacco leaf over a glowing ember until it is crisp, crumbling it in the palm of my hand, tearing a neat rectangle of newspaper, and rolling a firm but not too tight six-inch cylinder. If I inhaled shallowly, I could enjoy the flavor and the lift of the pure tobacco without inducing mild asphyxia and a fit of bone-rattling coughing. The coughing that the drifting smoke from the open fire sometimes caused me was less acute than that from carelessly inhaled tobacco, except for one incident in which damp wood raised a thick smudge that emptied both rooms of the house in a tumble of women, men, and children.

The table in my room was much too small to serve as a work space, and the room, admitting light only through the door and the window above the bed, was too dark anyway. Within a few days of my arrival, Kilibop produced a sheet of window glass he'd acquired somewhere that was perfect for a table top. Like many Kragur men, Kilibop can do a lot of solid carpentry with eyeball measurement and very few tools. He proceeded, with help from the teenage boys who often gathered to watch him work, to make me a very fine table in a few hours. With axe and bush knife, he hewed boards for the frame from small raw timbers, and when the frame was assembled, he installed the glass top and called on me to help adjust the table's height. Rokerai produced an old metal desk chair and I sat at the table, tried writing in my notebook, and then advised Kilibop on how many inches to trim from the legs. Two rounds of this sufficed to reach the perfect height.

Despite the uneven veranda floor and the makeshift measurement, the desktop turned out dead level according to the pencil-rolling test. Its only deficiency was that the glass top wasn't absorbent, so I had to put a sock under my forearm when I wrote to keep a pool of sweat from accumulating. I also often had to hold my pen without resting my hand on the page to keep from soaking with perspiration the paper on which I was about to write.

Nonetheless, the table provided a near-perfect work place for me, except for the fact that it abutted the household chickens' preferred route along the veranda railing to their nighttime perch under the western eaves of the house. A mix of white and dark but colorful birds, they spent most of their days foraging beneath the house for food scraps fallen between the slats of the floor, coconut gratings thrown there for their special benefit, and various insects. Strutting

Figure 8. The Egg Layer Folding Lounger with Flour Sack Pillow on Rokerai's veranda, 2008. Photo by the author.

along the veranda railing, silhouetted by the sea in the distance, they were very decorative. Once my table was installed, however, they found it convenient to use it as a shortcut to their perch, whether I was working there or not, and swats from my notebook seemed to give them little offense and make no lasting impression.

Kilibop had also salvaged from somewhere the metal frame of a folding beach chair, and he sewed a hammock-like seat for it from an "Egg Layer" chicken-feed bag and fashioned a plump pillow from a small flour sack. Worthy of an Ikea catalog, the Egg Layer Folding Lounger with Flour Sack Pillow was comfortable portable seating for attending and dozing off at outdoor charismatic prayer meetings on cool Wednesday evenings (fig. 8). Despite the joyful

noise raised to the Lord in song and shouts of praise at these events, the cool
night air and the deep shadows at the edge of the lamp-lit congregation, where
I usually sat, often lulled me to sleep, to be gently awakened by the handshakes
of fellowship with which the gatherings ended.

Despite Rokerai's veranda being open to breezes from land and sea, I sometimes still found it unpleasantly hot during the middle of the day. I often
napped during the hottest early afternoon hour or so, stretched out the width
of the veranda, comfortably aligned with the length of the bamboo, my feet
resting on the heavy timber at the veranda's front edge, my head on the Flour
Sack Pillow, and the bamboo screen that hung from the railing rolled up to
make way for stray zephyrs. But on still days, I sometimes woke up feeling like
someone had thrown a hot towel over my face while I slept. Nevertheless,
whether I was sitting at the table, napping, or sitting cross-legged on the floor,
Rokerai's veranda became my home in Kragur. Rokerai and Munbos allowed
me to make this major part of their living space relatively public. They understood that I wanted to be open to visitors from any part of the village and
sometimes from neighboring villages, and they even told people not to be shy
about coming up the stairs to see me.

Lodging with Rokerai and Munbos included a full range of services. Various young people made sure my two-gallon plastic jug was kept filled with
fresh water from the stream. Younger women of the extended family washed
my clothes in the stream and hung them on a line across the front of the veranda to dry, eventually, as the sun and rain came and went. Washing clothes
in the stream entails spreading them on smooth rocks, soaping them heavily—
if one can afford soap—scrubbing them vigorously, and rinsing them repeatedly in the clear water rushing around one's legs. This method is tough on
fabric, but it gets things clean. It is also a task of which I was very glad to be
relieved. Munbos also cooked large meals morning and evening, and she,
Rokerai, and Kilibop sometimes made coffee for my visitors and served it in
their disparate collection of mugs, often with a plate of navy biscuits or sliced
pineapple. Apparently no one in Kragur expects more than a single spoonful
of coffee powder in his or her mug, but my hosts knew that I liked two spoon-
fuls and they were always careful, when passing around the refreshments, to
see that I got the double-strength mug. In short, they did everything they
could to make my life comfortable.

I didn't do any physical labor for the household, but—as in my previous
stays in the village—I contributed in other ways, mostly by sharing the food
and other items I brought from Wewak. In fact, I prefer Kragur's taro, greens,
fresh fish, and other local food to white rice and canned mackerel, and I
planned on eating locally as much as possible and letting my hosts use the
bags of rice and cartons of canned fish as they pleased. This included contrib-

uting some of it to communal events that took place during my stay, such as feeding the mourners at a funeral gathering, as well as giving a lot of it to neighbors and members of the household's large extended family.

I did my best to be a considerate guest, although it was impossible to avoid disturbing the slumbers of other occupants of the house at times by my habit of talking at length in my sleep, often in a mixture of Tok Pisin and Kairiru. According to my Kragur housemates' reports, my knowledge of Kairiru is greater when I'm asleep than when I'm awake. Once in a long while I also throw myself out of bed, waking up to the feeling of my face crushed against the floor. I did this on only one occasion while in Kragur in 2008. The crash alarmed everyone in the household, but the flexible bamboo flooring proved a wonderfully forgiving landing place.

I had hoped to bring enough supplies with me from Wewak to last for my whole stay. But before May was over, it was clear I had underestimated how much of several items we were going to use—in particular, coffee and biscuits. Kilibop was able to get on a boat with other travelers to Wewak and bring back another smaller load of goods, and with careful husbandry this saw us through. By my last two weeks, however, I was stinting on hospitality for my visitors so I could feed my own coffee habit at my accustomed level in the privacy of the family.

I am probably fonder of privacy than most people, but I quickly grew pleasantly accustomed to the company and conversation of meals at Rokerai's house and to drifting off to sleep at night to the murmur of voices and the flickering firelight in the next room. That part of my life was routine and low-key. Other parts of my life, however, were not; like the heat, they sometimes made exiting without fanfare, if that had been possible, look appealing.

I sometimes grew weary of being treated as someone of special importance. I might not mind being famous, but I would prefer to be famous in part for staying out of the limelight. However, long-term visitors from distant lands are very much a novelty in Kragur, and American visitors are probably especially scarce. Most of the few Americans resident in PNG (only around two thousand in 2010, according to the US Department of State) are missionaries or members of missionary families, so a secular and skeptical American like me might be the very rarest kind of visitor.[10] Many villagers have also pointed out to me that it is a great novelty for a white person to mingle casually with them as I do, bathing in the stream, meeting and chatting with them on the mountain trail, sharing tobacco and betel nut (I don't chew anymore myself, but friends often give me betel to have on hand to share with others), eating the local food with them, and occasionally dozing on someone's veranda after a heavy meal. I hope villagers understand that I regard this as a privilege rather than a show of condescension; still, from their point of view, it's different.

Only a small part of my local notoriety, I think, is in recognition of my writings on Kragur, but this is changing. Many villagers didn't really understand what I was up to during my first stay there in the 1970s; but when I finally worked my way past my doctoral dissertation to a real book with a snappy cover, nice typography, and some photos and sent numerous copies back to Kragur, many villagers got to see the results of my many months of pestering them, even if in those days only a few of them could read the book. Years later, after several more visits to Kragur, copies of my second book arrived. This time, a lot more of the villagers who received copies could read it. So far, it looks like nothing I wrote in that book offended anyone egregiously or was seriously mistaken. A few people even told me that it was interesting and useful.

But Kragur has nothing like a library where copies of my books could be available to everyone. Some of the copies I've sent have passed from hand to hand; but it's still news to some villagers that they exist. And even some literate villagers who have heard of the books but not seen them aren't sure just what they are. I've been asked, for example, if the books are just for white people. I've been glad to be able to answer that they have been used as texts in some high schools and universities in PNG. They are, however, written in English that goes well beyond basic, which closes them to many villagers, although the general level of Kragur literacy is catching up fast.[11]

When I came back in 2008, I met many young people who could only vaguely remember my last visit. A few of these did know me as the author of books about Kragur. But many were impressed that I, a foreigner, could tell stories about their parents and grandparents and speak knowledgeably about local history and customs of which other visitors know nothing. My knowledge of a few key things about Kragur often distracts villagers from my profound ignorance about so much else. Still, a few men have honored me by calling me a *kokwal*, a term I'll have more to say about later, but which in some contexts means roughly a knowledgeable senior man.

In 2008, after worrying that Kragur people might be entirely indifferent to my visit or perhaps even find it an annoyance, I often found myself more an honored guest than I was used to. This included being asked to recount in public, for the benefit of those too young to remember the event, how and why I first came to Kragur. Kragur people are generally very good storytellers, packing their narrations of even mundane events with vivid details and dramatic action. Many Kragur men are also skillful and energetic orators (it is still unusual for women to speak at any length in public gatherings). Unfortunately, my public speaking and storytelling skills are, let's say, undependable. Many times as I recounted my first arrival in Kragur, I knew I was making pretty dull what is really a very good story, full of opportunities to drop the names of revered local people and both familiar and faraway places, flaunt some of my modest stock of local knowledge, marvel at the vagaries of chance, and give my wanderings in search of a research site a mythic flavor—most of which opportunities I chronically missed.

My limited capacity for eating, one after the other, plates of the best and biggest portions of special foods also suited me ill for local celebrity. The Sunday on which several families invited me to help celebrate their children's first Holy Communions, I had to beg off finishing several plates of taro prepared by pounding it with cooked bananas to a smooth pulp and rolling portions of it in grated coconut. Even so, I reached the evening feeling like I was about to give birth. Refusing food in Kragur can be a delicate matter, and I did so entirely on only two or three occasions when my body truly cried out against eating anything. Gifts of food, however, still had to be acknowledged, so on one of these occasions I was invited to come and simply view the plates of food laid out for me. On another occasion, when I was feeling quite ill, my disappointed hosts brought plates of food to Rokerai's house for me to see before I went back to my bed. The food, of course, doesn't go to waste, for there are always plenty of children and other family members to take up the slack.

I also fear that I tended to disappoint when villagers asked me for advice on how they could develop local businesses. Although I was happy to discuss with all comers ideas for improving village life, I could offer only very limited advice on how Kragur villagers could become more prosperous. Since I am much wealthier than any Kragur villager, some still assume that I must know things about how to make money that I am not divulging. Unfortunately, the thing I know best is that my own comparative prosperity depends much less on my personal wisdom and skills than it does on having been born in a prosperous society, with established commercial and legal systems, comparatively decent public education, and a variety of other functioning public services. I know some basic things about planning and running a small business, and I passed these on to anyone serious about such a venture. I hated the accounting course I once took, but I learned enough from it to offer sage counsel on the absolute necessity of understanding the true costs of your enterprise. And I'd learned from watching former employers about the dangers of getting too deep into developing a product before finding out if anyone wants to buy it. A lot of what I could advise, however, was irrelevant for people who didn't have a reliable way to take products to any but extremely local customers or bring customers to them, and most villagers knew this already.

In the 1970s, a lot of older villagers thought that getting money might be something like growing healthy taro gardens; that is, you had to put in a lot of physical labor, but the special ingredient that made it all come together was magic. In 2008, even some of the most sophisticated younger villagers also believed that to do a lot of important things right, you needed the right kind of magic. Almost everyone, however, realized that when it came to making money, one thing Kragur people really needed was less expensive transportation to the mainland or some way to bring buyers for goods to the island. I was not much help, then, as a development worker. But I did find myself doing a lot more work of other kinds than I had anticipated as a result of circumstances that deserve their own short chapter.

Chapter 4

Wu Wei Wu

Practice not-doing, and everything will fall into place.
—Lao-tzu

Feeling unequal to people's expectations, being too hot, and coping with too much celebrity occasionally made me want to pack my bags and steal away. But if I just wanted to be alone for a while in a cooler place, I could go down to the shore below the main part of the village. There was always a breeze here, and the sound of the waves on the tumbled boulders, the weathered chunks of coral, and the smooth driftwood logs drowned any sounds from the village. Trying, always fruitlessly, to sneak up on the tiny mudskippers darting from rock to spray-washed rock was also a sure distraction. Moments of uncertainty about what I wanted from this trip, however, were harder to escape.

The idea had started out simple. I wanted to see people and places I had grown fond of while I still had the necessary stamina and before the people died or the places became unrecognizable. I wasn't the only one who had this in mind. At least some Kragur people had repeatedly invited me to come see them again. Klarok, for example, had written to me in 2007, saying, "Old Sareo isn't very strong, so I'd like you to come and get some Kragur stories [that is, accounts of local history and what, in English, many would call myths] from him before he dies." I also wanted to see Kairiru again before, in my worst night-mares, gold mining permanently disfigured the island. (There is gold on Kairiru, but so far it has been deemed too costly to extract.) I think, however, that I also wanted to find out if I really cared about Kragur and Kairiru any-more, or if it had just been preying on my mind because I was so heartily sick of the shackles of the computer keyboard, the lash of the timesheet, and the slow death of spending my days separated from the outside world by sealed windows. If I didn't really care, I would at least have a good story to tell, and I would be saved any more trips to PNG.

I intended to keep a journal, of course, and I had a mental list not only of people and places I wanted to see and things I wanted to do but also of things about which I was especially curious. These included both things in Kragur life that had always seemed relatively fixed and unchangeable and things that had seemed to be changing particularly fast when I'd seen Kragur last. It was primarily my personal ties to Kragur, however, that moved me to make this trip. Beyond pursuing those, I expected to let events set most of my agenda. Although I probably should have, I did not consciously anticipate that once in Kragur I would quickly find myself caught up in complicated interwoven circumstances, which would reveal a lot about how Kragur was weathering its continuing voyage in the modern world and would also test my diplomatic skills.

Formal anthropological research requires gathering information systematically, through asking selected people carefully considered questions and making methodical observations of people's behavior, the way a natural scientist takes systematic samples of, for example, air, soil, or DNA. But one reason anthropologists typically live among the people they are trying to understand rather than dropping in on Wednesdays and Thursdays or sending them questionnaires in the mail—if they happen to have mail service—is that serious anthropological work also requires being around when things happen that you couldn't anticipate and being alert to what they can teach you. Ted Schwartz once told me about one of the most dramatic instances of this I've heard of among anthropologists in PNG, an incident he also recorded in a monograph published in 1962 by the American Museum of Natural History.

In 1953–1954, Ted and his wife at the time, Lenora, were working with Margaret Mead in what is now Manus Province, living among the Manus people Mead had first studied in the 1920s with her husband, British anthropologist Reo Fortune. Among their interests was piecing together the story of what anthropologists still commonly call a "cargo cult" that had been flourishing several years before in the area in which they were living. The story they finally put together from accounts after the fact was long and complicated, but at the core of the events they described was intense ritual activity intended to bring about a wholesale, supernatural transformation of the local society. Among the features of the new society would be easy access to large quantities of European goods—that is, the kind of goods that Europeans in Manus regularly received, with little or no apparent physical effort on their part, on cargo ships. What Ted and his colleagues didn't at first realize was that for some eight months, while they pursued their research on past events, another similarly dramatic event was taking place but concealed from them. The Australian administration had strongly opposed such activities in the 1940s, so, although hospitable in every other way, the Manus people involved in the rituals of the 1950s thought it best to keep their activities secret from Mead, Ted, and Lenora.

They finally began to discover what was going on when a young man un-guardedly asked Lenora if she had heard the whistles the previous night. She had not, but she said yes anyway. The young man, assuming she was in on the secret, then continued to talk freely about the ritual activities, which included interacting with spirits of the dead that communicated in whistles. As Ted later wrote, the people "had freely given us information on kinship, land ten-ure, language, and ideas on child rearing, and later even on the earlier cult episode. But they had withheld, until we seemed already to know of it, that which moved and excited them, that which had given promise and intensity to their lives during the time that we knew them."[1]

I haven't had similar revelatory experiences in Kragur. Maybe I've been privileged to see and hear about most of the things of major importance going on around me there, maybe there are dramatic revelations still to come, or maybe I will go to my grave ignorant of absolutely fundamental things about Kragur that villagers have kept from me, assumed I already knew, or simply thought I wouldn't find interesting. In the 1970s, I did learn without much fanfare that earlier in the decade, some of the people of Kragur had been in-volved in what could be called a cargo cult. That is, they were petitioning the spirits of their dead as well as, in some cases, the Virgin Mary, to send them money. Some hoped that the money would appear on top of the graves of their dead in the European-style cemetery near the small thatched church that stood at the eastern end of the village in those days. I first heard about this from villagers who had not participated in these rituals and who didn't mind embar-rassing those who had, most of whom were happy to forget about the episode. But, armed with a little knowledge of those events, I was able to engage some of the former participants in conversation, including a few who still thought that they had been on to something and might have succeeded if they only could have worked out some of the kinks in their methods.[2]

I would have learned less about such things, I think, if I had arrived in Kragur determined to root out any instances of money-procuring rituals, past or present, asking pointed questions on all sides. To some extent, in doing an-thropological research you have to practice what my Tai Chi instructor tried to train into the stiff limbs of his students: the art of wu wei wu—that is, "doing without doing." While I never perfected the wu wei wu of Tai Chi, in 2008 I couldn't avoid doing some of the anthropological work of unplanned discovery in Kragur. For instance, a couple of weeks after arriving I learned something extremely interesting about the symbolic meaning of left and right in Kragur simply by hiking on the mountain and getting a nasty bacterial infection.

Because my legs are not the powerful engines they once were and my feet not as sure, I brought with me to Kragur a pair of trekking poles. I highly recommend trekking poles to anyone who has ever felt a twinge of fear when

a foot slipped on a steep incline above a deep ravine or who has somehow
climbed to a spot where going back down looks as impossible as continuing
ahead. Of course, if you can't get poles, cut yourself a couple of sticks. My
high-tech poles (with contoured grips and "four-season, glove-friendly dual
FlickLocks") made me almost as stable and sure-footed, if not nearly as swift,
as I had ever been over the rocks and roots and mud. I quickly became very
fond of my poles and decided to name them. Many of the material things
Kragur people make and use have personal names, not only objects of political
or religious significance, like the carved wooden figures used in magical procedures, but also utilitarian objects, like wooden plates or taro pounders. I
decided to name the left-hand pole Harry, after my maternal grandfather, and
the right-hand pole George, after my paternal great-great grandfather. (I
skipped over my paternal grandfather and great grandfather because George
paired nicely with Harry as references to English kings. Also, I thought George
sounded more robust than either Earle, my paternal grandfather's name, or
Pinkney, Earle's father's name.) Harry and George, I told Kilibop, strengthened me, the way my maternal and paternal ancestors strengthened me. He
nodded in approval at the left- and right-hand poles in turn, saying, "Side of
the woman, side of the man."

It only flitted across my mind at the time—we were on our way to Iupulpul
and I was breathing hard and sweating harder—that Kilibop was referring to
a more general principal and not just to my choosing to honor both sides of
my family. The spatial arrangement of things has important symbolic mean-
ings in many societies, but this was only one of myriad topics to which I had
never paid much attention in Kragur. A few days later, however, it smacked
me in the face that Kilibop must have been referring to left and right as sym-
bolically female and male, respectively.

Practically overnight, insect bites on my leg and arm had turned into wet,
open sores, even though at the first sign of infection I had begun treating
them with antibiotic ointment. I washed, anointed, and bandaged them twice
a day for several days, but the sores kept getting bigger and uglier, and rough
circles of smaller sores seemed to be erupting around the originals. I finally
took a course of oral antibiotic, which started to dry them up overnight. Prior
to that, as I sat on the floor of the veranda late one afternoon, dressing my
garden of sores after a bath, one of my companions noticed that all the sores
were on the left side of my body. "Your wife must be worried about you," he
added. A rusty switch in my brain finally moved and suddenly anthropological
work had happened, or had at least begun. I didn't plumb this topic to my
complete satisfaction. People's answers to the few additional questions I asked
about male, female, and the spatial arrangement of the Kragur world did,
however, suggest that villagers are most likely to invoke the association of left

and right with female and male respectively when looking for a social cause—a disturbance in the patient's social relationships—for an illness or injury.

Further education in some other dimensions of Kragur life also pressed itself on me. I am fortunate that Kragur people who know my books, either at first or second hand, generally have been pleased that I wrote about Kragur and pleased with what I've written about it. When I visited Kragur in 1998, my first extended visit there since writing *Hard Times on Kairiru Island*, a lot of people assumed that what I saw and heard would go into another book, and some wanted to be sure that their points of view would be represented. *Village on the Edge* came out a few years later, so in 2008 a lot of people assumed that my visit was the prelude to a third book. The day after my arrival, as Kilibop and I sat chatting on the veranda of the guesthouse, we fell into conversation about the state of Kragur village leadership, and Kilibop offered his analysis of current issues. He concluded with very specific suggestions for what I should say about this subject in "the new book." (I took notes on what he had to say, but I reminded him that should there be a new book, I would present different points of view on contentious village issues, but, as in the previous books, I would not take sides.)

Not everyone was eager to be included in a new book. During one conversation on Rokerai's veranda, a Kragur man whom I did not know well suddenly broke off his account of a bit of local history, saying that perhaps this was something I shouldn't hear. Another of my visitors that day, however, reassured his companion that he could trust my judgment about what to write for the eyes of the world: "You go ahead and talk," he said. "Smith knows how to be discreet." That appeared to reassure him, and he went on with his story.

Most of my friends and acquaintances were less circumspect, and some even sought me out to make sure that any new book would get the facts straight as they saw them. Also, somewhat to my surprise, questions I had asked ten years before sparked a large part of the education pressed on me in 2008. Far from spending my days enjoying tropical beauty and vigorous outdoor life while reviving old friendships, I ended up part of a rather intense effort to record critical aspects of local history. This would not only demand of me considerable effort, it would pull me closer to the heated political contest then going on in Kragur and events that threw into sharp relief some of the dilemmas of being modern that Kragur people were facing.

Chapter 5

Is Kragur Poor?

At the outset it is but well to attend to a matter
almost indispensable to a thorough appreciative
understanding of the more special . . . revelations
and allusions of all sorts which are to follow.
—Herman Melville, *Moby Dick*

At this point, to help me tell my story, I need to consider a question that might at first seem simple: Is Kragur poor? Kragur villagers go barefoot, they cook over open fires, they have no indoor plumbing, and they eat mostly what they can grow, hunt, or gather themselves. Since we already know that Kragur is not an exclusive retreat for international elites seeking a restorative back-to-nature experience, this must be poverty. Although villagers bathe frequently in the stream, many make do without soap or towels. Most households have at least one kerosene lantern, but only the glow of a fire lights many houses at night, because its occupants can't afford kerosene. Store-bought items that bring joy to my daily life there, like coffee, are luxuries for most villagers.

A stroll through Kragur, however, leaves one with more mixed impressions of the material richness of the people's lives. A few houses list hard to one side because their support posts are weakening, rotting in the ground, and I've put a foot though more than one deteriorating patch of floor. Most houses, however, are in good repair, and the inventive uses of forest materials, the care given to fine points of construction (the fit of a hand-hewn beam or a window casement, the trim edge of the roof thatch, a cleverly fitted storage rack or shelf), and the structures' clean lines make newer houses handsome and inviting. The people are lean, but the children are bright eyed and lively, and adults in their prime stand straight and move with vigor. The pigs roaming free root muddy craters among the stony outcroppings of the village grounds and leave their excrement under foot, but they are fat and fertile, producing gaggles of scurrying shoats. Saying simply that Kragur villagers are poor leaves out a lot of important details.

Describing poverty in PNG as a whole also requires some nuance. In some situations, it's better not to use the word "poverty" at all. I was in a meeting of

World Bank representatives and PNG government officials in 1995 when one member of the bank's team referred to poverty in PNG. The government official interjected angrily that there wasn't any poverty in PNG because people could feed themselves from their own land and that PNG wasn't "like Africa" because "people aren't starving."

Some PNG politicians still react this way to foreign talk of PNG poverty. A tenacious reporter for the Al Jazeera English television network interviewed Sir Michael Somare, the most renowned figure in the nation's political history, in September 2009. In the course of her questioning, the reporter stated that there was "80 percent unemployment" in PNG and that "a majority of the population [are] living in poverty." Somare shot back that the majority of the people lived in rural areas and that they "always have their land." Further, he said, "In many other places they starve, they die in the streets. Papua New Guineans don't die in the streets." Not dying in the streets is a pretty low bar, but PNG's leaders also address the question of the country's poverty in a more affirmative way. For example, the PNG government ran a several-page advertisement for business opportunities in PNG in the *New York Times Magazine* in 2007. The advertisement acknowledged with little qualification that "according to the United Nations . . . [PNG] is . . . one of the poorest countries in the world," but it emphasized that the country had great potential because it was "blessed with a rich abundance of natural resources" and a stable government.[1]

Some academic experts also object to statements about poverty in PNG that overlook what is distinctively hopeful about the country.[2] There is no doubt, though, that the general welfare of PNG's people leaves a lot to be desired. The United Nations Development Program (UNDP) computes what it calls a Human Development Index (HDI) for the countries of the world. The index for each country is based on average life expectancy, adult literacy and enrollment in schools, and national income per capita. The UNDP Human Development Report for 2009 ranked PNG 148th out of 182 countries, just above Haiti and several countries of sub-Saharan Africa. (Norway ranked first, and the United States came in thirteenth.) Contributing to Papua New Guinea's low ranking was an average life expectancy at birth of around sixty-one years (135th place), an adult literacy rate of about 58 percent for people fifteen years old and older (129th place), a ranking of 167th for school enrollment, and a ranking of 138th in national income per capita.[3]

This is not good, but the HDI doesn't address access to land, starving in the streets, or simply getting enough to eat. It *is* true that most people have access to land and grow most of their own food. According to the 2001 edition of the *Papua New Guinea Rural Development Handbook*, published by the Australian National University, about 85 percent of the country's people live in rural areas, on their own land, and they get about 80 percent of their calories from locally grown food. Most land—about 97 percent of all land in the country—is held under what is called "customary title."⁴ This means that the basic principles governing access to most land in PNG today are very much what they were before European contact. I say basic principles rather than rules because people are quick to work within general principles to create specific ways of allocating land adapted to changing circumstances. In general, however, customary systems effectively guarantee some kind of access to land to everyone. As anthropologist Alex Golub has commented, it would have been beyond the means of the small Australian administration that governed PNG for most of the colonial epoch to meddle much with local land systems, but it was also wise not to do so. Colonial powers also took very little land out of the hands of indigenous people, in sharp contrast to the practices of colonial powers in many other parts of the world.

Customary title is protected by PNG law, but the government does not routinely demarcate land or issue written titles. Before and since national independence, there have been many proposals for and experiments with introducing more formal systems for demarcating and documenting land rights, but the issue is extremely complicated and sensitive. Some government-overseen avenues for formalizing land rights are available, but they remain voluntary.⁵

Unfortunately, simply having access to land and growing most of their food doesn't guarantee that PNG's people all have enough to eat. Studies in the late 1990s showed that in both rural and urban areas, "average calorie availability" stood at around 2,660 calories per person per day. This is a healthy amount, even for people living physically active lives, but the research also showed that not everyone in PNG was getting a full share. About 42 percent of the population got less than the 2,000 calories a day considered the "target requirement."⁶ Also, urban people consumed about 50 percent more cereals, fats and oils, and meats than rural people, in large part because they had higher cash incomes. This difference between urban and rural diets is one reason that urban PNG is considerably plumper than village PNG. Many high government officials and successful businesspeople even sport impressive paunches and correspondingly ponderous gaits. The studies showed, however, that the more varied urban diets also contributed to the fact that children in urban areas were much less likely than those in rural areas to suffer from stunting (low height-for-age ratios). In fact, according to the same studies, about 40 percent of rural children suffered from stunting.⁷

The general physical well-being of urban and rural people in PNG contrasts in a number of ways, but there are also significant differences in people's circumstances within the country's majority rural population. Politically, PNG is divided into nineteen provinces, and each province is divided into several districts. The *Rural Development Handbook* indicates that the people of Kairiru and neighboring Mushu are only "marginally disadvantaged" in comparison with the rest of rural PNG in terms of agricultural resources, population density, access to services, incomes, and child malnutrition. Among the particular disadvantages they suffer, lack of income stands out, with "very low" annual average incomes per person of from zero to 20 kina. The *Handbook*'s index of disadvantage considers incomes per person per year of greater than 200 kina "very high."[8] (In 2000, 200 kina equaled less than US $100.) Remember that we're talking here about incomes in *rural* PNG. Most Papua New Guineans who earn—or otherwise acquire—real money live in the urban areas.

The country boasts some conspicuously high rollers among its political leaders. An Australian newspaper raised some dust in PNG in 2008 when it reported that Prime Minister Somare had purchased an apartment in the Australian city of Cairns for the equivalent of about US $360,000 (about 900,000 kina), and his son had purchased a house just outside Cairns for the equivalent of about $630,000 (about 1,575,000 kina). The leader of the parliamentary opposition, Mekere Morauta, demanded that the Somares make more information on their assets public. It then came to light that Morauta had purchased a mansion in Brisbane under his wife's name for 3.6 million Australian dollars (somewhat less than the same amount in US dollars). The minimum wage in PNG at the time was 37.2 kina (about US $15) a week.[9] The growing gap between rich and poor in PNG is one of the circumstances that can make the country's glass look half-empty. (Americans who tut-tut over this, however, should recognize the damage growing income inequality is doing to their own country.)[10]

I know only a little about how much money Kragur villagers were earning in 2008. The last time I got anything near complete information on villagers' incomes was in 1981, when producing copra was the major source of cash income, other than whatever relatives working in towns sent home. When I searched the records of the Copra Marketing Board in Wewak that year, I found that Kragur villagers had earned an average of no more than about 20 kina (equal then to about US $25) per person in 1980 from copra sales. Within a few years, the international price of copra had fallen so low that no one in Kragur bothered to produce any at all. In 1998, what little money people earned came largely from selling betel nut and garden produce in the Wewak market and occasionally selling garden produce to the hospital and the hotels in town. From this, it was rare for a family to earn more than 100 kina, even in a good year, and most families earned far less. During the short-lived vanilla boom, one Kragur man, quick to get his plantation started, earned many hundreds of kina, and a few others had earned smaller amounts, but most vanilla planters missed the boat entirely.

In 2008, a number of villagers were placing their hopes for regular cash incomes on growing cacao beans, and a few were making some money from this. Here too, however, the cost of transporting their crop to sell to a fermentary on the mainland, where the process of turning the beans into chocolate starts, was taking a big bite out of their earnings. There are parts of the East Sepik Province much farther from Wewak than Kairiru where virtually every village has a fermentary,[11] and I was told that there were several fermentaries on Mushu Island. Kairiru, however, was entirely without.

Kragur villagers can still get by day-to-day with very little money, but every time I go back I can see that this is getting harder. While opportunities for earning regular incomes have never lasted and cash incomes have been more or less stagnant, the prices of manufactured goods, including store-bought food like rice and tinned fish, have continued to increase.[12] A special burden since around the year 2000 is the soaring world price of petrol, which has made it more expensive than ever simply to get to town.[13]

Even being a full participant in the life of the Catholic Church was getting more costly in 2008, although not necessarily because of world economic conditions. One Sunday late in June, a local leader of a church service at Bou read to the congregation what he said was a message from "Bishop Tony" (Bishop Anthony Joseph Burgess, an Australian who served the Catholic Church in his natal country until appointed bishop of the Wewak Diocese in 2000). The message reminded the members of the bishop's flock that they were responsible for helping support their parish priests financially, including helping to pay for fuel for their travel among the many villages of their parishes. The local leader said that the message came entirely from the bishop, but he delivered it with a heavy dose of personal passion and, I strongly suspect, personal embellishment. "Don't come to Mass empty handed!" he harangued. "How much should you give? Ten, twenty, thirty kina! Forget about ten or twenty toea! That's the price of a betel nut!" He went on to remind the congregation that each family also was expected to make a Thanksgiving offering of 16 kina a year, in two installments, and that the Bou church needed repairs that would cost about 10,000 kina. The parish also was asking each village to contribute a substantial amount toward festivities to mark the ordination of a Mushu man as a priest later that year.

"The Lord loves a cheerful giver!" the pastor of the First Presbyterian Church in Holt, Michigan, my hometown, used to say, as the ushers passed around the collection plate. The bishop's message that Sunday in June (as delivered by the messenger, we must remember), however, made many Kragur people anything but cheerful. One leader in Kragur church affairs told me later that "the people would like to give, but where would they get the money?" Others were more critical, such as the devoted participant in Kragur church activities who said it sounded like the bishop was saying that you couldn't be a good Christian unless you had money. Another man took the bishop's message even more amiss, remarking that if the bishop insisted on making such demands for money, he should be the first in line to burn in hell.

Yet the parish priests of the Wewak Diocese and the bishop himself lived in great simplicity by Yuropian standards, nor did the contributions of barefoot villagers go to purchase silk vestments and elaborate church furnishings. Also, the Catholic Church has done more than any other institution to bring schooling to the East Sepik, and in 2008 the church still surpassed the government in providing health services in the province. Encouraging greater local financing was part of the larger effort to transform the Catholic Church from a missionary endeavor, which technically it had ceased to be years before, into a locally rooted institution. Nonetheless, when Kragur villagers first agreed to be baptized in the 1930s, many people probably thought that because this was the religion of the wealthy Europeans, it might make village people wealthy too, perhaps quickly. Some have been surprised to receive a bill.

Educating their children, however, probably places more immediate financial pressure on villagers than any other expense. Virtually all Kragur villagers hope that their children will do well in school and that at least some of them will be able to get good urban jobs and send money home. But even primary school in PNG isn't free. Villagers told me in 2008 that it cost a family 80 kina (about US $32) a year to send a child to grades one through five at Bou and 180 kina (about $72) a year for grades six through eight. High school, for which children have to leave the village, costs a great deal more, but even paying for eight years of schooling at Bou is a heavy burden for many families.

A few people told me that they had saved enough that year to pay school fees from selling betel nut, tobacco, taro, and other local produce to other villagers in the small market now held a couple of days a week in Kragur. A regular public market within the village was something new since 1998. In that year, a lot of people were buying and selling betel nut within the village, but in an informal way, often sending small children clutching a few coins to ask at someone's door if they had a few betel nuts to spare. Even this was more commerce among villagers than I'd seen in previous years. In the 1970s, I saw nothing like this, and many villagers at that time insisted that they simply didn't buy and sell among themselves; it wasn't how the ancestors lived and, many said, it wasn't how good Catholics should behave.

The effort to keep the use of money out of the village drew on older beliefs that generosity was essential both to individual well-being and collective prosperity, as well as on local interpretations of Christianity.[14] Despite the growth of commerce within the village, generosity is still highly valued in Kragur—and not simply in order to get along well with others. In 2008,

Kilibop spent several days carving carefully shaped wooden gun stocks for several young men, who then added loops of surgical tubing to make spearguns, or arrow guns, as they called them (and which I first misheard as "aeroguns"). I asked Kilibop if the young men paid him anything for his work. He said that they didn't, but when he had a big job to do, like clearing a fallowed garden plot or cutting timbers for a new house, he could count on them for help. Also, he said he feared that if he took payment for his work, he would lose his skill. I think it's fair to say that he regarded sharing his skill as a moral obligation and feared that asking payment could bring retribution from the ever-present moral watchdogs, the spirits of the dead. He would be following his father in that. Old Stephen Umari's children still reminisce about how they and their mother sometimes used to upbraid him for giving away most of the fish he caught; Umari would answer, "Don't you think that the ancestors can see what I do?"

But even with attitudes about using money within the village loosening, in 2008 there wasn't nearly enough cash coming into the village from outside for many people to profit from trading with each other. One man told me that he'd paid for schooling for his children in 2007 by selling two fat pigs to someone running for political office who fed the pigs to his supporters at a campaign event. In 2008, a few families were raising pigs for the same purpose, but you have to have the money to buy a young pig before you can grow and fatten it, and a big sale isn't a sure thing. Many villagers rely on urban kin to pay for their children's education, but this isn't a sure thing either. Some families have many children but few or no money-earning urban kin, and the urban kin have to send their own children to school, too. Schools allow students to continue attending for a time while their parents seek money to pay the fees. Many families, however, have to withdraw their children from school temporarily while they find ways to raise money, and many whose children qualify to continue to higher grades simply can't find ways to pay for it.

Whether people *feel* poor or not is sometimes as important as how much money they have. Kragur people don't feel completely downtrodden. They are proud of their self-sufficiency, and, a bit like some high national officials, they sometimes focus on their potential rather than on current travails. As village elder Godfrey Siliau Kavi (Siliau) put it on one occasion, "Kairiru Island doesn't lack anything. We have everything here. But we don't have the tools!" When it comes to money, however, Kragur people generally do feel poor in relation to PNG's *susok* people—and even in comparison with the people of villages located closer to government services and towns where they can sell the things that they grow or make.

In addition to feeling poor in money, many Kragur people feel isolated. The immediate reasons for this are obvious. Boats, motors, and fuel are expensive.

For many years, anyone could get a round-trip boat ride between St. Xavier's High School and Wewak for only 5 kina, but the capacious *Tau-K* has been out of service for a long time now. In 2008, to ride as a passenger with no cargo to and from Wewak on one of the local small boats could cost as much as 40 kina. Ironically, before the advent of motor boats, Kragur and other Kairiru people weren't hemmed in by the ocean. They moved around on it quite freely, albeit at the stately pace of outrigger sailing canoes. During the early years of European colonization, the people of the Sepik coast and of the islands both close to the coast and far out at sea were still engaged in a complex network of sea trade.[15] In fact, Kragur people sailed to Wogeo Island (clearly visible from Kragur on a clear day, about fifty-five kilometers [thirty-four miles] away) to trade as recently as 1958. That is not long ago at all; I was nine years old then, riding in the back seat of my parent's 1955 Chevy.

Some Kragur people still have the skills to sail an outrigger canoe to the mainland, and there is still some small sailing canoe traffic among the islands off Wewak. But it is a major undertaking to build and maintain a sailing canoe large enough to carry more than a handful of passengers and their cargo. Also, I'm quite sure that no one in Kragur has ever built and sailed a voyaging canoe simply in order to earn money. In the glory days of canoe sailing, the trading voyages were part of a system through which important men built prestige and alliances, and they were occasions for major feasting, song, and dance. In 2008, some older men who could remember the festivities that were part of this voyaging couldn't talk about them without tears in their eyes.

Even if it were easier for Kragur people to travel to Wewak, it would ease only one dimension of their isolation. In the days of voyaging, they were not cut off from the political, economic, or religious center of things, because—judging from what contemporary Kragur people say—many Kairiru people probably considered their island the center not only of their own lives but also of the world in general. Such a view of the world was by no means universal in precolonial PNG.[16] It was not, however, uncommon. In the 1930s, Ian Hogbin wrote the following of the people of Wogeo Island: "The local notion is that the earth is like a huge platter with raised edges and the sky above a shallow upturned bowl. At the center of the bowl, is Wogeo itself. . . . Radiating outwards are the other islands and the moon and the stars."[17] My mentor Ted Schwartz observed that Manus islanders entertained a similar notion of the world in years past.[18] Kairiru people undoubtedly recognized places of historical and supernatural importance on other islands and the mainland, as many do today; I'm quite sure, however, that they didn't see themselves as off to the side.

When colonial powers took over what they called New Guinea, they established a few political, economic, and religious centers (that is, government stations, commercial centers, and missions; Wewak became all three). This effectively pushed everyone not already located near the new centers into the hinterlands. So, in spite of the speed of the motorboats, airplanes, cars, and trucks that eventually came with the colonists and the wonders of instant communication via radio and telephone, in 2008 Kragur was in a very real way more remote from the center of things than it was in the days of the sailing canoe and the drum signal.

Kragur people have not been entirely resigned to this. In the 1990s, as part of a larger reorganization of government structure, provincial governments created new local government electoral units. An initial proposal would have created electoral areas in the East Sepik Province that divided the islands off Wewak among areas dominated by mainland populations. This incensed island political activists, who objected that it would make it extremely difficult for islanders to combine to press for attention to their shared problems, including, of course, transportation and communication with the mainland. Kairiru Island activists, such as Patrick Beka of Bou Village, were in the thick of the fight, under the banner of "Island Dignity!" They got their way when the boundaries of electoral areas were finally drawn and the islands off Wewak were grouped together, distinct from any mainland locales. The struggle for "island dignity," however, in the shape of better access to political and economic opportunities, continues.

There is, of course, movement between the mainland centers and island hinterlands. Among other things, a few Kragur people who have lived large parts of their lives in one town or another have moved back to Kragur. The most affluent families in the village in 2008 were those of Kragur people come home to live after retiring from urban careers, such as teaching or the military. They were able to afford more luxuries than their fellows; some had used manufactured materials—corrugated metal, milled lumber, plastic piping to bring water to the house from the stream—in building their houses, there were books and magazines in their homes, and they often had tea, coffee, and sugar on hand. The retirees, however, had to adjust their attitudes toward money when they moved back to Kragur. One, for example, told me that he learned fast that it was easy to alienate others by spending too much money, even when he shared small luxuries with friends and family members. Another told me that after leaving the village for boarding school when quite young and living for decades on a salary, it had taken him several years back in Kragur to realize that many villagers simply had no money at all.

Some of the retirees hoped to use their urban savvy and their urban contacts to get the provincial and local governments to pay more attention to improving services to the islands off Wewak, including improving access to markets for whatever crops they can grow. Just having a few more affluent families in the village, however, isn't likely to change things much, and most of the Kragur people doing well in PNG's towns are probably going to stay there for the duration. As one villager said to me, if they do come home, it will be "only in their coffins." Some urban Kragurs have told me as much themselves, and some are clearly too much at home in the urban world ever to leave it except under duress.

A few *susok* people have told me that when they come back "home" to visit, they quickly tire of the physical discomforts of village life. I can certainly understand that. And some may find themselves tiring quickly, if not actually going berserk, from "the excess of attentive neighbors," the thought of which made Vojtech Novotny shudder. I can understand that, too. But I can also understand why some *susok* people have come back to Kragur to stay. Having whined at length about how hot it is and piled up statistics about rural PNG poverty, I still have to say that Kragur is in many ways a pleasant place to live, especially if some retirement savings or a pension relieve you from depending entirely on the sweat of your brow to feed your family and you can afford to get to town when you want to.

Among other advantages of Kragur life, there is virtually no violent crime of the kind common in all of PNG's towns, and the environment is generally conducive to good health. A pillar of good health in Kragur is the reliable supply of cool, clean water. I've stayed in a number of villages in PNG where if it didn't rain for several days in a row, there wasn't enough fresh water to bathe in, or where the river, stream, or spring from which people got their fresh water was either very unreliable or ridiculously far from the village—or both. This was not so in Kragur. Brother Matthew Bouton, an administrator of National Catholic Health Services in the province, told me that during the drought of 1997–1998, while many rural parts of the province had suffered from outbreaks of diarrhea, especially among children, because people were reduced to drinking contaminated water, the increase of reported cases on Kairiru had been very small. On Kairiru, the water level in Kragur's principal stream went down, but the stream continued to flow, and some Kragur people said that of all the villages on the island, only Kragur and Baru (on the mountainside not far east of Kragur and effectively a hamlet of Kragur) enjoyed uninterrupted water supplies.

A 1997 report on the feasibility of installing a small hydroelectric generator suggested that Kairiru's springs were probably fed by rainwater caught and concentrated by the island's geological structure.[19] This water supply, however, isn't invulnerable, and fortunately many villagers know it. In 1998, Michael Washol Waibai (Washol), Kirar's father, told me that the mining company that had recently been prospecting on Kairiru had left behind open exploratory trenches and that erosion was cutting them deeper and wider. He also told me that waste from the exploration had fouled one of the island's streams, and the prospectors had told people not to use its water for a year. He was rightly concerned that any further exploration or actual mining could damage Kragur's main water source. (Subsurface mineral rights in PNG belong to the state, which can approve exploration, but mining can't go ahead without reaching agreement with local landholders on financial and environmental issues.) It has been well over ten years since the mining companies dug their trenches on the mountain, but mining companies still have an eye on Kairiru. A June 2009 article in *The Australian* on the doings of several coal and mineral mining operations included mention of gold prospects on "two small islands," one of which was Kairiru, where "encouraging gold grades" had been found.[20]

From my first arrival in 1975 through every trip I've made to Kragur, I've drunk the water from the stream without treating it in any way, and while this may account for my benign amoebas, I've never had more than a minor gastrointestinal problem in the village. Still, before I left for PNG in 2008, I asked some of my Kragur correspondents if the stream water near the village was still clean enough to drink. Two villagers said it was just fine, although Herman suggested that to stay on the safe side I might want to get my drinking water from Nar, where water flows directly out of the mountainside into a rocky channel in green shade. Shortly after arriving, I raised Herman's suggestion with one of my hosts, but he brushed it off, saying that all the water in the stream comes from Nar, so what's the difference? Well, the difference is that it travels some distance from Nar before it reaches the outskirts of Kragur. Villagers are, however, very careful to avoid polluting the water and very careful where they take water for drinking and cooking. The water also gets well aerated as it tumbles over the rocks. During my visit in 2008, someone did find a large dead python in the stream, which he quickly removed. But it was fresh, he said, and hadn't started to decay, so there was nothing to worry about.

The World Health Organization/United Nations International Children's Fund (WHO/UNICEF) program for improving water and sanitation would count the Kragur stream as an "unimproved" water source, because it is "subject to runoff, bird droppings, or the entry of animals."[21] To count as "improved," the spring would have to be protected by channeling it directly into a spring box (that is, a small closed reservoir) and from there to "a pipe or cistern." Strictly speaking, Kragur people are among the small percentage (approximately 33 percent, according to WHO/UNICEF) of rural Papua New Guineans who *do* have access to "improved drinking water sources." In the early 1990s, a Kragur *susok* person obtained funds from WHO to install a system that diverts water from the stream to a tank just above the village and pipes it to a half-dozen water taps conveniently located among the houses. But in 2008, villagers told me pointedly that the water from the taps was okay for washing yourself or cleaning dishes, but not for drinking, because sometimes it stood in the tank or the pipes too long. Drink the water from the stream, they said.

I arrived in 2008 armed with compact water purification equipment and purification tablets just in case I discovered that the stream water wasn't as pristine as it used to be. My plan was to drink the untreated water and start purifying it only if I had gastrointestinal problems. This was a demonstration of my tremendous faith in local judgments of the water. You could also call it careless and stupid. My wife conveyed her low opinion of my plan with a penetrating and unforgettable look when I explained it to her while we were shopping for supplies for my trip. Even fast-moving, crystalline water can convey serious ailments that don't respond to the kinds of remedies for gastrointestinal problems I carried with me or that show up only months or years later. I strongly recommend that the reader not do what I did. In the end, however, my faith was justified (or, my carelessness went unpunished). I got only pleasure from drinking the cool waters directly from the stream during my stay and passed with flying colors a thorough search for gastrointestinal infestations after my return.

My own health aside, dependable good water is enormously important. Unclean water and inadequate sanitation account for a major share of illness in places like PNG.[22] Fortunately, Kragur's "unimproved" water seems to be serving the village well. I learned a lot more about Kragur people's health in 2008 than ever before, mostly from the attendant at the village health clinic. The clinic, located at the west end of Kragur, is part of the provincial public health system. It had been established since my last visit and served several nearby villages as well as Kragur. In the 1970s there had been a one-room medical aid post (as rural medical clinics were then called) at a place called Masu, on the edge of Shagur. The attendant was equipped to stitch up wounds (no small thing) and give injections of procaine penicillin, a kind of shotgun remedy, helpful for a variety of painful conditions, but usually given without diagnosing underlying problems. Attempts to establish and maintain more modern services had all foundered until local community will and government resources came together in the 1990s. I'd taken photos in 1998 as Kragur men cleared the ground and cut and carried the timbers for a local-style house for a clinic attendant and a small separate timber and thatch building for a consulting office and single-bed infirmary, although at that time no attendant had yet been assigned to Kragur.

When a clinic attendant was assigned in 1999, Kragur was lucky to get someone with considerable paramedical training. Vincent Kasian, originally from a mainland village east of Wewak, had served several years in the PNG Defense Force as a medic, and he'd received additional instruction not only from the provincial health service but also from members of a US Special

Forces unit on a training mission in PNG. Vincent used as his principal medical reference the very fat "U.S. Special Forces Medical Handbook." His military medical training included combat lifesaving, which he said had proven
useful in treating some of the kinds of injuries people get in village life. I've
seen some bad injuries in Kragur myself: legs cut by axe strokes gone awry,
feet lacerated on sharp stones while traversing mountain trails in the dark,
and backs damaged and bones broken by falls from trees. The reader may be
wondering what tasks take Kragur people up trees. Munbos was picking edible
leaves when she fell and broke her leg. Others I know have fallen while cutting
bunches of betel nuts from high on the tall, slender betel palms or while gathering green coconuts. One lesson these latter incidents teach is that one should
never use both hands to try to pull loose a bunch of betel nuts or a coconut;
always keep one hand for the tree.

Vincent married a Kragur woman, Pauline Pileng, and together they trans-
formed the originally bare clinic grounds into a garden of crushed coral terraces and paths, stands of betel nut palms, and hibiscus hedges. An outdoor
plaza of crushed coral with log seating around its edges is the clinic's waiting
room. Vincent also set a good example by piping water from a stream to a tap
just outside his well-built outhouse, so people could wash their hands immediately after using the facilities.

Vincent told me that waterborne diseases and diarrhea were "very rare"
among the people he served. The most common complaints, he said, were sore
backs and knees, the result of the heavy work of everyday village life and the
steep climbs and descents required to travel almost anywhere outside the village, except along the trail to Bou and Shagur. (Indeed, most villagers over
about forty I know complain of sore knees, but they have no choice but to keep
on climbing and descending anyway.) Malaria was also very common, he said,
and I saw that a number of villagers were incapacitated briefly by malaria
just during my few weeks in Kragur. Villagers generally have strong resistance
to malaria and take no preventive medication. Most adult villagers can quickly
recover from bouts of malaria that, without medication, would kill me. Over
the years, however, multiple malaria attacks take a toll on their health. Malaria
is also a serious danger to small children. Tuberculosis was the leading cause
of death among his charges, said Vincent, but asthma, bronchitis, and pneu-
monia were also common, which he attributed to smoky household fires and
heavy tobacco smoking. Indeed, several people my own age who had been hale
and hearty ten years before were in 2008 emaciated and brutally short of
breath from chronic asthma or emphysema, both called in Tok Pisin *sotwin*
(short wind).

My casual impression in 2008 was that there were more nonsmokers in
Kragur than there used to be. For instance, I didn't see any preschool children

with tobacco-leaf cigars clamped in the corners of their mouths as I sometimes did in the 1970s. And one evening at Rokerai's house, two or three of Munbos' grandchildren decided to chide her about her smoking, telling her that it would give her *sotwin*. She protested that, in fact, smoking made her stronger. This reminded me of her late husband, Stephen Umari the elder, who—when we took breaks during our treks on the mountain—usually pressed me to smoke in order to "strengthen" myself for the next steep climb. By 2008, however, younger people sometimes shook their heads in disapproval when they saw me rolling a *brus*. "That stuff will kill you!" one young man exclaimed in surprise (and in English) when he saw me retrieving a partially smoked *brus* from my shoulder bag and lighting up one day as we sat in the shade watching a volleyball tournament in Shagur. I appreciated his concern, and it was good to know that my example wasn't leading him astray.

In addition to dispensing medications for the major local afflictions, such as acute malaria attacks, Vincent also provided family planning services, delivered babies, stitched up wounds, and treated a great variety of other ills. His consistent treatment with antibiotics of yaws—a common children's disease, which can permanently damage bones and joints (and perhaps a contributor to the many bad knees among my middle-aged Kragur friends)—had virtually eliminated it in Kragur, Vincent said. The supply of drugs from Wewak could be erratic, but the clinic was clearly a great boon to Kragur and other area villages. Incorporating an English expression, Siliau told me that "Vincent's work is 'up-to-date.' I think a lot of us would die without this clinic."

In one of our long discussions about local health issues, ranging from the regular allergy season caused by flowering trees to his concerns about the possibility of HIV infections on the island, Vincent told me that malnutrition wasn't a problem.[23] That speaks well for the way people are managing their land and sea resources. It doesn't, however, necessarily mean that there is always plenty of food for everyone. I've kept up a correspondence with Brother Herman for many years, and in his letters he has mentioned on several occasions that, at the moment, there was not enough food in Kragur. There is always plenty of food in the homes where I stay, because making sure of that is part of my being a good guest, but I've never looked into Kragur nutrition systematically. I know firsthand, however, that on some days some families do not have food in their houses. Whenever I'm in Kragur, there are people who come ask me quietly for some rice or a tin of mackerel because, they say, they have no food that day. I also know that food was short both during the 1997–1998 drought, because there was too little water, and in the months after the drought broke, because the rains returned in excess and soaked the island so thoroughly that some crops rotted in the ground.

Historically, occasional food shortage due to drought, frost, or other distur-

80 Chapter 5

bances in growing conditions are nothing new in most parts of PNG. Food supplies have generally improved since European contact, because new food crops (such as cassava, potatoes, African yams, maize, pumpkin, and a new type of taro) have given people a wider range of food sources to rely on, and many people can earn a little money with which to supplement the food they produce themselves when they need to.[24] If Kragur is suffering from more than occasional food shortage, lack of regular money incomes certainly enters into it. It's also possible that a growing village population is pressing on the amount of good land available, even though from a distance Kairiru looks largely unoccupied and uncultivated. Stands of sago palms (the pith of which is rich in carbohydrates but requires laborious processing), mature gardens interplanted with a variety of crops, or cacao trees grown in the shade of the forest are next to invisible to the untrained eye. Also, not all the unused land is necessarily well suited to cultivation, and villagers who told me that there was still plenty of land for everyone often referred to places high on the mountain and difficult to reach. This is much like the situation of PNG as a whole, in which, according to the *Rural Development Handbook,* about 70 percent of the land has very limited potential for growing food or cash crops because it is too mountainous, weather conditions are unsuitable, or it is subject to frequent flooding.[25]

A sign that good garden land conveniently located is getting scarce in Kragur is that, according to what several villagers told me, people weren't letting land lie fallow between periodic cultivation for as long as they used to. Younger villagers spoke of this in terms of the number of years elapsed between leaving off cultivation and clearing and planting again. Older villagers said that in the past they let garden plots lie fallow until they had to fell sizable trees in clearing it, but today plots were cleared when the new-growth trees were still small.

A growing village population could easily account for this more intensive land use. In the 1970s, there were only a couple of hundred men, women, and children living in Kragur. By 1998, the population had grown to 350 or more, according to a count Kirar made to assist the elected village leaders. In 2008, people told me that the population was over six hundred, and it was obvious that the village was much bigger than before. I didn't count the people, but I was able to compare the number of houses in the village with the number ten years before because Kirar had made a map of the village for me in 1998, and in 2008, both Kirar and Kilibop's son David Watar Umari (Watar) drew maps of the village for me. Comparing the maps showed that the number of houses had increased from about 80 to about 124 in ten years, mostly by extending the area of the village rather than by crowding more houses into the same space.

Yet despite a changing ratio of people to good land and the disappointments of copra and vanilla, many Kragur people remain alert to new possibilities for producing both money and food from their land. As I mentioned, in 2008 numbers of families were already producing some cacao. Lucas Saulep, formerly of the Papua New Guinea Defense Force, was using his relative affluence to buy cacao seedlings and give them to people who couldn't afford to buy their own. He and some others were also experimenting with growing different kinds of rice, in the hope of diversifying village food sources.

Regarding villagers' health, it's worth mentioning how Kragur people care for the infirm elderly and people with psychiatric problems. Men and women keep contributing to household welfare as much as they can for as long as they can, doing a little work in the gardens, gathering firewood (mostly a woman's task), or watching young children while their parents go to the bush or to their garden plots. Villagers speak very harshly of people who don't care for their disabled elders, although I know of a few cases in which strife in the family led to elders being badly neglected. It is unheard of, however, for anyone to go homeless.

In the few cases I've seen, extended families also cared well for members with psychiatric problems. The psychiatrically impaired, like the physically disabled, contribute what they can, and unless they prove dangerous to themselves or others they are allowed to go their own ways. One tall and good-looking young man occasionally visited me and told me he was God and that Jesus was his son. He also occasionally announced that he wanted to fight. But he always smiled when I welcomed him, and to my knowledge he never started a fight or tinkered frivolously with the cosmos. He went to the gardens with his family regularly, and people said he was a strong worker.

The low cost of living compared with town life, lack of crime, dependable clean water, a relatively healthy environment, the support an extended family can give in times of need, and perhaps the opportunity to take part in building a more prosperous village—all these things contribute to Kragur's attractions. There is also, of course, the pull of family past and present, which is in some ways inseparable from ties to the land. Many Kragur villagers I've known over the years have held that Kairiru Island is not just where their ancestors settled but where they came into being. As one man put it many years ago, when the island came into being, so did its people. While this belief may have been more common in the past, it is by no means completely antique.

One afternoon in 2008, Leo Tirom, a tireless picker of my brain for information of all kinds, asked me what I thought of the contention that the original peoples of both Australia and PNG had migrated from Asia. He knew, he said, that some scientists said that this was the case, but he'd also heard that a lot of Australian aboriginals denied it, saying that their ancestors originated right there in Australia. "That's right!" said Alois Kitok Flal (Kitok), who was sitting with us: "The original people of Australia emerged in Australia and the people of Kairiru originated on Kairiru!" In 2008 some villagers also still made the claim, one I'd heard many times in the past, that Kairiru was the first landmass to have appeared on the vast expanse of water that is the world as seen from Kragur.

More immediately, the village grounds are where several generations of ancestors are buried, some at the edges of the village, some alongside houses, and some in places now forgotten. In some contexts, when villagers refer in Tok Pisin to Kragur's *graun*, they mean not simply its ground, the dirt and stones on which the village stands, but also the ancestors interred there. I noted earlier that many villagers say that spirits of the dead, roused by the anger of their living kin, can make people sick unto death. In Tok Pisin, they call such illness *sik bilong graun;* that is, illness emanating from the *graun*, where the ancestors are buried. Many villagers also hold that the support of one's own deceased ancestors is essential to success in gardening, fishing, and other vital pursuits. In short, the village land is not inert; it is, to many who live there, an active part of village life. An attachment to the village, then, can be not only an emotional attachment to living family or fondly recalled scenes of one's youth; it can also be a link with previous generations that still wield influence in the present.

Some anthropologists go much further than this in describing the significance of the places they are born and raised to indigenous people of the Pacific Islands in general (including, of course, PNG). In a common Pacific Island view, they say, not only does your native place nurture you through the food and water you consume, through living there you incorporate into the core of your being the substance of the place, and you share this substance with the other people of your place, regardless of your genealogical relationship to them. So, as anthropologist Martha Ward has written of the people of Pohnpei, "People are in places, but places are also in people."[26]

In the words of Sherlock Holmes, "These are very deep waters." If this is what Papua New Guineans are like, their relationships to places go far beyond the powerful nostalgia I feel for the house where I grew up, which my grandfather built, and the land on which it stood, which he planted with tall spruce windbreaks and dozens of fruit trees. After my father died, we thought of scattering his ashes in the apple orchard there, but we refrained because we knew we would eventually have to sell the house and land out of the family, losing all material connection to it despite generations of building and cultivating. Yet it's very easy, I think, to propose too stark a contrast between Papua New Guineans and, in particular, westerners (in Kragur terms, Yuropian people). Consider the people of American towns deserted by failing industries, who stubbornly stay on after the factories have closed and the jobs are gone, so that they can be near friends, family, and, yes, the graves of their ancestors. And consider the urban Papua New Guineans who are likely to return to family lands "only in their coffins."

Yet there is plenty of easily understandable nostalgia for some aspects of village life among Kragur's permanent migrants to urban life. Everyone at the table looked a little wistful when at dinner one evening in Moresby one long-term urbanite recalled the pleasures of bathing in the stream, "letting the water flow over you and scratching your back against a rock." And some Kragur *susok* people may also find ties to the village hard to describe in the language of nostalgia, family sentiment, or economic interests. Some may doubt that Kairiru was the first land to emerge from the sea, that the ancestors emerged with the island, or be puzzled by the notion that her or his body and the land of Kairiru share core substance. But even as a less-than-conscious symbolic system or simply as metaphor, a concept of people bound to and through land is strong stuff, and a little could go a long way. Such an attachment to the land may well be among Kragur's riches for some and help keep them there or draw them back.

Chapter 6

Ancestors on Paper

Druids aren't allowed to write anything down, it's against
the rules. . . . Once you write something down it becomes
fixed. It becomes dogma. People can argue about it,
they become authoritative, they refer to the texts, they
produce new manuscripts, they argue more. . . . If you
never write anything down then no one knows exactly
what you said so you can always change.
—Bernard Cornwell, *The Winter King: A Novel of Arthur*

If land is at the heart of village life, family ties—sometimes through marriage but primarily by descent through males from a common male ancestor (patrilineal descent)—are at the heart of questions about land. This helps account for how questions I'd asked in 1998, rather too innocently, in 2008 sucked me into both deep discussions of local history and the push and pull of intravillage rivalry. I arrived in Kragur in 1998 thinking I understood how kinship and leadership were related in the traditional system, but I almost immediately bumped into something that seemed to contradict a lot of what I thought I knew. Trying to dispel my confusion, I started asking questions. I went home without having satisfied my curiosity, but the discussion I started was there waiting for me in 2008.

In 1998, I heard a lot of people referring to Kitok as Kragur's chief. People who don't live in villages often assume that people who do live in villages usually have chiefs or something like them; that is, paramount leaders, often determined by heredity, with broad powers, a bit like European royalty but on a smaller scale. But this isn't as common as the *susok* people of the world think, and I had never before heard anyone in Kragur speak of anyone as a chief. Rather, even the people with the most power and authority in the village generally had emphasized that there was no single leader but instead several leaders with complimentary spheres of authority. Also, many Kragur people had always been quick to opine that villagers would work together toward common goals more readily if there *were* a single leader. Having a single leader, they often said, was the Yuropian custom. They may have received this impression from the fact that rigidly hierarchical ecclesiastical and business organizations—that is, the Catholic Church and the German New Guinea Company—provided the earliest examples of European life in much of coastal and island New Guinea, followed by an Australian colonial bureaucracy.

In 1998, it looked as if Kragur people had decided since my previous visit to designate one of the men of authority as a kind of first among equals and call him chief. According to some villagers, a group of the influential traditional leaders got together and decided that one of them, William Pileng, by virtue of the status of his male ancestors and his own knowledge and leadership ability, should serve as "chairman" (the English word was used) of the traditional leaders. Not long thereafter, however, Pileng died. Kitok was asked to take his place, again by virtue of hereditary status but also because he was willing to take on the role, which brings responsibility as well as prestige. Kitok himself told me that there were others better versed in the lore of a traditional leader than he, but they had preferred to stand aside.

To the best of my knowledge, however, no one had suggested that anyone be called chief until Kitok stepped into this leadership role. A few villagers said that they didn't know who had picked up the English word "chief" to label a Kragur leader—or why. As one man said to me, "It's the way the white people talk. They call their boss 'chief.'" The Kairiru language, some pointed out, had its own words for leaders, most common among them *ramat wolap*. *Ramat* means "man" and *wolap* means "big," so this means "big man." Villagers translate *ramat wolap* into Tok Pisin as the single word *bigman,* a Tok Pisin word for traditional leaders used in many parts of PNG that anthropologists have incorporated into their own vocabulary.

One version of events has it that a villager known for his sense of humor (which, as ever, not everyone appreciated to the same extent) took to calling Kitok "chief" in jest, a jest that depended in part on knowing of white people's penchant for assuming that villages have chiefs. Not everyone, I hear, got the joke, but they did become accustomed to calling Kitok chief. There was also quiet debate in some circles about who would take Kitok's place as first-among-equals in Kragur when he died. But for his lifetime, the title "chief" and Kitok's right to it seemed to be well established.

Kitok, however, wasn't necessarily *the* chief. I found in 2008 that as people became accustomed to speaking of Kitok as chief, some also started to use this title for others who qualified as *ramat wolap*. In fact, several months after I got home from PNG, I received a letter about recent village events signed by several influential men, including Kitok, their signatures all in a column under the heading "Chiefs of Kragur." The only return address given on the envelope was also "Chiefs of Kragur." I left the envelope casually placed but highly vis-

ible on my desk at work for several days, just to let my colleagues and employers know they were dealing with someone with powerful friends.

Although I thought I knew a lot about Kragur ancestors, when villagers
tried to explain to me in 1998 what gave both Kitok and his predecessor, Pileng, their high hereditary status, they spoke of ancestors I'd never heard of
before. In the 1970s I had figured out the basics of how Kragur people sorted
themselves into groups when the occasion required. I say "when the occasion
required" because in daily life, the people most important to villagers are the
members of their immediate households and the closer members of their
extended families, on both the male and female sides. But when villagers talk
about the village as made up of different groups, more often than not they talk
about groups based on descent through males from male ancestors. Of course,
groups defined by such patrilineal descent include women as well as men.
Women are members of their fathers' descent groups, but their children become members of their husband's groups; lines of patrilineal descent stop
with women and continue through men. I had to know this much to understand virtually anything of village life.

But who were these ancestors whose names I'd never heard before? I spent
several hours in 1998 with older Kragur men adding to the information I'd
collected in the 1970s but still didn't learn enough to grasp the historical roots
of Kitok's high status. I did, however, discover that some of the senior men of
the 1990s, unlike the elders of the 1970s, had started putting down on paper
what their elders had conveyed to them only by word of mouth. In addition, the
questions I put to them about their ancestors seemed to encourage them to
record more of what they knew about the forebears of their respective groups.

By 2008 it had become very common for Kragur people to speak of these
descent-based groups using the English word "clan" or the Tok Pisin word
klen. In the 1970s, the preferred term for such groups had been the Kairuru
language word *koyeng*, and almost no one said clan or *klen*. Many people still
said *koyeng* in 2008, but the new terms were taking over fast. Kragur people
have been worrying about the declining importance of their clans for as long
as I've known them. One thoughtful young family man in 1998 spoke of the
clan system as virtually a dying institution.[1] Yet in 2008, many villagers
quickly engaged with my interest in learning more about the most ancient
members of their clans. In fact, my plan to ask just a few more questions to
clarify why some of Kragur's several chiefs were more prominent than others
turned, by popular demand, into an effort to record on paper the male ancestors of all the Kragur clans.

When I met Ralph and John for breakfast at the Hideaway Hotel the day I
left Moresby for Wewak, I brought with me a deep box of black and white
photos of Kragur people that I'd taken in the 1970s. I had sent a large box of

photos to the village after I returned from Kragur in 1976. I figured that by 2008 a lot of these prints would have decayed or been lost, so I had brought along a duplicate set. I also brought to breakfast a copy of the charts of clan ancestors I'd put together based on my information from the 1970s and 1998. People had given some of this information to me for my eyes only, so above the title of the document ("Notes on Kragur Genealogy") was blazoned, in both English and Tok Pisin, the warning, "Confidential: Do not read without permission" (in Tok Pisin: *"Em i tambu: Yu no inap lukim sapos yu no kisim finis toksave olsem em i orait"*).

Ralph and John were eager to see the pictures and suggested that rather than my taking them to the village, where they might end up lost or decayed again (although a number of people, I found later, had preserved them in albums), I leave them with John, who would scan them and make a digital record for a longer posterity. And Ralph and John saw in my incomplete clan history charts the prospect of having a relatively complete written record of the ancestors of the village clans. "We don't have anything like this," Ralph told me, and he and John thought it was high time they did.

They hoped that I would pursue this, but I knew I could take it only so far. Many Kragur people hold information about their clan ancestors very close to their chests. I knew some villagers were averse even to sharing parts of what they knew with members of their own clans. And although a few people were already writing things down, it was entirely possible that others would be shy of this, in part because writing things down can make it harder to keep them secret.

Keeping knowledge of ancestors secret can be important because it leaves more room for strategically unveiling particular bits of knowledge, while keeping the big picture vague, in the heat of a dispute over, for instance, who settled which part of the island first or which clan has primary rights to an important kind of magic by virtue of acquiring it in the deep past from a spirit being. Some villagers with considerable genealogical and historical knowledge also feared that if the stories of their ancestors became too widely known, unscrupulous members of other groups could incorporate parts of them into their own histories in order to make unjustified claims for land, status, and authority. Many other villagers, however, were eager to compile and record clan histories precisely because they are at the center of such controversies, not only within the village but between the village and other villages or, perhaps, government agencies or mining companies. As Rokerai put it, such knowledge is "the spear of the village" (*spia bilong ples*).

I knew that this project could become controversial, but I figured that it probably couldn't add more than a snowflake to what was already a constant flurry of controversy over village leadership. In the past, I'd heard lots of fireside talk of who was presuming authority he didn't have or who should be exercising more vigorously his true responsibilities. By 2008, some Kragur people had already started taking some of their chronic arguments about clan primacy into a much wider arena. A brief article appeared in one of PNG's major daily newspapers, the *National,* in May 2007, during the campaign for the parliamentary seat that Moses Manwau eventually won. The headline read, "Islanders install Saulep as chief," and the article went on to say that in a ceremony on Kairiru Island, Ralph Saulep, one of Moses' opponents for the Wewak Open Electorate parliamentary seat, had been "bestowed with the chieftainship title formerly held by his uncle, the late paramount chief, Joachim Waibai Tirom."[2]

Some readers of the *National,* however, took issue with this, and a subsequent edition of the newspaper included a letter headlined "Stumped by chief's appointment," submitted by a resident of Kairiru writing, in English, under the pseudonym "Junior Custom Loya"—that is, a junior expert in customary law. The writer diplomatically noted that "the issue of attaining chieftainship is a touchy subject, not only on the island of Kairiru, but elsewhere in Papua New Guinea." He then put diplomacy aside to state emphatically, "As far as I am aware, there isn't anyone outside of _____ clan who would become paramount chief of the village."[3] (I've deleted the name of the clan in this quotation because, although the letter is part of the public record, I think most Kragur people would prefer to keep specific clan rivalries out of the public spotlight.)

The writer also questioned a number of other items in the newspaper account of Saulep's installation as chief, including the rights of the members of Ralph's clan to what the newspaper report called a "ceremonial spear." This ceremonial spear is probably what is called a *sukup* in the Kairiru language. I understand that a *sukup* is indeed an attribute of authority, rights to which are handed down patrilineally. *Sukup* are among the items that have personal names, so a clan doesn't simply have hereditary rights to a *sukup,* it has rights to a particular named *sukup.* I am also quite certain that only some clans in Kragur can claim rights to their very own *sukup,* and I understand that only certain senior members of these clans have the authority to use the *sukup.*

A physical *sukup,* carved from wood and perhaps decorated with shell ornaments and cassowary feathers, doesn't last forever, but when it wears out, the name lives on and can be attached to a new material home. In the proper hands, a *sukup* has the power to attract wealth. Members of a clan with rights to a *sukup* would certainly have taken it on the long-distance trading voyages of the past, standing it in one of the canoes to help ensure that their trading partners would be generous. But, as I understand it, a *sukup* is powerless in the hands of someone without hereditary rights to use it. Its power, like that of magical procedures, comes in part from its association with the ancestors, and the ancestors only lend their weight to the work of people with valid claims to their help. As one villager once put it, speaking of magical procedures for enhancing the fertility of gardens, if a man uses magic to which he doesn't have rights, *"graun em i no inap harim em"*—that is, "the ground won't hear him." Again, the "ground" here isn't just the dirt and stones, it is the earth in which the ancestors are interred and, ultimately, the spirits of the ancestors themselves.

Ralph had run for parliament in the previous election (in 2002) as well, and I have one of his posters from that campaign. It bears a head shot of Ralph in a crisp white shirt, red tie, wire-rim eyeglasses, a neatly trimmed moustache and goatee, and an expression of calm seriousness, framed by a panoramic view of Kragur atop its high cliff. The poster's text tells voters that business development is the way to secure their self-determination, health, and security, and states Ralph's commitment to and ability in promoting business opportunities. The poster is headed by the slogan, "Toward True Business Independence!" (*"Long Trupela Bisnis Indipendens!"*) In short, it shows a man at ease in the modern world bearing a message of economic promise to the folks at home. But, presenting Ralph with a *sukup,* as described in the newspaper, was also making a strong statement about the authority due him as the descendant of a long line of ancestors with their own kind of power to attract wealth.

I won't comment on the pros and cons of either Ralph's or the Junior Custom Loya's competing claims. That presumes a lot more understanding of politics both traditional and modern in Kragur than I have, and it would align me with one of several clans in what is still a hot debate. But when I read the newspaper articles, the kinds of claims and counterclaims being aired in this national forum sounded very familiar to those often aired within the village. The newspaper exchange also confirmed the wisdom of my staying as close as possible to the role of simple recorder of whatever information on their ancestors people wanted to divulge and far away from any presumption to judge their claims.

The enthusiasm of some Kragurs for making written records of ancestors in 2008 flowed in part from concern with defending claims to land if the discovery of gold on Kairiru ever led to attempts to conclude a mining agreement with islanders. But rights to resources that confer power and leadership within Kragur were also at stake. These included rights to items laden with symbolism and power (like a *sukup*); rights to certain utilitarian articles (such as particular types of canoes or fishing nets); rights to practice or oversee the practice of certain skills, such as carving the large, elaborately decorated log drums known in Tok Pisin as *garamut,* or the human-like figures used in some magic, known in the Kairiru language as *kaikrauap* (or *keraikrauap*); rights to present particular song and dance performances (in Tok Pisin, *singsing*); and rights to use magic that increases the fertility of food crops and the productivity of hunting and fishing or—the dark side of this—that can destroy food sources. Knowledge of magic for killing people, or sorcery, is also a resource passed down through the generations.

People, almost exclusively men, who have the hereditary rights to use magical power don't always know how to conduct the magical ritual. In recent generations, this is most often because they were away from the village working for wages at a time in life when, in the past, they might have been learning magical skills from the older generation. Nevertheless, even having only the rights without the full technical knowledge still brings status, and someone with the technical knowledge but not the rights could get into big trouble for employing magic without the permission or oversight of the hereditary owners.

When Kragur people explain why rights to magic and other aspects of status are distributed as they are, they invariably invoke sequences of male forebears receding far into the past. In 1998, I found that a great many Kragur villagers had adopted a Tok Pisin version of the English term "social structure" to talk about these lines of descent, referring to them as *straksa*. This part of the contemporary Kragur vocabulary may have come from the *susok* Kragur people in towns, who are quite familiar with the English term. At least one village resident also had studied social science as a seminary student. In any case, it provided a concise label for the project of recording knowledge of clan ancestors that some of us had undertaken together, which my Kragur collaborators called the *wok bilong straksa*—that is, the "work of structure," or simply *straksa wok*, or "structure work." One product of the *straksa wok* is a set of charts showing sequences of descent through males reaching many generations into the past. Almost as important as these records of the ancestors' names are the stories that go with them, stories about the migrations and other exploits of the ancestors that eventually brought them to what is now Kragur and through which they acquired whatever knowledge and rights they passed down to their descendants.

A lot of what the villagers involved in this effort told me I have to keep secret. Although a few villagers thought it would be a great thing to have a single document in which the histories of all the clans were recorded for all future Kragur generations, it was pretty clear from the beginning that this would be out of the question. Even so, I was flattered that Kragur people trusted me enough to put all this information in my hands, relying on me to conceal or reveal it only as they instructed.

Granted, not everyone jumped on this bandwagon immediately. Nick Kung Urim (Nick), a leading man of the Ku clan, told me one evening, when we had already been working on the Ku descent record for a couple of weeks, that some villagers thought I was probably going to take this information and somehow make money from it. He had assured them, he said, that this wasn't my intention. Nevertheless, this did concern me, so I explained just what a money-losing venture my years of visiting and writing about Kragur had been. Among other things, I told him how much I had earned in 2007 from the sales of my books about Kragur, noting that it was about enough to pay for a couple of nights in one of Moresby's better hotels. Nick had worked on merchant ships that took him as far away as Vanuatu, Hong Kong, and Calcutta before marrying and settling down in the village, so he knew something about the prices of things in the larger world, and he agreed that I was earning a pitiful amount from my efforts. I also told him he could assure worriers that very few people in America were interested in the secret details of Kragur clan ancestry, so there wasn't much scope there for making money even if I wanted to.

Still, different views of just how much to trust me were never completely reconciled. During one long meeting with the knowledgeable men of a large clan, one man stopped another from pronouncing the name of a distant ancestor, saying, "This is secret! Smith can't hear it!" Almost simultaneously, however, someone else was saying that it was okay to tell me, and someone else was blurting out the name. It turned out that yet another man had already given me this name prior to the meeting.

Carrying out this project, I saw how much literacy had become part of daily life in the village in comparison with twenty or thirty years ago. Quite a few men showed up at the discussions of their clan histories with written records of the information they had received from their elders, and some of them had even charted the relationships among their ancestors, connecting the names of fathers and sons with vertical lines and the names of mothers and fathers with horizontal lines. A lot of men also brought pencils or ballpoint pens and tattered notebooks to the meetings to make their own records of the discussions (fig. 9). Fortunately, I was well supplied with writing materials, so I could pass around pens and sheets of notebook paper to those who needed them. I didn't have handy everything that a scribe needed, however, so some men used the straight backs of knife blades to draw connecting lines for their own charts, and a few used the keen edges of their heavy bush knives to sharpen their pencils.

Something else I saw for the first time was the knowledgeable men of particular clans comparing and debating the bits and pieces and versions of their clan histories that they had learned from their elders. Doing this on such a scale was new to Kragur people as well, I gathered. At the beginning of the first meeting of the representatives of one of the larger clans, one of the senior

Figure 9. Godfrey Siliau Kavi and Joe Shorai on Rokerai's veranda, recording the history of their clan, 2008. Photo by the author.

men pointed out that in the past, individuals had kept most of their knowledge to themselves, passing it on only to their immediate descendants. Sitting down together to share their knowledge, discuss it, and come up with a version on which they could agree was completely new, he said.

With the tools of literacy long at their disposal, why *hadn't* anyone done this before? A big part of the reason, I understood, was fear. Knowledge of the ancestral lines of descent is not only important, it is also powerful. It isn't only vital in weighing claims to land and aspects of leadership, some of it is subject to more sinister uses. In 1998, a man of one prominent clan told me the names of two of his most ancient forebears in a whisper so low I could hardly hear him. He also forbade me to repeat them, stopping me short even when I tried to whisper them to clarify their pronunciation. This was, he said, because these were names sometimes called on when performing certain kinds of magic, and they shouldn't be spoken frivolously. He added, however, that it might be alright to speak about them openly after a certain individual of another clan had died. As he said this, he nodded in the direction of the major concentration of the houses of that individual's clan.

I knew that for decades many villagers had suspected the person in question of using sorcery against his enemies, and my companion that day didn't want to take even the slightest chance that he might overhear or in some more esoteric way ascertain the names of these powerful ancestors, giving him the opportunity to use their power for evil rather than good. By 2008 this individual was dead, and somewhat to my surprise, those who had once only whispered the potent names of their ancestors were now speaking them quite freely, at least among members of their own clans.

Some dangers nonetheless remained, including the danger that people with no rights to them might appropriate the names of ancestors of one clan to embellish the histories of their own and make illegitimate claims to status and authority. Or, there was the danger that too much discussion of clan histories could result in bitter arguments even among people of the same clan. In several of the *straksa* project meetings, some of the men made a point of inveighing against giving in to such fears. They warned that passing on records of their histories was too important to leave to chance. The world was changing, they said, and sometime soon they might have to assert the claims not only of the individual clans of Kragur but also of the village as a whole against outsiders. "We can't be afraid!" Munuo pronounced in one *straksa* project meeting, and Kitok declared in another that "The time for fear is over!"

Kitok even went so far as to tell me that the whole tradition of secrecy about such things was misguided and that the leaders of the past should have shared their knowledge more widely, instead of each group trying to keep its knowledge to itself. I recalled later that Kitok had said pretty much the same thing to me thirty-two years before, lamenting that if people insisted on hiding their knowledge, they would find one day that they had no "history." His use of the English word "history" seemed then to suggest that he meant not just strategic knowledge of clan ancestors but a larger, shared story of Kragur's past.

Kitok's was an exceptionally democratic vision. In 2008, it was in tune with the way some villagers saw the campaigns for elected leaders that were then under way; that is, as ways to break away from concentrating leadership in the hands of a few, chosen on the basis of their ancestry. Both in the election and the *straksa* project, however, I could see that this vision had vocal opponents. While some collaborators in the *straksa* work emphasized the value of the results to all of Kragur's future generations, others were prone to speak of what immediate advantage their own clans might obtain from it. "We'll see who wins and who fails" when all the clans have recorded their stories, said one eager participant in the project. Another equally eager participant suggested that once we had recorded the *straksa* of all the *klen*, we should press ahead to look at the "*straksa bilong vanu*"—that is, the *straksa* of the village (*vanu* in the Kairiru language). Then, he said, we'd see "who's the boss."

Some of the participants in the project even saw the *straksa* work itself as a contest. They kept track of which clans were closer to completing the work of recording their histories, and they were pleased if they found that their own groups were making faster progress than others. I tried to stay as clear as possible of this kind of thing, refusing to discuss how the different groups were progressing and keeping mum when people started comparing the numbers of generations of ancestors that members of the different clans could name. Fortunately, many villagers understood clearly that I was not trying to find out who the "boss" was or which clans were more knowledgeable about their pasts. At the beginning of one of the early gatherings of the learned men of one of the clans, when someone started to make unflattering remarks about the ancestral knowledge of other groups, another man quickly interjected that this wasted the time they should be spending organizing their own knowledge, and in any event, Smith hadn't come to weigh the knowledge of one group against that of another. Still, I often felt rather uncomfortable in the role I'd taken on, and I took pains to explain, when the occasion arose, that I really, really didn't care who could name the most ancestors and which clans could claim the most types of magic and other resources. The American sayings, "I don't have a dog in this fight" and "I don't have a horse in this race," translate very easily into Tok Pisin, and I used them several times.

Of course, as an anthropologist friend of mine pointed out, I shouldn't be surprised if I find that in a few years or even sooner people no longer agree on what they agreed upon in 2008. Or they could continue to agree on the details of clan histories but change their views on their significance. For example, suppose someone were studying the ancestors of Michael French Smith and how Smith and his siblings and cousins formed groups on the basis of common ancestry. My great-great grandfather George Smith had several children, but for the sake of this example, let's say he had only two sons, Snowden and Pinkney, known as Snow and Pink to friends and family. (These are actual Smith family names.) Now, let's say that for generations no one had questioned that the descendants of Snow and Pink formed two separate clans, the Snow-Smiths and the Pink-Smiths—that is, that the clan split after George. But it isn't impossible that, a generation or so after my brother and I and our cousins all left the scene, the descendants of the Snow-Smiths and the Pink-Smiths decided to emphasize their common descent from George and forget about the split between Snow and Pink, a split that once had seemed immutable. Or we could imagine that for generations everyone had treated all the descendants through males of George Smith as a single, indissoluble unit; but in 2025 they decided that it was important to distinguish the descendants of Snow from those of Pink.

People in PNG sometimes tinker with their *straksa* in more radical ways than these. I haven't seen anything in Kragur that seems to point in such a direction. But in other parts of PNG, people have changed the significance they assign to their relationships through common ancestors, marriage, or other sorts of connections to adapt to new circumstances in which it is advantageous to form new kinds of alliances. Anthropologists Martha Macintyre and Simon Foale have documented how people's ideas about "clans" and their relations to resource rights have changed over the course of the development of a large gold-mining project on the PNG island of Lihir, in New Ireland Province.[4] Anthropologist Colin Filer also observed that, during that same period, Lihirians created a Council of Chiefs, even though outside observers concurred that Lihirians had never had a system of hereditary chiefs before. The Lihirians explained that they were modeling their Council of Chiefs on those found in Fiji.[5]

In short, Lihirians changed their *straksa* because they found it useful to do so. In this way, they are anything but "traditional" in the sense of being bound by rules laid down in the distant past. But, if we hung around to watch long enough, we might find out that such flexibility is a fundamental feature of their "tradition." Their *straksa* is not simply a creature of the past, and they do with it what they like to make it at home in the present. And so can the people of Kragur, I imagine, if they see the need, no matter what is written on paper. The word "structure" or *straksa,* of course, seems to imply stability, but stability isn't necessarily rigidity. Water has structure, but it flows.

The process of the *straksa* project was as interesting to me—maybe even more interesting—than the supposedly stable charts of ancestors that it produced. I have spent perhaps too much of my life scheduling meetings, sitting in meetings, and trying to keep meetings from going on until everyone died of exhaustion. I admit that on hot, humid afternoons during some of the *straksa* project gatherings, I sometimes felt as if I needed a couple of sturdy house timbers to keep my eyes open. But these meetings were, as far as I know, different from any meetings ever held before in Kragur. They were certainly different than any I've ever attended there, and they are worth a few words in the next chapter. Also, some details about the kinds of things ancestors bequeath to their descendants will help show why the Kragur people who worked with me took this work so seriously.

Chapter 7

Meetings and Magic

Now, as the business . . . is a very ancient and interesting
one, let us in some measure expatiate here.
—Herman Melville, *Moby Dick*

It took no effort on my part to get the *straksa* work started. The day I arrived in Kragur, a Saturday, several men approached me to say that they were ready to continue the discussions we'd started in 1998. By early afternoon of the following Wednesday, a small group of knowledgeable men from one of the clans had gathered on my veranda to start the kind of discussion of their ancestry none of us had ever had before. Representatives from a second clan met with me the following Sunday.

A senior man started off one of these meetings by producing a dog-eared notebook from the small *bilum* (Tok Pisin: a string bag, woven from handmade cord) he always carried and opening it to a page bearing a list of ancestral names he'd learned from senior men gone before. He had shown me this book in 1998, but he'd told me then that its contents were secret, known to him alone and the elders from whom he'd received the information. In 2008, however, he opened it in front of those gathered on my veranda without any comment.

These prompt gatherings and the fact that some men were clearly coming forward with information they had once held in confidence were a propitious beginning; but, to borrow from the words of the Gospel of Matthew, "where two or three are gathered together," there will be a lot of talk before reaching any conclusions.[1] At the Sunday meeting everyone agreed on the major task at hand, but there was considerable talk of just how to start. The men eventually decided to focus on the line of male ancestors leading directly to the current Kragur clan members, to get the names straight first, then go back and sort out where they had settled, their movements from place to place, and the stories explaining some of these migrations.

The question remained of just how far back to go. Someone said we needed to begin by identifying the very first human beings, not just the most ancient direct ancestor known. Some thought they could trace a line of named ancestors directly to these beings, but the general feeling was that this was a discussion, perhaps even a debate, for another time. Even within clans, claims to knowledge about the first human beings can be controversial. "No one knows what happened back then!" one man blurted out when the same topic arose in another *straksa* meeting. "Did anyone see it? Did God make these first people? Did the ground open and they emerge? We don't have a book that tells us about this!"

Also, no one seemed to be completely sure where to draw the line between the earliest *laif man* (Tok Pisin for living or mortal people) of the clan and what some of those gathered called *spirit man* (Tok Pisin for spirit people). Others spoke of the beings that preceded ordinary mortals as *masalai*, a Tok Pisin word that refers to supernatural beings usually associated with a particular natural feature, such as a stream, a cave, or the swirling currents at Point Urur. The most famous *masalai* on the island is the *masalai* Kairiru, who created the lake on top of the mountain. In the end, we recorded the names of several spirit people at that first Sunday meeting, the men acknowledging that we weren't going to agree that day on exactly how they were related to the deepest mortal ancestors but that they were somehow part of the clan heritage.

These first meetings—and later gatherings of representatives of other clans—proceeded with a good deal of decorum. I sat with my pen poised to take notes, but the men ran the meetings themselves, sometimes turning to me and saying that I needn't bother to write anything down until they had hammered out whatever point they were considering. Occasionally one of the men also recording the proceedings would call for a pause in discussion to read back and confirm what he thought had been decided so far, or several men would compare the numbers of generations they had each recorded and then put their heads together to reconcile their counts and their lists of names. They handled most disagreements very diplomatically:

"I disagree a little with that."

"Let me clarify what I said."

"I think you're mixing stories there."

"I support that."

"Thank you for mentioning that point."

"Let's cross-check our lists."

"That's another clan; forget about that."

"We're stuck again."

"We're going to need some help on this."

As in almost any meeting anywhere, however, patience sometimes wore thin, and decorum slipped:

"I'm tired of this."

"My ass hurts."

"You shut up!"

"Fuck you!"

Amid all this, clouds of tobacco smoke rolled off the veranda, older men with weak teeth ground their betel nut with powdered lime (made by incinerating coral or shells) in small wooden mortars before popping the mixture into their mouths, and quarts of red betel nut juice were spat over the railing or between gaps in the flooring to the ground below. When I lost the thread of the discussion and sat waiting until a difficult point had been sorted out, I would enjoy a few puffs of local tobacco and a short coughing fit, or I would just stare out to sea, perhaps watching someone fishing from a canoe bobbing just offshore or observing the progress of a freighter moving almost imperceptibly along the distant horizon.

Frequently, meetings ended with someone's promise to seek out an absent elder for additional information to bring back to the group at the next gathering. In only a very few cases, someone directed me to a woman for information on a particular clan, but I'm pretty sure that women advised some of the men behind the scenes. Some women know a lot about these matters, but it isn't the custom to include women in decision-making gatherings. During one of the meetings, Margaret Kanis, Kilibop's wife, sat in the doorway of Rokerai's house with a baby on her lap, listening to the men get tangled up in differing versions of the order of their ancestors, and she tried to choke back her laughter but failed. "We're doing this for your own good!" one of the men reprimanded her, and she managed to retreat to a quiet smile. A few weeks later, however, working on the history of Margaret's patrilineal ancestors, we had to consult her for critical details.

While members of some of the clans pushed ahead with the *straksa* work spontaneously, a few clans kept their distance. Getting relatively full accounts from all the clans would be nice, but it wasn't worth making a major nuisance of myself, so I didn't press anyone. One of my professors in graduate school had advised us to "badger your informants," if that's what it took to get your research done. But even during my anxiety-fraught dissertation research, I'd been a very reticent badger. Several men, however, were quite concerned that I get the whole picture from all the clans and took it upon themselves to recruit knowledgeable contributors from, as far as I know, all the clans in the village.

This did not go entirely without a hitch. On one occasion, I returned to Rokerai's house from a recreational scramble up and down a muddy, red-clay trail to find Kitok waiting for me on the veranda with two men from clans with which I was already working but who hadn't been part of the discussions so far. One of them, I know, had been away from the island when the work with his clan started. They had gone to see Kitok to ask just what I was doing and tell him they were worried that I would get their clans' stories wrong or be careless with their secrets. Kitok brought them to see me. I explained the *straksa* work, assuring them that anything anyone wanted kept confidential would be kept confidential. One of them asked to see the descent chart that his group had produced. He looked it over at a leisurely pace, carefully concealing from the others the section a clan member had outlined in heavy red ink and marked "Itambu!" ("Secret!"), and then he handed it back to me without comment.

I knew that this didn't necessarily mean that he agreed with everything he saw, but I made then and I make now no claims that these records represent anything other than faithful accounts of what the villagers involved agreed on and told me to record. I took pains to record exactly who helped prepare the records of each clan, and I took photos of all the participants for good measure. Everyone involved agreed that this was the right thing to do, because Kragur people judge the validity of genealogical information in part by its source. One of the most frequently asked questions in the *straksa* work meetings was, "Who told you that?"

The records that resulted from all this give me a much firmer grip not only on who, past and present, was affiliated with each clan, but also on how the various clans in the village fit together, in some cases through descent from common deep ancestors or, for comparatively recent settlers in Kragur, through some form of adoption into lines already established there. Putting it all together, I can build at picture of the *straksa* of the village as a whole. I can't put this down on paper, however, for any eyes but my own, because so many key parts of the separate clan histories are confidential. So, my big picture is a tentative one that I can't submit to villagers for confirmation. Even if I could, getting representatives from all the clans to agree on a single version of the big picture would probably be harder than the original *straksa* project and more likely to stir up controversy.

Although some villagers know only their corners of the big picture, others do understand—and better than I—how all the pieces fit together; but they too would be reluctant to pronounce on this in public, because no matter how much you know about someone else's ancestors, in most situations it is bad form to air that knowledge in public. Each clan's story is its own to tell. Kragur people, however, do generally agree that in some way they are all kin, and that if they could trace their ancestors back to the very beginning, they would find that all the descent lines go back to the original inhabitants of Kairiru.

The records of clan ancestors were the major part of what the *straksa* work was about, but they were not the only part. Some men were also eager to record stories about their ancestors' exploits. Although Kragur itself was established only a handful of generations ago, some clan histories stretch much further back in time. Over the generations preceding settlement in Kragur, ancestors of its current population lived in various places on Kairiru, on Mushu, and even on the mainland. The stories I've heard explaining the movements of these ancestors virtually all concern people seeking refuge from warfare or looking for a place to weather one of the great famines that are part of the area's oral history. Such stories not only give life to the bare lists of ancestral names, they also make them more credible in villagers' eyes. As one of the men said, anyone can list names, but do they know where these people lived and what they did in life?

Among the things ancestors did that are vital to the status of their descendants were clearing and planting land and acquiring rights to other kinds of property, some of which in English we might call intellectual property. The most fundamental principle on which claims to the use of a piece of land rest is that a patrilineal ancestor was the first one to clear it of forest for gardening or to plant useful trees there, such as coconut, sago, or betel nut palms. In many cases, of course, this happened a long time ago, and descendants of the first ancestor to *katim rop* ("cut the vines"), as one says in Tok Pisin, have multiplied since then. Hence there are often numbers of people who have some sort of claim on the use of a parcel of land, so the distribution of land is a matter of balancing claims and needs, not a matter of anyone having exclusive ownership in the Western sense. Even so, there are still many arguments about rights to particular plots of land. If it gets easier to make money growing cacao or other crops, villagers will have a greater incentive to try to accumulate control over land at others' expense, and questions of land rights could become more contentious.

The intellectual resources that the ancestors acquired and passed on to their descendants are another matter. Unlike the things you can get from land, such as cash crops or gold, they don't have any value in the world's money economy, despite their great importance in Kragur. For example, the forebears of one clan have passed down to them, among many other things, the rights to several *singsing*, each with a name and its own distinctive kind of costume; rights to a canoe of the large, elaborately decorated kind used for long-distance trading voyages; and rights to smaller, less elaborate canoes, for fishing but not voyaging, that also bear personal names. Like *sukup*, the ceremonial spears that are also passed down through the generations in several clans, particular physical canoes wear out, but the names endure and attach to new material canoes. Rights to performing a *singsing* or building and using a named canoe usually include rights to use magical spells that, for example, give dancers vitality or make canoes more seaworthy. Possession of the rights to such objects and all their immaterial accoutrements enhances the prestige of a clan. The most important rights passed down within clans, however, are rights to magic that can make crops flourish or wither, bring schools of fish to the nets or disperse them, or even bring peace and harmony to the village or allow discord to flourish.

Villagers often speak of such rights as belonging to a particular clan, although it's more accurate to say that they are passed down within a clan, and within any generation particular clan members control them. In the 1970s, people used the Kairiru language word *tiptip* to refer to all such rights. That is, to have rights to something was to have *tiptip* for it. When I used this term in 2008, people understood what I meant, but they were much more likely to use the word *kokwal* in speaking of such rights. I can't account for the apparent falling out of use of the term *tiptip*. A lexicon of the Kairiru language compiled by linguist Richard Wivell in the late 1970s contains the word *tiptip* but defines it only as an "ancestral term . . . exact meaning unclear" (Wivell 1981b). So perhaps it was already going out of use when I first learned it—but why, I don't know. Like *tiptip*, *kokwal* implies knowledge of something, rights to its use, and leadership in activities that require its use. But the villagers I worked with on the *straksa* project also spoke of a person who was such a knowledgeable leader as a *kokwal*. In short, having *kokwal* makes one a *kokwal*—that is, a particular kind of leader.

I have always found one kind of magic especially interesting. In Tok Pisin, villagers call it the magic for *strongim ples* or *passim ples*—that is, magic to strengthen (*strongim*) or secure (*passim*) the village. As Kilibop explained it to me in 1998, the magic safeguards not only village harmony but also village health and prosperity, so that "you can't be hungry, people can't run away, people who are far away must return, no one can break up the village." If used for evil, however, white-bearded elder Peter Kaur added, the result is "everything drifts now. The children, the pigs, the dogs, they fly away. The village falls apart, people are hungry, people fight."

The proprietors of this magic, those who hold *tiptip* or *kokwal* for it, don't perform it very often, in part because it is a weighty endeavor. Not only do the lead magician and his assistants have to observe many taboos, so do villagers in general. This means that it's pointless for the lead magician to put in the effort if people aren't going to support him. Among other things, if people argue and fight, the magic won't take. This means that villagers have to keep discord in check in order to put up a stronger barrier against discord, and in any group of people this can be hard to do for more than a very little while. The words of the Gospel of Matthew again come to mind.

The *strongim ples* magic was performed once during the year I spent in Kragur doing my dissertation fieldwork. Benedict Manwau (Manwau)—father of Moses Manwau—was among the first villagers to make me welcome when I first arrived in the village. He was not only good company, he was also a very influential man and a proprietor of much important magic to which his clan held rights, including the *strongim ples* magic. Our friendship didn't get me an inside look at everything that went into performing the magic, but I joined the rest of the village in observing, from a distance, the public finale. This took place in a large open area—an expanse of stony ground punctuated by protruding black boulders—sloping down toward the edge of the cliff, often used for public meetings in those days. Villagers gathered around the edges of the area, while Manwau, gray, lean, and bent, squatted on a large rock near its center. I could see his lips moving—intoning a magical spell, I assumed—and we all watched as he bit off small pieces from the spicy root of a wild ginger plant, used in magic in many parts of PNG, chewed it, and turned stiffly to spit the juice on all sides.

I was standing near another senior man of Manwau's clan while this was going on and asked him if it was alright for me to take a picture. He nodded his assent, so I snapped a photo. In 2008 when I was talking about the *strongim ples* magic with Rokerai and two or three men his age or younger, I mentioned that I'd seen Manwau perform the magic and taken his picture squatting on a rock spitting ginger. Manwau died only a year or two after I left Kragur in 1976. His name, however, still meant something in 2008. When I told stories about him, some of these young men seemed as impressed as if I'd told young baseball fans in the United States that I'd shaken hands with Ted Williams or Mickey Mantle.

Later on, however, a man old enough also to have seen Manwau performing the magic in 1976 asked me quietly if it was true that I had taken a picture of Manwau on the rock. When I said that it was, he suggested that I not show it to anyone, because it could be dangerous to reveal exactly which rock it was. I hadn't really thought of the rock as an essential part of the magic until I described the scene to Rokerai and his friends, who had nodded knowingly. It made sense, however, that magic to strengthen the moral and material foundation of a village, and a village built on rocks to boot, would incorporate a rock in its symbolism. The identity of the rock was public knowledge at the time, but more than thirty years later at least some villagers thought it was possible that someone wishing to do the village harm could incorporate the same rock in magic to undo Manwau's work and the work of those who had performed the magic since.

Kokwal for the most important kinds of magic (such as that affecting gardening, fishing, weather, or village harmony) confers considerable authority in Kragur. The ability to use it for good makes a man (again, this is almost inevitably a man) a potential public benefactor, and the ability to use it maliciously makes a man potentially dangerous. Over the years, villagers have suspected a few *kokwal* of straying to the dark side, but I have never met a *kokwal* who didn't vehemently deny anything of the sort. Even so, there is often caution as well as respect in attitudes toward *kokwal* endowed with control of the important forms of magic.

Rights to magic and named utilitarian or ceremonial objects are sometimes passed between clans. It is very common for the clan of a woman to give such rights as a kind of marriage portion to the groom's kin when she marries. Since Kragur people traditionally marry outside their own clans, this has spread many kinds of rights quite widely within the village and beyond, because marriages outside the village are not uncommon (in which case the bride almost invariably goes to live in the groom's village). It is well understood, however, that primary authority over the use of magic stays with the clan in which it originated and that the recipient of magic as a marriage gift can use it without the permission of the original *kokwal* only within limits.

Some clans have also obtained rights to such things as *singsing* and named sailing canoes, with all their accoutrements of distinctive costume, decoration, and whatever magical spells enliven the dance or speed the canoe, from beyond the village. Kragur men obtained rights to such *singsing* as Sia, Sangal, and Imundru and the canoe Urimterakau, for instance, from other islands or places on the mainland to which they had traveled. When people describe these acquisitions, they often use the Tok Pisin word *paim*, which sounds as if they mean that their fathers, grandfathers, or more distant ancestors purchased the rights to things. But these transactions in *kokwal* are quite unlike cash-and-carry purchases. Although the recipients of *kokwal* give something in return (such as pigs, taro, and shell ornaments, often in the context of a feast), what's going on is usually best described as an exchange of gifts between men that forms or cements a kind of political alliance. When I finally heard a thorough and authoritative account of Kitok's ancestors, I learned that the contemporary status of his clan and his status as chief rested in part on the fact that several generations ago, before there was a village at Kragur, his ancestor Benau presented a feast (a *worap*) to the ancestors of another of Kragur's contemporary clans. Benau's effort impressed his guests so much that they gave him rights to the powerful food production magic belonging to their own clan.

People describe some of the things in which they hold rights as though the ancestors had created and christened them. Regarding other items of their heritage, however, they are very clear that they were not ultimately human creations. Some *singsing*, as one man put it, were part of the original creation on Kairiru: "When the ground emerged, so did these *singsing*." People say that their human ancestors also obtained certain important magic from *masalai*, the spirit beings mentioned earlier. I've been told that human beings obtained the magic for taro fertility from the *masalai* Kairiru and that the ancestor of a clan rich in *kokwal* obtained a number of kinds of magic through cunning from a *masalai* who appeared to him in both human form and as a large snake.

Although people can still accumulate secondary rights to magic and many useful and prestigious things through marriage or gift exchange, the days when the ancestors in one way or another established rights to the most important kinds of magic appear to be over. People just have to live with whatever legacy, rich or poor, their ancestors left for them and whatever status it entails. Kragur people seem rather uniformly proud of their ancestors, but a scion of a clan particularly favored with *kokwal* once told me that he felt sorry for people whose ancestors hadn't left them equally rich heritages. What were their ancestors *doing*, he wondered aloud, when his ancestors were on the alert for opportunity?

There is no simple answer to the question of how Kragur people understand that magic works. Knowledgeable people can tell you what steps to take to make it work and explain why sometimes it fails to work, but I don't think there is a common theory of *how* magic works. Manwau himself explained to me in colorful terms how certain kinds of magic worked—how, for example, magic to spoil pig hunting drives the wild pigs into enclosures in trees. But then he laughed and said that this, of course, was just what is called in Tok Pisin *tok piksa*—that is, "picture talk" or metaphor. Pigs, he said, can't really go inside trees. He and another noted magician of his day, Albert Wagari, also told me, however, that when they performed magic they called on the spirits of their ancestors for help and that certain kinds of magic invoked the power of such beings as the *masalai* Kairiru. In 2008, a young man who had assisted his elders in performing the taro fertility magic told me that the taro magic, for example, acts directly on the taro because the magicians know how to communicate with the taro in the taro's native tongue.

Some kinds of magic employ carved wooden male and female figures called *kaikrauap* in the Kairiru language. These, I was once told, don't have any power in themselves, but through performing the proper ritual they become embodiments or vessels of Wankau. Wankau is the name of an important spirit ancestor, but villagers have also described Wankau to me as a kind of mystical essence pervading everything in nature, or the "spirit behind the spirits" of all individual things, as one man put it. Once it is infused with Wankau, the magician uses the *kaikrauap* to perform magic.

One thing about magic in Kragur I am quite sure of is that, while someone using magic maliciously does so secretly and alone, magic performed to benefit the entire community is almost inevitably a collective effort. Observing a taboo is one aspect of the community cooperation such magic requires. Villagers occasionally make a collective taro garden to prepare for a special event—such as a feast commemorating the death of a leader and marking the succession to his position of one of his heirs—or perhaps to make a ceremonial gift of taro to the people of another village to settle a dispute. They always call this a "big garden," although each participating family actually makes a garden on its own land, and men with rights to apply the magic for increasing the fertility of taro gardens oversee all the separate gardens. A "big garden" made in 2002, I was told, included fifty-two separate gardens. According to some accounts, the 2002 garden wasn't as productive as people hoped it would be, because some of the village people didn't observe the taboos (*tambu* in Tok Pisin) that help give the magic its full strength. The leaders themselves have to submit to especially strict prohibitions on certain behavior, such as having sexual relations, accepting food from the hands of fertile women, eating food boiled in water, or drinking coconut water, which is said to "cool" the magic.

I got to see a similar collective effort to magically improve the fishing in 1976. This stretched out over several weeks, but villagers were very disappointed with the results. The final diagnosis of the magic's failure was that the village had not been harmonious enough. Over and above some taboo violations, a lot of villagers believed that the magic had failed because too many people had been harboring unresolved anger toward others. Had they really wanted the magic to work, they should have come forward to air and settle their grievances.[2]

Not everyone agrees on exactly why magic for the common good requires social harmony. I heard it said in 1976 that if the people couldn't gather together, the schools of fish wouldn't gather together; that if the people couldn't cooperate among themselves, the ancestors wouldn't cooperate with the people; and that God and the Virgin Mary wouldn't grant their favors if the people fought among themselves. Whatever the details, it is very clear that magic for the common good is something more than manipulating nature or activating supernatural powers using some kind of spiritual technology; they are demonstrations of the village's collective moral worth.

Every time I go to Kragur, however, I find some who worry that the power of the *ramat wolap* or *kokwal* is waning, in part because belief in the power of magic, what some call in Tok Pisin *tumbuna save* (ancestral [*tumbuna*] knowledge [*save*]), is declining. I've heard a few young people in Kragur dismiss the reality of magic on the grounds that science offers better explanations of things, but the influence of Catholicism is probably a bigger threat to adherence to *tumbuna save* than is the influence of science. I recall a strong advocate of Catholicism in Kragur in the 1970s, Michael Saulep, father of Ralph, saying that he had no fear of sorcery, not because sorcery wasn't possible but because the power of the Catholic deity was superior. And one man told me that the 2002 big garden had been a disappointment in part because many women ignored the taboos, thus undermining the magic. They did so, he said, because they claimed to have "new life." That is, the women believed that the blessings of the Holy Spirit they received through Catholic Pentecostal worship freed them from the power of other spirits and, hence, many of the obligations of the old ways.

It also may be, as one man suggested to me in 2008, that many people have so lost touch with *tumbuna save* that they don't realize when they are violating some of its tenets and putting themselves at risk by doing so. Most villagers are at least guardedly optimistic about the effects of electricity provided by the promised hydroelectric generator, and I expected only crabby old people to share my concern that cheap electric power will mark the end of Kragur's peaceful nights. So, I was surprised when a friend about half my age said that a lot of villagers may be unpleasantly surprised at what happens if, when they get electricity, they start playing radios and electric guitars until the wee hours. His father's generation, he said, had been quick to admonish people who made too much noise at night, because it "disturbed the stones" that support the village. And he told me of how his father had upbraided the first young man to bring a guitar to Kragur and sit up late into the night strumming it, "krung, krung, krung!" I quickly realized that he was talking about the *strongim ples* magic and saying, metaphorically, that his elders believed— and he did, too—that too much noise at night weakened the magic and made the village vulnerable to unrest and disorder.

One man told me in 2008 that he thought that a "majority" (here he inserted the English word into his Tok Pisin) simply no longer believed in the *tumbuna save*. He wasn't happy about this, but I think he may be overstating the case. I know that it's not only the elders who take pride in the number and kinds of magic to which their clans hold rights; the younger men who took part in the *straksa* project also took their magical heritages very seriously. A clan's magical heritage can inspire fear as well as respect. Villagers fear the leaders of certain clans, I've been told, because they believe those leaders have magical power over the fertility of key garden crops and other food sources. And I know that many villagers are scared of the leaders of particular clans because of their alleged knowledge of sorcery.

But whatever villagers think about the power of ancestral magic, Kragur people know that they face more and more problems that *tumbuna save* can't remedy—including fluctuating prices for their market crops, steadily rising school fees, and the indifference or ineptitude of provincial and national governments. This doesn't necessarily mean that *ramat wolap* or *kokwal* can't help, or even lead, in addressing such relatively new challenges. But if rank-and-file villagers aren't certain just how such leaders are relevant in the changing world, neither are many of these leaders. I've heard a man whom many call a chief announce in public that there are no longer any real bigmen. The same man plunged enthusiastically into the effort to document his own clan's traditional rights to leadership, but he is also active in some of the many committees springing up in Kragur to manage such nontraditional institutions as schools, Catholic worship, and the health clinic.

Whatever uncertainty villagers may harbor about the current relevance of *ramat wolap* or *kokwal,* they at least agree that they were once powerful and essential. They are not yet sure that new kinds of leaders are up to contemporary challenges. This skepticism encompasses those elected to represent them in national and local governments, but it didn't stop villagers from casting their votes and even getting seriously excited about the 2007 (national) and 2008 (local) elections. And despite all the talk about the fading significance of the inherited *tumbuna save* that is still the primary source of clan status, clan affiliation played a major role—too major, some thought—in these exercises in free choice.

Chapter 8
Preferential Ballots
and Primeval Brothers

It is the fashion of a certain set to despise "politics" and the
"corruption of parties" and the unmanageableness of the masses;
they look at the fierce struggle, and at the battle of principles
and candidates, and their weak nerves retreat dismayed from
the neighborhood of such scenes of convulsion. But to our
view, the spectacle is always a grand one.
—Walt Whitman, editorial in the Brooklyn *Eagle*

I have never visited Kragur for more than a few days without getting the sense that I was arriving at a particularly intense time in village life. I did arrive in Kragur for the first time, in November 1975, just a few weeks after Papua New Guinea achieved national independence; and in 1998 I arrived just after the end of a major drought. I know, however, that I get this feeling at least in part because being in Kragur is always a particularly intense time in my own life. Things also may seem especially intense to me in Kragur because people there live their lives more in public than most people in America do.

In Kragur, you can hear the sounds of family quarrels from several houses away, public meetings are held in the open air, and people arguing—about everything from who broke the axe handle to the foibles of the nation's prime minister—sometimes seem to want as many others as possible to hear their shouted accusations and rejoinders. During the day and into the evening, if people are at home they generally leave their doors and widows propped open and exchange greetings with people who pass by on paths often just a few feet away. In addition, virtually everyone in the village is some kind of kin to virtually everyone else, and what concerns your kin will sooner or later—generally sooner—concern you.

Still, there was in fact a lot going on in Kragur when I arrived in 2008. Many villagers were watching every step of what they hoped was Moses Manwau's progress toward the Wewak Open Electorate seat in parliament, and all the people of Kairiru and other area islands were in the middle of a campaign for the office of president of the Wewak Islands Rural Local Level Government. Back in the United States, the campaigns for party nominees for the 2008 presidential election had been in full swing when I'd left, so the atmosphere in Kragur was familiar in some ways to that I'd left behind. At home in the United States, of course, public contests didn't project themselves into my house unless I invited them.

During its many years of governing the Territory of Papua and New Guinea, in service of its mandate to prepare the country for independence, Australia introduced elections for positions of local, regional, and national leadership. The PNG governmental and electoral system, of course, has evolved since then. The main elements of local and provincial elected government in PNG today start with village councilors, each of whom represents a ward (one or more per village, depending on village size). The councilors direct basic village public works, such as keeping main trails cleared or helping maintain the buildings and grounds of village schools, and they represent their wards in aspects of the administration of Local Level Government Areas (LLGs), including decisions on allocating funds for local development projects. The funds come from higher levels of government and from local head taxes. Each LLG is led by a president, who is elected by all adult citizens over eighteen. The presidents of the LLGs represent their constituents in the provincial assemblies. Each province sends representatives of the several electorates into which each province is divided to the national parliament in Moresby. A representative to the national parliament elected by the voters of the province as a whole also serves as provincial governor.

Kairiru falls within the Wewak Islands Rural LLG, which includes islands relatively close to the mainland—Kairiru itself, Mushu, Tarawai, Walis, Kerasau, and Yuo—and islands considerably farther out to sea, such as Wogeo, Koil, Wei, Kadovar, Bam, and Blupblup. (Blupblup is the name given this tiny island on many maps, but Kragur people call it Ruprup, which is still the kind of name that makes you want to jump in a boat and go see what's there.)

One of the first things I noticed when I arrived in Kragur in 2008 was the campaign posters thumbtacked to the walls of many of the houses, displaying the faces and touting the virtues of candidates for Wewak Islands LLG president (fig. 10). Campaigns on behalf of candidates for councilors of the two wards between which Kragur is divided, Wards 11 and 12, were also under way, but there were no posters for the contestants in these neighborhood races, who—as far as I could tell—spent no money on their campaigns. These candidates, of course, were also already well known to the voters. In contrast, while some of the sixteen candidates for Wewak Islands LLG president were Kairiru islanders and well known to Kragur people, others were from islands hours away by boat. The spread of this LLG area over so many miles of sea

Figure 10. Campaign posters for candidates for president of the Wewak Islands Local Level Government, Patrick Beka and Philip Numbos, 2008. Photo by the author.

meant that a serious candidate had to spend considerable money to make a showing in the election, not only for posters and handbills, but also for transportation from island to island to campaign in person. I was told that one prominent candidate spent 7,000 kina (about US $2,800) in the 2008 campaign. In the Wewak Islands, this is no small amount.

Although I'd been in Kragur during elections for village councilors before, I'd never seen the relatively new LLG election system in action. The professionally printed campaign posters alone were something radically new to my eye. They all followed the same pattern: a full-front photo of the candidate's face, with the candidate's name prominently displayed; the number that voters should check on the ballot to vote for the candidate (although ballots included candidates' names, too); and some statements about the candidate's platform. Most posters were brightly multicolored, but many campaigns had also posted dozens of black-and-white photocopies of the colored originals.

Elections were old hat in PNG by 2008. The proclamations and promises on many posters (usually in both Tok Pisin and English) wouldn't have been out of place in elections in almost any Western political campaign. One poster, for instance, announced, "Village people need a leader who knows how they live, and shares their concerns" (I translate freely here from the original Tok

Pisin: "*Ol man bilong ples i nidim lida i save long sindaun, slip na wari bilong ol*"). Another proclaimed, "A man who can make things happen, he doesn't just talk. Enough is enough!" ("*Man husat i ken mekim samting kamap, i no toktok nating. Inap em inap!*").

The posters also included advice on what to do if the candidate wasn't your first choice. In 2003, PNG adopted a limited preferential voting (LPV) system at all levels of elected government. This means that voters pick not only their single favorite candidates but also mark their second and third choices. If no candidate gets a clean majority (50 percent plus one vote) of first choices, then second and third choices are weighed to determine the winner. This solved what had been a vexing problem in PNG elections—competitions among large numbers of candidates yielding winners who had mustered only small pluralities of the vote, sometimes largely members of their own ethnic groups, and who therefore had only narrow support among their constituents. The posters for candidates for LLG president often asked voters for their second or third choice votes, even if the candidate wasn't a voter's first choice.

It wasn't just this voting system that was relatively new in PNG in 2008. The posters plastered all over Kragur assumed a much higher level of general literacy than thinkable in the 1970s, although even in 2008 some older villagers couldn't read either English or Tok Pisin. The emphasis on the numerical possibilities of LPV voting also assumed a certain level of comfort with arithmetic. It wasn't necessary, however, that everyone in Kragur be adept at fathoming the subtleties of the LPV system because many of the strongest supporters of each of the candidates were masters at calculating what combinations of first, second, and third choices their candidates would need to surpass the opposition. Village-level campaign committees sometimes met far into the night speculating on from which parts of the Wewak Islands electorate their candidates could expect to get what portions of first, second, and third choices. Then they spent many daylight and evening hours in the slow, face-to-face task of explaining to local voters why, even if their first choices went elsewhere, it would be to their advantage to throw a second or third choice to the campaigner's candidate.

Papua New Guineans started having Western-style elections when the first local government council was established in 1958 in the highlands region of the country. Australia slowly established this system of local elected leadership throughout the country as a first step toward building a national, democratically elected parliamentary government. According to scraps of government records I was able to find in 1976, Kragur held its first election to choose a local councilor in 1961, selecting Joseph Kashau. (Kashau was serving as councilor again when I first arrived in Kragur. He was among the village leaders who weighed my request to stay and work in the village, and he became my friend and a font of knowledge about Kragur's past and present. He was old and ill when I visited Kragur in 1998 and had died by 2008.)

Not long after Kragur elected its first councilor and before local councils had even been established in most parts of the country, the Australian administration established a national House of Assembly. The first cohort of representatives was seated in 1964. In 1967, during the first term of the House, seven Papua New Guinean and two Australian members joined with a group of educated Papua New Guinea public servants to form the first political party in PNG, the Papua New Guinea National Union or PANGU party, with a platform of rapid movement toward home rule. Although many Papua New Guineans were very nervous about the prospect, the country did move rapidly in this direction. Self-government in internal affairs was granted in 1973, and the country gained full independence in 1975, the House of Assembly morphing into a national parliament.[1]

The governing of Papua New Guinea hasn't always run smoothly since then, but the country has clung fast to its constitutional system, and power has changed hands only as the result of elections rather than through coups or popular uprisings. Even so, the parliamentary elections, which lay the groundwork for selecting a prime minister, have often been rough-and-tumble affairs. Political parties are numerous in PNG, but party affiliation often means very little to candidates and even less to voters. What historians James Griffin, Hank Nelson, and Stewart Firth wrote about the first election for members of the House of Assembly in 1964 could apply almost as well to many parliamentary elections following national independence: "People voted for individuals. There were no 'national' issues, except that most [people] looked to the government for more 'development.' They wanted a representative to persuade the [government] to provide them with more roads, [medical] aid posts, schools, airstrips and opportunities to enter the cash economy."[2]

There was also a tendency in 1964—which has remained—for clans, villages, or regional groups to vote together, a practice known as "block voting" (in Tok Pisin, *blok voting*). Block voting contradicts the ideal of individual political choice, but it also arouses consternation because of the methods many candidates have used to achieve group unity. In parts of PNG, candidates have gone beyond simply appealing to group loyalty to using bribery and intimidation, including violent retaliation for voting outside the block. In addition to block voting, elections for many parliamentary seats have been tainted by ballot box stuffing, ballot box theft, vote buying, padding the rolls of registered voters with "ghost voters," and other kinds of blatant manipulation.

For instance, Bill Standish of the Australian National University was an observer of the parliamentary election in Simbu Province in 2002 and wrote that at one polling place, "the procedure was largely supervised and carried out by tough young men who were the candidates' supporters, as much as by the polling officials."[3] The 2002 election might have been a low point in the history of PNG democracy. It has been described as the "all-round worst election" in PNG's history,[4] and "a major embarrassment" for the country.[5] Rather far beyond embarrassment, it was also reported that election-related violence resulted in dozens of deaths.[6]

In addition to instituting the LPV system in 2003, prior to the 2007 parliamentary contests the government of PNG took a number of steps to try to prevent a debacle like that of 2002, such as trying to correct voter registration rolls, providing better security at polling places, improving methods of moving polling teams around rural areas, and providing more voter education. What I know of the voter education effort comes from the PNG Electoral Commission posters in Tok Pisin affixed to the walls of the veranda of Rokerai's house, along with a poster displaying the pictures and ballot numbers of all the candidates in the 2007 race for parliamentary representative from the Wewak Open Electorate.

One voter education poster lists the "Good Ways" (*Gutpela Pasin*) for participating in the election, illustrated with colorful, well-composed photographs of cheerful people exhibiting proper behavior on the campaign trail and at the polls. The other poster provides the same for "Bad Ways" (*Pasin Nogud*), acted out for the camera by the same troupe of people but this time wearing expressions of fear, anger, and suspicion.

The "Good Ways" poster urges candidates and voters to act as follows:

- Speak Well to Win Votes [that is, win votes by persuasion] (*Toktok Gut long Winim Vote*);
- Vote According to Your Own Preference (*Vot long Laik bilong Yu Yet*);
- Leave the Voting Area in Good Condition (*Larim Vot Ples istap Gut);*
- Vote Only Once (*Vot Wanpela Taim Tasol*);
- Leave the Ballot Box with the Election Workers (*Lusim Balot Bokis wantaim ol Ileksen Wokman*); and,
- Vote Only for Good Candidates (*Vot long Gutpela Kendidates Tasol*).

Finally, the poster reminds people that "Men and Women Have the Right to Vote According to Their Own Preferences" ("*Manmeri igat Rait long Vot long Laik bilong ol Yet*").

The "Bad Ways" poster warns against contrasting behavior:

- You Can't Fight with Guns to Win Votes (*Noken Pait wantaim Gan long Winim Vot*);
- You Can't Intimidate Men and Women Who Are Voting (*Noken Poretim ol Manmeri long Vot*);

- You Can't Wreck the Voting Area (*Noken Bagarapim Ples*);
- You Can't Vote Several Times (*Noken Vot Planti Taim*);
- You Can't Steal the Ballot Box, or the Ballot Papers (*Noken Stilim Balot Bokis, wantaim ol Balot Pepa*); and,
- Candidates Can't Buy Your Vote (*Kendidet Noken Baim Vot bilong Yu*).

Mirroring the final injunction of the "Good Ways" poster, it closes by enjoining against trying to deter people from voting their individual preferences: "You Can't Bribe or Intimidate Men and Women to Vote the Way You Want Them to" (*"Yu Noken Grisim o Poretim Manmeri long Givim Vote long Laik bilong Yu"*). In case there was any doubt about the leading principle of good campaigning and voting, the bad-behavior poster states at the bottom in bigger, bolder letters, "All men and women have the right to vote according to their own preferences. It's the individual's choice" (*"Ol manmeri igat rait long vot long laik bilong ol. Em laik bilong wanwan"*).

By the time of the 2007 parliamentary election, although the LPV system was in place nationwide, some election officials were still concerned that people would find it too complicated. By and large, however, Papua New Guineans handled the system well and it seemed to accomplish what it was intended to. That is, it prevented candidates from winning elections with only tiny pluralities of the vote and made it necessary for candidates to reach beyond their own clans and communities for support.[7]

Only three years later, in 2010, the American Academy of Motion Picture Arts and Sciences instituted a similar preferential voting system for choosing recipients of the Academy Awards, or Oscars. Many American movie industry observers were at least as concerned as PNG election officials that the voters (the members of the academy) would find such a system dauntingly complex; "Oscars' New Voting System a Real Puzzler," read a headline in the newspaper *USA Today*.[8] Fortunately, the members of the academy proved as adaptable as PNG villagers, and the awards were presented on schedule and with no more controversy than usual.

The 2007 PNG election was far from perfect, especially in some highlands provinces, but some observers described the campaign as "the quietest in recent PNG history." By all reports I heard, the 2007 election was also relatively quiet and orderly in the Wewak Open Electorate, in which two Kragur men—Moses Manwau and Ralph Saulep—were among the candidates. I learned from one of Rokerai's election posters that there had been forty-three candidates for the Wewak Open seat, making the wisdom of the LPV system evident. Thirty-two of the forty-three candidates ran as independents. The remaining eleven candidates each represented a different party. In the country as a whole, only one woman won a seat in the 109–member parliament in the 2007 election: Lady Carol Kidu, an incumbent member. (A number of Papua New Guineans bear the honorary titles "Sir" and "Lady" because PNG is a member of the British Commonwealth of Nations. Membership in the Commonwealth also explains the stamps issued in honor of Queen Elizabeth's birthday and those commemorating the rare visit from a member of the royal family.)

The 2007 election also went quite smoothly within Kragur, despite the homeboy competition. Someone did tell me that at one point, some of Ralph's and Moses' supporters almost came to blows, but this is a vast distance from systematic intimidation and violent retribution.

Ralph was the candidate of the Pan-Melanesian Congress. His campaign posters listed a number of specific projects he planned to promote in parliament, such as building a new hospital at Cape Boram, bringing telephone service to the offshore islands, and improving programs for area youth. The core of his platform, however, was his experience as a business lawyer and his insistence on the need for business development, not only to increase cash incomes but also as a foundation for improving education and family health and achieving "true independence."

Moses, for whom this was the third effort to win a seat in parliament, ran as a candidate of the PNG Party. Under the headline "Mr. Wewak," one poster from Moses' 2007 campaign sets a head-and-shoulders photo of him—wearing a startling yellow, red, and blue polo shirt—against the background of a Wewak beach, with a glimpse of Mushu and Kairiru in the distance. Moses, a medical doctor who is known around Wewak and even in Kragur as Dr. Moses, made no explicit promises on his poster but emphasized his oneness with the local people. He "Lives with you all the time; Feels pain with you; Has worries and sorrows like you; Gives his time to listen to you" ("*Stap olgeta taim wantaim yu; Pilim pen wantaim yu; Kisim wari na hevi olsem yu; Save givim taim long harem yu*"). Moses also told me that he favored placing health and education above other policy concerns. One of his major aims if elected, I heard, was to work to become minister of education and from that position to seek to lower school fees.

A lot of Kragur people had a healthy skepticism about campaign promises. Rokerai's attitude toward one common campaign claim crossed over from skepticism to cynicism. All the candidates, he said, always vowed that they were honest, but everyone knew that this couldn't be true. And if it were true, then it wouldn't help you choose among them. If there were a candidate who said he was a liar, mused Rokerai, he'd be tempted to vote for him, because he'd know that he was honest. For his part, Watar had a pretty low opinion of parliament members in general, and he mused about starting a new political party with a name more honestly reflecting what he regarded as their principal activities. His party would be called either the Sindaun Nating Pati (Do Nothing Party) or the Raun Raun Nating Pati (Wander Aimlessly Party).

But the campaigns churned ahead anyway. In 2007, candidate Jim Simitab was declared the winner in the race for member from the Wewak Open Electorate and was seated in parliament. But in 2008 the election still wasn't over as far as Moses and his supporters were concerned. Moses had come in a close second to Simitab, and he almost immediately filed a petition for a review of the results, charging Simitab supporters with ballot box tampering. Simitab and members of the electoral commission fought his petition in a court battle that was still in its childhood when I arrived in 2008. It wasn't until the middle of 2009 that a court ruled that Moses even had a right to apply for a review of the evidence.

I believe even Ralph's supporters were pleased with the news that Moses could take his complaint to law; better one Kragur man in parliament than none at all, many figured. And Ralph quickly pitched in to help Moses with his case, even meeting him and his supporters at the airport in Moresby when they first arrived to take their cause to the next level after having been granted a right to petition for a review. Apparently trying to ease the friction between his and Ralph's supporters, Moses included some of Ralph's village backers in this delegation to the national capital.

Despite the widespread hope in Kragur that Moses would eventually prevail, there was some grumbling about the entire episode. Look how close the election was, a few villagers said to me; if Ralph and Moses hadn't divided the Kragur and Kairiru votes, one of them would certainly have won outright. I understand that they did try to reduce the effect of their competition on their respective chances by each urging his supporters to give their second-choice votes to the other. And they understood well that in an LPV system, attacking your opponents too strenuously can backfire, because it can ruin your chances of getting their supporters' second- or third-choice votes. Despite all this, it looked as if some voters had brought either less sophistication or more bitterness to the polls and declined to give any support to their local favorite's opponent.

One Kragur analyst held that this must have been so because—according to his calculations—if everyone in Kragur had given their first- and second-choice votes to Ralph and Moses in any order, Moses would have won even without the relatively few disputed votes for Simitab. I don't use the word "analyst" lightly here, because I've seen this young man expertly calculate with a scrap of paper and a stub of pencil several different possible distributions among a list of candidates of first-, second-, and third-choice votes to assess their effects on the outcome.

Kitok told me that he had counseled Ralph and Moses not to compete against each other. I am almost certain that they wouldn't have done so if they had been members of the same clan. Ralph and Moses are not only of different clans (each very proud of its heritage), they are also on opposite sides of a larger division of the Kragur population. Kragur's clans are divided between what anthropologists call *moieties*. Moieties are groups formed by sorting a larger group into two complementary smaller groups. In Kragur, one moiety is called Seksiek and the other is called Lupelap.[9] Each moiety is said to comprise the descendants of one of two brothers, the Lupelap descended from the older brother and the Seksiek from the younger. These brothers were the offspring of a spirit being in a very ancient time before Kairiru was populated by mere mortals. The descendants of the two brothers who eventually settled in Kragur established there a distinction between the descendants of the elder and the younger.

This division was very important, I'm told, when indigenous religious practices were in full flower; that is, before Catholic missionaries got a grip on the Kragur imagination in the 1930s. The Catholic mission and its early local converts suppressed the Kragur version of what anthropologists often call a men's cult—an institution common throughout a large part of PNG in the past and still active in some places in the present. When the Kragur men's cult was still a center of village life, it was the rule for people to take their spouses from the opposite moiety and for the men of each moiety to initiate into the men's cult the young men of the other, who were their kin by virtue of cross-moiety marriage. Initiating the young men into the cult included imparting knowledge of ritual for relating to the powerful spirits, known in Tok Pisin as *tambaran,* to which the ceremonial houses of the men's cult were dedicated and engaging in ritual activities to impart to the initiates full masculinity. Although cult activities focused on men—enhancing the power of senior men who directed them and imparting full masculinity to boys—in many communities, men and women agreed that keeping good relations with the *tambaran* spirits contributed to the welfare of the entire population.

I understand that by the 1940s Kragur people had abandoned at least the public aspects of cult activity, but at least one of the ceremonial houses— much larger than an ordinary house, with high, sweeping gables at each end—remained standing until Allied bombing of Japanese camps on Kairiru in World War II destroyed it, along with much of the rest of the village. In the 1970s, a few of the oldest men in Kragur had vague memories of being shown the sacred interiors of the ceremonial houses, but no one was still alive to whom the secret *tambaran* knowledge had been imparted.

Kragur people do, however, still recognize the division between Suksiek and Lupelap. They talk about clans as belonging to one or the other division, and some even refer to the two council wards as "the Seksiek ward" and "the

Lupelap ward" (although there isn't an exact fit between the ward division and the distribution of moiety households). While I am virtually certain that Ralph and Moses would not have challenged each other if they had belonged to the same clan, I also think it's highly unlikely that they would have challenged each other if they were members of the same moiety. But I'll probably never know for sure if intramoiety competition in parliamentary elections is off limits in Kragur. It's rare enough for a village as small as Kragur to field two candidates for parliament in one election, let alone often enough to test a hypothesis. Clan loyalty, however, clearly played an important role in the 2008 local elections, the topic of the next chapter.

Chapter 9

A Clean Election and
Its Messy Aftermath

How soothing it will be to get away from all this complexity
of personal relationships to the simplicity of a primitive
tribe, whose only complications are in their kinship
structure and rules of land tenure, which you can
observe with the anthropologist's calm detachment.
—Barbara Pym, *Less than Angels*

There is a lot more to democratic government and a democratic society than voting, but the difficulties of conducting any sort of plausible popular voting are considerable. From what I saw in 2008, I'd say that Kragur people and the government election officials from Wewak managed it very well, and this is no small compliment. Not, however, that everything was sunshine and smiles.

The elections for ward councilors and Local Level Government area presidents were supposed to take place nationwide at the same time as the 2007 parliamentary elections, but they were postponed until 2008, probably because preparing for the parliamentary elections under the new LPV system with hopes for better logistics and security than in 2002 was a big enough task in itself. So I arrived in Kragur in 2008 when the campaigns leading up to the polling, to be held in early June, were still in progress.

The council election I observed decades before in 1976 involved no apparent public campaigning before the day of the vote. It was such a low-key affair that if not for the public polling, I almost could have overlooked it. All of Kragur was a single council ward in those days, and when a challenger edged out the incumbent councilor, the two candidates shook hands in the center of the village and I saw or heard no protests or complaints afterward. If there was any public campaigning for the council election in 2008, I didn't see that either. I know that there was a lot of quiet counting and recruiting of supporters behind the scenes, but it was only after the election that I could see how intense some people's feelings were about the contest.

I missed a lot of the public campaign for LLG president, but I arrived in time to see some of it. On the morning of Wednesday, May 14, just four days after my arrival, a candidate from one of the larger villages on Mushu Island visited Kragur, and I got to see my first PNG campaign speech. Someone rang the village bell at about 7:30 a.m. to call people to the assembly. This was the same rust-coated propane cylinder left over from World War II that probably had been hanging from the curving trunk of a large coconut palm near the center of the village since the late 1940s, but its clanging still easily reached all corners of Kragur. A sizable crowd had gathered by about 9:30, villagers responding to the bell at the same leisurely pace with which they still responded to any official summons. It had rained hard in the night and it was still drizzling lightly, and people sheltered as best they could under the spreading trees surrounding the meeting ground.

Years ago, Kragur people had abandoned an open space just up from the edge of the cliff as the favored public meeting spot. They now held most outdoor public assemblies on a flat rectangle of ground farther up the slope and directly in front of the small prayer house where those who were too sick or elderly to walk to Bou on Sundays held services. A bench of bamboo logs squared one of the meeting ground's corners at the end opposite the prayer house, and people also found places to sit on the verandas of neighboring houses, on rocks and bamboo logs under the overhanging thatch at the front of the prayer house, and on the boulders forming the lower boundary of the meeting area. I brought my folding, three-legged camp stool and found a place under the corner of the prayer house eaves. Immediately to my right, Peter Kaur seemed perfectly comfortable arranging himself under the scant protection from the rain of a tall palm, squatting with his lean buttocks resting on two adjacent stones, a method of seating I could never learn to tolerate for more than a few minutes.

By the time the candidate stepped forward, in clean shorts and sport shirt but barefoot, the sun was coming out and the sweat glistened on his face as he stood in the center of the meeting ground and began his presentation in Tok Pisin. Kairiru is not the indigenous language of the candidate's home area on Mushu, but I found in the coming days that even Kairiru-speaking candidates chose to orate in Tok Pisin.

The candidate began by saying that unlike some other candidates, he couldn't afford campaign posters. Today, he said, he was his own poster. To emphasize his connections to Kragur and Kairiru, he pointed out that he had been a student at St. Xavier's secondary school and his father had once been the pilot of the now-retired St. Xavier's boat, the *Tau-K*. Although he'd also attended a Catholic seminary, he said he hadn't felt the call to a lifetime of church service and had returned to his village. Therefore, he continued, he understood village problems and the problems of islanders, and he could "feel [their] pain." I'd already seen the same claim to empathy with other's distress on Moses Manwau's campaign posters. On hearing it from the mouth of a second PNG politician, it was impossible not to think that Bill Clinton's rhetorical style was becoming as ubiquitous as the swan maiden story—but at the much faster pace of electronic communications media.

The candidate made no soaring promises, but he assured people that he stood for "honesty and equality." He would, he said, represent all the people of the area, not just Mushu. He would also make sure that all ward councilors had a voice in the LLG proceedings, help councilors prepare proposals for LLG funding of local community projects, and visit all the council wards in the area. This was a platform short on policy specifics but perhaps attractively modest to people who had heard many over-the-top promises in the past, like that of the 2002 parliamentary candidate who had promised to build a bridge linking Wewak to Kairiru and provide Internet access in every village.[1] More interesting to me than the candidate's presentation, however, was the lively discussion that followed. The Kragur people here on this day were anything but passive players in a mysterious foreign ritual; they were knowledgeable, probing, and outspoken participants who took what was going on very seriously.

Paul Bashu, in white shirt and dark pants for the occasion, began the discussion by addressing the full meeting rather than questioning the candidate. He reminded everyone that this was the only LLG candidate from Mushu, but there were seven from Kairiru who might split the Kairiru vote among them. This would increase the Mushu candidate's chances considerably, as Kairiru and Mushu were the largest and most populous islands in the Wewak Islands LLG area. Although horse racing is known to most people in the area only through the news and the televised races at a betting parlor in Wewak, Bashu then turned to the candidates to say, "We [Kairiru islanders] have seven horses in the race, but you're the only horse from Mushu and people say that you're the hot favorite," all of this said in Tok Pisin except for the English phrase "hot favorite." I think he meant this as much as a warning to Kairiru people as encouragement to the Mushu candidate. One of the candidate's traveling companions, however, picked up the horse race image and pointed out that if people bet on the wrong horse, they wouldn't win, as he put it in English, the "goods and services" that an LLG president could deliver. Since the candidate himself had just promised that if elected he would not practice favoritism, I hope he reminded his entourage of this on the boat trip back to Mushu.

Nick Marai, a retired Wewak police officer, then pursued Bashu's line of analysis a little further, asking the candidate how many eligible voters there were in his own village and if they supported him. There were several hundred, the candidate replied, and he had entered the race at their urging. Another Kragur man then rose to say that he supported the Mushu candidate and that people shouldn't throw away their votes on candidates who couldn't win. Before the meeting adjourned, sitting Ward 11 councilor Gabriel "Gabby" Kareo reminded everyone that "the time of politics is a time of lies," so they should be sure to question everything any candidate said and make up their own minds. The assembly concluded on another note familiar from political campaigns in America, where belief in God seems to have become a requirement for public office at all levels. Someone in the crowd declared that "a man who fears God will do good work in public office," and another advised the dispersing crowd to "listen to the voice of the Holy Spirit!"

Although there were several candidates from Kairiru, I had a chance to hear only two of them campaign in Kragur, and it looked as if these two men between them commanded the allegiance of most Kragur voters. Retired school headmaster Philip Numbos was one of these; Patrick Beka of Bou Village was the other. Beka had worked for the area health department for several years, helped start the Wewak Islands LLG after the provincial government reorganization of 1995, and served more than once as councilor for Ward 13, which encompasses Bou and Shagur. On Monday, May 19, Beka came to the village to make his final plea for Kragur votes.

Someone rang the bell about 8:00 a.m., but at 9:00 the crowd was still pretty sparse. A loudspeaker had been hooked up to a car battery for Beka's address, and someone used it to boom across the village an irritated reminder that it was time for the meeting. Beka was there already, sitting in the shade, looking relaxed and quite accustomed to waiting patiently for such events to begin. Not everyone shared his patience, however, and a middle-aged man finally got up and made an angry, unamplified speech about people not responding to the bell. Then he took the loudspeaker microphone and let loose again. When he told everyone who was still lingering in the outhouse to hurry it up, he drew some laughter, so he worked that message into his harangue a couple more times, then turned to the crowd and, smiling broadly, said, "Thank you!" with a slight bow.

A few men in the crowd shouted to him in Tok Pisin, "Yu boi tru!" I hadn't heard this expression before, but in 2008 it was very much in vogue. It translates as something like "What a guy!" or "You're the man!" or, among my wife's people, "You're a mensch!" In the colonial era, many whites used "boy" as a demeaning term for any indigenous man, whatever his age or status. In contemporary PNG, however, while the term *boi* can connote youth, it isn't usually used pejoratively. It's a good thing for a man to be counted among "we Kragur boys," and an especially good thing to be a *boi tru*. It's also good to be a *boi stret* (boy straight), which is about the same thing (and has nothing to do with sexual orientation).

Before the morning campaign proceedings began, one of Kragur's Catholic leaders took the opportunity to make a rather lengthy series of announcements about church events, including the coming Feast of Corpus Christi, in celebration of which a statue of the Virgin Mary was to be carried in procession throughout the island's villages. And before Beka finally stood to speak, one of his supporters offered a prayer asking for guidance for the candidate. He followed this, however, by a thoroughly secular admonition that people shouldn't be constantly inquiring about a candidate's "base vote"—that is, the number of firm supporters, usually from the candidate's own village or island, that a candidate could count on. Rebutting those who recommended voting for the candidate who had the best chance of winning, he said that the point wasn't to pick the winner but to pick the candidate you wanted to win.

Finally, Beka took the floor—that is, the hard-packed earth meeting ground—barefoot and wearing long pants, a sport shirt, and an "I ♥ Jesus" baseball cap. The cap, however, was the only reference to things religious in the rest of his presentation. He had a long political career behind him and reminded people of his accomplishments, emphasizing his successful efforts to keep the Wewak Islands together in their own LLG area rather than parceled out among several mainland-based areas. He spoke also of the need for better, more honest money management in the LLG, the need for representation for island women in local-level government, and the need to root out nepotism. As he spoke, he paced back and forth underneath what felt to me like a truly punishing sun, dismissing at one point a suggestion that he move into the shade. Staying in the shade, however, would have required him not only to move out of the center of the meeting ground but to stand in one place, which would clearly have cramped his energetic style. He finished by asking for people's number two and three votes if they couldn't give him their first choices. Then he called for the sitting councilors from Wards 11 and 12 to come forward. Standing between them, he clasped each by the hand and pledged that he would work in solidarity with whomever the councilors were after the election.

The discussion that followed wasn't a question and answer session with the candidate but—again—an exchange among villagers about how to allocate their votes. Yes, someone said, block voting is a bad thing, but look at the result of splitting the Kairiru vote in the parliamentary election. Bashu again analyzed the distribution of candidate support and said, in English, that the election was a "numbers game." There was definitely strong sentiment in this crowd for a Kairiru candidate, and several people suggested that it would be wise to give their first and second choices to Beka and Numbos, in whatever order they saw fit. A Beka supporter then rose, promising that he didn't have much to say but holding several pages of closely written notes, which looked ominous. He didn't get far, however, before someone picked up the loudspeaker again and boomed, "Keep it short!" Seeing he was losing his audience fast, he rushed to finish his remarks, and the meeting soon drew to an end.

I noted that the final speaker had delivered almost half of his foreshortened remarks in English. Other speakers, too, larded their remarks with long passages in English, in addition to such short phrases as "hot favorite" and "base vote." I wasn't sure if I was seeing evidence of a leap ahead in English literacy or a growing communications gap between the younger and better educated and the older, less cosmopolitan villagers.

The other Kairiru candidate, Philip Numbos, didn't hold his last rally in Kragur until the evening of Sunday, June 1, the day before the election officers were scheduled to come from Wewak to begin polling in Kragur, first in Ward 11 and the following day in Ward 12. Numbos' father had been a *ramat wolap* of the old guard and Numbos' own speaking style had in it a good deal of the traditional bigman's self-assurance. But in addition to pointing out the ways he had already helped the village, he struck a note of humility by saying that after five years living in retirement in the village, he realized that there were "haves and have-nots" (he used the English phrase) in Kragur and that he and the other educated Kragur people had been too interested in their own advancement and hadn't combined their efforts to improve the lot of the village. In making this point, he produced a copy of *Village on the Edge* and cited the statistics I'd included demonstrating that the average level of schooling in Kragur was much higher than the average for PNG as a whole. Kragur, he said, was full of educated people, but someone needed to organize them, and he proposed to do just that. He closed by calling on people to have "Kragur pride" (in English again) and to hold fast to the tradition of generosity and hospitality that sets Kragur people off from others wherever they are found. "Kragur's way beats them all!" he concluded, this time in pure Tok Pisin ("*Fasin Kragur i winim ol!*").

Bashu then contributed his numerical analysis, going over the numbers of eligible voters on other islands and noting how Kairiru's population gave its candidates an advantage if the islanders used their votes wisely. And if you can't read and write, he said, be sure to get someone to help you mark your ballot, a practice that is permitted in PNG elections if done under the supervision of a polling official who ensures that the helper doesn't influence the voter. Philip's campaign manager (Peter Kaur's son, Peter Chapuan Kaur) followed Bashu's remarks with his own analysis, arguing that the chances that one of the two local Kairiru candidates, Numbos or Beka, would become LLG president were good if everyone made them either first or second choice on their ballots.

With that, the public campaigning was over, although I knew there would be a lot of private campaign activity far into the night. From what I saw, however, the candidates had given Kragur people a lot to think about, both regarding voting strategies and reasonably tangible differences between the candidates. None of them pleased Rokerai by announcing that he, the candidate, was a liar, but I judged that most villagers took all political promises with more than a grain of salt. In fact, Kragur was already breeding its own political satirists. While sitting with Rokerai, Munbos, and several others, waiting for the bell to call us to the Numbos campaign event, Benny Sogum (the young man who occasionally announced that he was God), who had been sitting by the fire smoking, rocking, and grinning, began suddenly to deliver a typical campaign speech, full of familiar promises and pleas for second- and third-choice votes. His phrasing, cadence, and intonation were pitch-perfect, and he drew a hearty round of applause and several promises of votes if he could get on the ballot.

Despite the ease of mocking the candidates in general, I didn't have grounds to question their sincerity. A smaller thing, however, did bother me, and that was just how much of the oratory and subsequent discussion older or less-educated villagers had really been able to understand. Mixing the Kairiru language with Tok Pisin and English is common in Kragur, and I'm not sure that what is going on should be construed as "mixing" rather than simply linguistic evolution. I occasionally jotted down examples of the blended language some villagers often used. One of my favorites was one man's remark in a public discussion that was wandering from its alleged point. Yielding to his frustration with this, he broke in on a speaker to say, "*Kiau umashul bihainim agenda!*" That is, "I say" ("*Kiau umashul,*" which is pure Kairiru) "follow" ("*bihainim,*" which is Tok Pisin of considerable vintage, although derived from English) "the agenda" ("agenda" is straight English, but only for a little while longer because it is rapidly becoming part of the Tok Pisin vocabulary). I've heard numbers of villagers complain about the way younger people in particular grab whatever word is handy without care for distinguishing languages, but this trend is likely only to gain speed.

I'd never heard more English thrown around publicly in the village than in the 2008 campaign events. Some speakers lapsed into long passages of English, and as I said, the candidates themselves were prone to lace their remarks with English, including phrases such as "haves and have-nots," "educated elite," and "bottom-up planning." I remembered years ago an older villager laughing at a visiting Kragur townsman who had lectured a public meeting on the need for "compromise" on some village issue and telling me that at least half of the people who heard him probably didn't know the word "compromise." Regarding "bottom-up planning," one elderly man told me that he liked the idea because he assumed that it meant going back to the ways of the ancestors.

Whether the candidates had made themselves clear or not, polling for ward councilors and the LLG president began on June 3, a Wednesday. The team of three election officers (a presiding officer and two assistants) had intended to begin polling in Ward 11 the day before, but they had been unable to leave Wewak on schedule because they didn't receive their stipend for boat fuel in time. When I walked down to the polling area (the meeting ground in front of the prayer house) on the morning of June 3, a large number of villagers had already gathered, and the voting apparatus was in place. Most of the meeting area was roped off, and signs—one professionally printed and the other hand-written—indicated the entrance and exit from the area: "This Way In" and "This Way Out." Two tables were set up for the election officers in the shade near the entrance to the voting area, where they would sit in the red plastic chairs they brought from Wewak to check people's names against the ballot rolls. In the sunny middle of the area stood two voting booths. These were collapsible cardboard devices, set up on tables to form three-sided cubes within which people could mark their ballots in privacy (fig. 11). Each booth bore boldly printed text: "Election Booth / Election Commission Papua New Guinea / 'Make Your Mark For The Nation'." Two metal ballot boxes sat on the ground a few steps from the booths, not far from the way out, marked with handmade signs on sticks, one for "Presidents" and one for "Ward Councillor."

No stranger could ever walk through Kragur without being noticed, but the polling officers also wore T-shirts identifying each of them each as a "Polling Official PNG Elections." Other than that, they could almost have passed for local rural Papua New Guineans. One of them, the presiding officer I believe, had come supplied with an enormous bunch of betel nuts, into which he dug deep over the two days of the Kragur polling. One of his assistants, however, was smoking filter cigarettes from a pack, marking him indelibly as a townie.

A separate area was roped off under the eaves of the prayer house, just beyond the ballot boxes, for the scrutineers, a number of local men seated on stones and bamboo logs. Each candidate for ward councilor or LLG president was entitled to a scrutineer to watch the polling booths and the ballot boxes, alert for any signs of irregularity, much like the poll watchers who perform these duties in US elections. Kirar, himself a scrutineer, told me later that they had the authority to stop the voting if they thought that, for example, someone assisting an illiterate or blind voter was trying to influence that person's vote. The scrutineers also inspected the ballot boxes before voting began and after the boxes were emptied for vote counting to be sure nothing had been slipped in or left behind, and they witnessed the sealing and unsealing of the boxes with plastic fasteners, confirming by the numbers on the fasteners that the boxes had not been tampered with and resealed during any pause in voting.

The two polling days were festive occasions. Many villagers wore their

Figure 11. A Kragur villager marking ballots for Local Level Government president and ward councilor in a portable voting booth, 2008. Photo by the author.

newest, brightest clothes, as though they were going to church; they came early, and many stayed after voting to socialize and watch the proceedings. When occasional voters got confused and tried to leave the polling area through the entrance rather than the exit, the onlookers laughed and called out to correct them. A number of women offered taro, betel nut, tobacco, and other goods for sale near the polling site, laid out on pieces of cloth spread on the ground. Just downhill from the meeting ground, I could see villagers coming and going on a wide, gravelly path that led between two houses up to the polling area. Several women had laid out goods for sale on either side of this passage, at the front corners of the adjacent houses, and along the walls of the houses in a row of dwellings just below. The scene startled me for a moment, because it didn't look like the Kragur I knew, innocent of commerce; it reminded me instead of a Latin American village on market day where, at the intersection of two streets, a stream of pedestrians passed to and fro, pausing to eye wares for sale, chat with the vendors, and move on.

Several members of the Kragur auxiliary police in full uniform added color to the larger scene. I learned from John Belal, the leader of this small group of volunteers (I counted nine members), that the East Sepik Province had started forming village auxiliary police units in 2004 and that the program had come to Kairiru and Mushu Islands in 2006. Originally, he said, the village units had reported to the ward councilors, but earlier in 2008 they began working with a "field commissioner" (Belal's English description), a member of the regular police force stationed on the mainland side of the island. There were even plans, he said, to build cells at the field commissioner's headquarters. Street scenes out of Latin America in Kragur were one thing, but I found it painful to picture people in cells on Kairiru, and I hoped it would never come to that.

Kragur had, however, encountered problems in the last couple of decades for which local police had apparently come in handy. In 1998, numbers of villagers told me at length about the spreading popularity, especially among young men, of drinking home-brewed alcohol (called *hombru*—that is, home brew—in Tok Pisin) and of how some young men became violent, abusive, and impervious to the authority of their elders when they drank. Periodically, the ward councilors and the bigmen were able to get the problem under control, they told me, but it had a way of coming back. In 2009, the Kragur auxiliary police had apprehended three men for home brew infractions and taken them before the regular authorities in Wewak, who sentenced them to community service work in the village ("work at the school, the clinic, repairing roads," said Belal), supervised by the auxiliaries. There were also young local marijuana smokers to be dealt with. Apparently they couldn't be satisfied with getting quietly high and wandering the village looking for something sweet or spicy to eat. Rather, I was told, they got rowdy just like the home brew drinkers.

The election officers enlisted the auxiliary police on both polling days to help monitor people helping others to vote and to keep spectators behind the boundaries of the polling area. (The officers, however, permitted me to wander in and out at will to photograph the proceedings from all angles.) One of the auxiliaries also sat with the election officer as he checked off voters against the official roll, confirming their identities and helping the officer interpret spellings of voter names that didn't clearly suggest their proper pronunciation. On the second day of polling, there was also a break at midday to clarify, with the auxiliaries' help, some of the names on the voting roll that didn't match what the villagers in question actually called themselves.

The auxiliaries stood out in a crowd when they suited up (fig. 12). The provincial program didn't provide them with uniforms, but someone in one of the Kairiru or Mushu units knew someone in Wewak who knew where to get pieces of discarded regular police uniforms. On the two polling days, most of the Kragur auxiliaries dressed in light blue uniform shirts still bearing the sleeve patches of the Papua New Guinea Royal Constabulary. They complemented their shirts with a mixed bag of long pants, military-style web belts, and black shoes. A few of the auxiliaries also sported berets with Royal Con-

Figure 12. The Kragur Village Auxiliary Police, 2008. Photo by the author.

stabulary patches. Kilibop was a member of the unit, but he saved his one pair
of black shoes for his church duties. For his work with the auxiliaries, he had
pieced together with needle and string a single pair of jungle combat boots
from three different pairs in varying states of collapse. (Late in my visit, he
also saved my hiking shoes by sewing the soles back on with string when the
island's stones began to tear them off.)

The climax of the voting was counting the ward councilor ballots. (The
ballot boxes for LLG president remained sealed to be opened and counted in
Wewak along with the LLG ballots from the other villages and islands.) The
scrutineers checked the number on each ballot box before an officer unsealed
it, then an officer emptied the box on the presiding officer's table, after which
he displayed the empty interior of the box to the scrutineers and onlookers.
The officers then tallied the votes, recording the numbers of first, second, and
third choices for each candidate on a large hand-lined and hand-lettered poster.
The results wouldn't be official until they were confirmed and announced in
Wewak, but the counts were unambiguous. In each ward, one candidate received well over the 50 percent plus one of the first-choice votes needed to win
without involving second- and third-choice votes. Sitting Councilor Gabby
Kareo was returned from Ward 11, and Lucas Saulep upset the sitting councilor
to win in Ward 12.

Voting on each day proceeded with no greater disturbance than a few shouted complaints about the procedure from the sidelines that the election officers immediately rebutted. As the second and final day of polling ended and the officials were gathering up their paraphernalia, I approached one of them to say that I was very impressed by the efficient and professional way they had administered the process. As we were speaking, we heard a chorus of angry shouts rising somewhere beneath us in the village, followed by the sound of stones hitting houses. I raised my eyebrows, but the polling official just laughed and said, "That's all part of it!" Unfortunately, however, that wasn't going to be all of it. While I stand by my judgment that both villagers and officials managed the voting admirably, and I know that the results endured, some ugliness followed in the election's wake.

When the shouting and stone throwing started, I was inclined to veer toward it on my way back to Rokerai's house to see what was going on. Friends, however, steered me along an upper path, away from any possible danger. Kragur people sometimes speak metaphorically of throwing stones when talking about casting aspersions, as native English speakers do, but the agitated men below were casting actual igneous, metamorphic, and possibly sedimentary rocks. Sitting on Rokerai's veranda shortly thereafter, we could hear angry young men roaming through the village, passing close to our house at one point.

There had been room for suspense in the ward councilor voting, but I don't think anyone could have found the results a great surprise. The outcomes, for example, matched local pundit Benny Sogum's predictions for both Kragur wards as well as for Ward 13 in Shagur, and both of Kragur's winning candidates won by clear majorities. Gabby Kareo's supporters had projected the number of first-choice picks he would receive within five votes. I had to wonder why objections erupted as soon as the final results were announced.

The day after polling concluded, one of the losing candidates told me that some of his supporters had made a public fuss on election day simply because they were disappointed. I soon learned, however, that some protesters thought the election—which looked very clean to me—was tainted. There were rumors, for example, that one of the auxiliary police assisting in the polling had gossiped about how some people cast their votes, and that a couple of people who helped others vote had marked the ballots contrary to the voters' instructions. None of the scrutineers had protested such alleged incidents during the voting, and the auxiliary police said that the accusations were sheer fantasy.

A few villagers, however, found the accusations credible. The specter of block voting also raised its ugly head. I heard that one or two losing candidates had berated close kin for "breaking the vote"—that is, not voting for fellow clansmen—and that some of the supporters of losing candidates had even harassed clan bigmen for allegedly committing the same offense. I know that one disgruntled youth threw a stone at Godfrey Siliau, a leading *kokwal*. Another bigman told me that an angry young man had confronted him as he walked home one evening and had even taken a swing at him. He had been forced, he said, to put the young man in his place with a solid blow.

The bright side of all this was that while some villagers seemed committed to block voting, even more, it appeared to me, found this misguided. In 2008, both Kragur villagers and candidates for office in the larger Wewak Islands area often invoked the principle of personal choice in voting. Under the LPV system, of course, unless you know you have an exceptionally large natural "block" in your corner, it is to your advantage to remind people that they don't have to vote the same way as everyone else in their clan or village. But men talking politics on my veranda also frequently spoke of personal choice in voting as good in principle, not just as the basis of a good LPV campaign strategy. Personal choice, some said, was a "democratic right," using an English phrase that is being rapidly incorporated into Kragur Tok Pisin vocabulary. Even Munbos, born long before voting became routine for Papua New Guineans, declared energetically one evening that her vote was hers alone to do with as she pleased.

I couldn't say if commitment to individual choice in voting in Kragur was also encouraging people to act more as individuals in life in general and to rely less for their identities on their ties of descent, marriage, or perhaps shared substance derived from the land.[2] The idea of individual choice in the political sphere, however, clearly had a strong foothold in the village.

This issue probably is more complicated for women, because—although they are born into their fathers' clans—after marriage they become identified with, although not technically members of, their husbands' clans, especially after they have borne children. If I were a Kragur woman, I think I'd be glad to be able to invoke my "democratic right" to vote as I saw fit, rather than be subject to competing claims for loyalty. Following the 2008 election, there was at least one man who couldn't forgive one of his female kin for straying from his idea of proper allegiance.

Late in the afternoon of the final polling day, I was writing at my table on the veranda waiting for things to quiet down so I could walk to the stream for a bath without encountering a knot of angry young men, armed as I would be with only a towel, albeit a large towel, and a bar of soap—only a small one. Munbos was in the main room of the house with a visitor, an elderly female friend, mother of several grown children, married into the clan whose main residential area abuts that in which Rokerai and Munbos live. What happened next was over in a flash. A young man dashed up the stairs and into the main room of the house, seized Munbos' visitor by one of her thin arms, pulled her out to the veranda, and started dragging her down the stairs. Munbos, how-ever, had quickly latched on firmly to her visitor's other arm and pulled back. On the lower rungs of the stairs, three or four men tried to get hold of different parts of the would-be abductor's body, slippery with sweat, and pry him lose from his victim.

Suddenly, the intruder lost his grip and Munbos pulled her guest back into the house. The intruder then bolted up the stairs again and, standing at the door, began shouting accusations that Munbos' visitor had let the winning candidate buy her vote, turning her away from a candidate of her husband's clan. By this time—only seconds later, if that—I had stopped gaping and stood up, considering the best way to thwart more violence, if necessary. Then I clearly heard the intruder pronounce the name "Smith" in the midst of his tirade. I didn't think I could let this pass, so I stepped up behind him, placed my hand on his shoulder, and said, in my best John Wayne voice, low and slow, "*Taim yu tokim nem bilong mi, yu tokim isi isi*"—that is, "When you say my name, say it nice and easy." He turned, surprised, and protested that this had nothing to do with me. I replied that if he was going to go around shouting my name, it did, and I advised him quietly to go home, which, to my great relief, he immediately did.

That wasn't quite the end of it. When I got up in the morning, I couldn't open my door. I pushed harder and when the obstacle blocking it began to grunt I realized that Kilibop's son Watar had slept in front of the door, for "security," he said, in English. Although I slept soundly that night, others in our household told me that the sound of stones hitting the walls had awakened them in the small hours.

I didn't think I really needed a security guard, and I was allowed to wander about at will by myself after that first night of the troubles. I knew, however, that my name had come up in the previous day's ugly incident because there was a rumor going around that not only had one of the ward councilor candidates paid people to vote for him, he had done so with money I had given him for another purpose, shortly after I arrived in May.

This wasn't the first time I'd heard rumors that money I'd given to villagers for community purposes had been misused. The principal rumors concerned money I'd sent to be used, in one case, to repair the broken-down medical clinic boat and, on a second occasion, to buy picks, shovels, and other tools to help set the village right after the 2002 earthquake. The requests I received seemed completely legitimate, and I made sure to inform others in the village regarding to whom I'd sent the money, just to keep things open and above-board. On both of these occasions, the recipients of the money also sent me store receipts for their expenditures.

Many villagers knew I'd sent money on these occasions, and some gave me credit for efforts to contribute to the common good, but some thought I'd been a chump. Even before I returned to Kragur in 2008, I received a letter suggesting that the money I'd sent for tools and boat repair had been misappropriated. I wrote back, sending copies of the receipts and hoping these would put the gossip to rest. I found out in 2008 that they hadn't. I heard from several people a complicated story of how, despite the receipts, others had managed to wrest personal profit from my donations. Although teasing apart the tangled threads of a dispute usually provides a useful lesson in the fine points of community life, after several villagers repeated these accusations to me I cut off any further attempts to discuss it.

It looked as if there were older and more far-reaching animosities here, and any hint I might give of partisanship would only exacerbate them. Rokerai agreed that this was the right thing to do, but for a different reason. Once a *kokwal* makes a gift, he said, it's beneath him to worry about what becomes of it.

I was sure, however, that I hadn't been chumped into financing bribery in 2008. I found it hard to believe that the person accused would do such a thing; but I also knew that I hadn't given him any money in May, as his accusers claimed. Yet there were other rumors of election bribery going around as well and other grievances to keep the pot of postelection discontent boiling for a while longer. I've already mentioned the anger in some quarters over lack of clan loyalty, an issue that didn't pass quickly. One man left his own house, which stood in the midst of those of his male clan fellows, and went to live with more distant kin for several weeks after the election. Some villagers also feared that voting for the candidates of their choice might anger people suspected of having knowledge of sorcery. And some blamed several cases of malaria in the village on the election. "The time of politics," one man said, "is a time of illness," because many people get angry and "the ground has ears."

If all this makes Kragur sound like an unusually fractious place, I need only remind American readers of the seas of vitriol that washed across the country during the American presidential election of 2008 and the midterm congressional elections of 2010. To compare Kragur with a community of a somewhat more similar scale, I can look back at the local politics of my hometown in Michigan, which had a population of about five thousand when I was growing up there. Among those quiet streets and modest homes, contests for school board membership and leadership of local commissions were marred by religious prejudice, thinly veiled blackmail, accusations of communist sympathies, and blatant greed. True, I don't think anyone in Holt feared or was accused of sorcery—but perhaps only because no one thought of it.

In Kragur, we didn't hear the final results of the voting for LLG president until June 22. On June 20, we heard that although Numbos was out of the race,

Patrick Beka was running neck and neck with the sitting LLG president, Toby Samet of Wogeo Island. Neither Beka nor Samet had received the 50 percent plus one first-choice votes needed to win outright, so it had come down to a tally of the second-choice and maybe even the third-choice votes. Someone told me that the results wouldn't be broadcast on the provincial radio station, a government-owned operation, because the electoral commission, also a government agency, couldn't pay for it. Whatever the reason, people were not turning to the few radios in the village for news. The evening of June 20, just before dark, we watched from the veranda as two boats passed along the coast heading for Shagur. We could hear the engine of a third boat that hadn't appeared yet, and then we heard its engine die, as if the boat were pulling in just east of Kragur. Rokerai ran down to the shore to see if anyone was landing who had news of the election from Wewak, but the only passenger getting off knew nothing of it.

By the evening of the following day, news had made its way to Kragur that Beka had lost to Samet. Beka's supporters in Kragur, who were many, were upset. Some may have blamed bribery or cheating, I don't know. It was refreshing, however, that some of his strongest supporters simply blamed Kairiru and Mushu voters for not using their second- or third-choice votes to strengthen a local candidate, whoever their first choices might have been. "Stupid Kairiru! Stupid Mushu!" fumed one Beka activist, but that was the strongest open display of anger that I saw or heard regarding the outcome of the LLG race.

Some villagers, however, were still grumbling about alleged injustices in the ward councilor race when I left Kragur in early July. Nick Urim and his close patrilineal kinsman Jack Mari told me that this had been the most disruptive ward councilor election they'd seen in Kragur. Kragur can be pleased, however, that it preserved greater decorum than some other Kairiru villages. I had it from a reliable source that during the polling in one of the villages on the landward side of Kairiru, supporters of one candidate were walking around near the polling place with bush knives in hand. Some Kragur partisans may have continued to nurse their grievances, but the results of the election stood, and before I left the newly elected councilors took up their official duties without opposition.

Chapter 10

Life Goes On

Lala how the life goes on
—John Lennon and Paul McCartney, "Ob-La-Di, Ob-La-Da"

The 2008 local election was under way when I arrived, and its repercussions were still percolating when I left. It was only months later that a letter from Kragur told me that the social mess the incident on the stairs to Rokerai's house left behind had been at least formally put to rest. But if I've given the impression that everyone in Kragur was entirely focused on the election during my stay, I need to correct that. Some villagers appeared to enjoy the break from routine that the election brought but didn't seem to care much about the results. One of my middle-aged male friends was as quick as anyone to attend every election event, but when I tried to draw him into conversation about the postelection rumors and conflicts, his only comment was that he was "happy for everyone"—for the winners, who had something to celebrate, and for the losers, who had something to complain about.

Some villagers were growing weary of it all even before the voting. In spite of her enthusiasm for voting her personal preference, one night two days before the polling Munbos just couldn't take any more of the political conversation going on around her cooking fire. "Enough politics!" she exclaimed. "You show me some food!" We had just eaten a generous meal, but I think Munbos meant that all the politicking hadn't yet made her days of gardening, gathering firewood, and cooking any easier.

While the public events and private drama of the election went on, people still had to see to all the ordinary daily chores. While hiking up and down the mountain during the last days before the election, I met many villagers going to and from gardens or sago palm stands. A common sight was a family making its way up the trail, the husband in front, often carrying an ax and a bamboo- or wire-pointed spear in case there was a chance to bag a tasty marsupial, such as a tree possum, tree kangaroo, or bush rat. The wife usually came behind, often with a baby in a sling, a bark-carrying basket on her back, and one or two preschool-aged children bouncing along lightly beside her. Two or three lean, yellow-brown dogs with long backs and necks and short coats sometimes ranged around the family group, noses alert for game.

In the 1970s, I paid close attention to how Kragur people organized their daily activities and how much time they spent in different kinds of tasks. I went about this very systematically, making observations several times a day for a week at a time of what everyone in a single geographic area of the village was doing, sometimes spending entire days with family work groups, taking detailed notes on their activities. While villagers almost never seemed to be in a hurry, their days in the 1970s were very full. Women were more obviously busy than men, in part because they did most of the child care. The biggest difference between men's work and women's work, however, wasn't in the number of hours they were occupied but in the kinds of tasks they performed. When making a new garden, for instance, men cut most of the large trees and women cleared the smaller brush; while women gathered many of the materials for building houses, men did almost all of the construction; and making canoes, a frequent activity in Kragur in 1976, was almost exclusively a job for men.

Probably the most conspicuous difference between men's and women's work was that men kept in their hands most of the work of politics, governing, and keeping things straight with the spirit world. Women sometimes commented that attending meetings dedicated to curing illness, settling disputes, or conducting magical rituals wasn't very taxing compared with weeding taro gardens and breaking up firewood. Men, however, didn't necessarily agree that they were getting off easy. Lots of younger men told me that sitting in meetings bored them and they preferred physical work; and older men, the usual leaders of men's political and ritual activities, often found these gatherings very stressful, because missteps could create rather than resolve problems and stir anger that could cost people their health or their lives.[1]

My casual impression in 2008 was that the general pattern of work in the village hadn't changed a lot from the 1970s. Women's work of harvesting and preparing food, washing dishes, and gathering and breaking up firewood was relentless (fig. 13). No matter what political crises were shaking the village, women kept their houses scrupulously neat, with everything in its place and the floors swept free of food scraps, tracked-in dirt, and the sawdust sifting down from the steady work of the carpenter ants able to survive the smoke drifting up through the rafters. Meanwhile, men still took the lead in things that required a lot of sitting and talking.

Since the village was in the middle of an election campaign, there may have been an unusual amount of sitting and talking going on in May and June of

Figure 13. Life goes on, and women keep hauling firewood:
Christine Mokish in 2008. Photo by the author.

2008. Nevertheless, our household stayed well fed. The stock of tinned fish
and rice was drawing down more rapidly than I'd anticipated, but I gave Munbos money to supplement it—and the family's own taro, yams, cooking bananas, and sweet potatoes—with garden produce from the Kragur market. For
protein, there was a steady trickle of fresh fish and at least one sizable marsupial, bagged by a group of young men using Kilibop's arrow guns.

    I had mixed feelings about eating marsupial. I don't mind the strong flavor,
but in my experience it takes rather a lot of chewing. Also, in 2008 I met a
marsupial—a very young tree possum—up close. On my way to Bou one day,
looking for Patrick Beka, I ran into Valentine Monup, who invited me to take
a slight detour to see what amounted to a small menagerie. In front of his

house he had dug two deep and wide pits, kept filled with water by a bamboo pipe from a nearby stream, in which he was raising large, colorful Japanese carp, the founding stock provided by Brother Herman. An electrically pink, red, orange, yellow, blue, green, and black bird wandered the veranda of his house, picking bits of shredded coconut from the flooring. Bruce Beehler, an American friend who knows vast amounts about PNG fauna, identified this from my photo as a western black-capped lory (*Lorius lorius*). Also on Monup's veranda, a tawny juvenile tree possum with huge eyes and a silky coat—a young northern common cuscus (*Phalanger orientalis*), according to Bruce— was happy to climb on my shoulder or search through my clothing with its delicate hands for anything edible. Monup explained in English that he loved taking care of animals because they were "part of God's creation." This encounter did not prevent me from partaking of the northern common cuscus served to me at meals in the days to come, but only because I was sure that I was not eating "Tricks," as Monup had named his pet.

The only local food I declined to eat was a type of marine snail, because it reminded me of scallops, to which I am very allergic. Snails, however, weren't often on the menu, and a number of villagers complimented me on my taste for local food. I'm especially renowned for my fondness for sago. It's usually prepared by mixing the powdered pith of the sago palm with boiling water and forming the results into slightly translucent, moonlike globs. These are served arrayed on a plate in a single gelatinous layer and topped with a tasty sauce, cooked greens, and fish or meat of some kind if it's available. I like it, but I understand that it's an acquired taste.[2] Some villagers enjoyed telling me of Western visitors to Kragur who turned down not just sago but every other local food they were offered with looks of distaste, which they imitated with malicious glee; and they implied that I was much superior to such people in my eating habits.

In truth, on days when the effects of malaria medication, heat, and humidity were souring my stomach, I sometimes wanted to wave away forever any more chunks of smoked fish or plates of steaming taro. When people complimented me on my enjoyment of local food while I secretly yearned for a bowl of cold yogurt with fresh strawberries, preferably eaten in the total anonymity of a posh hotel restaurant somewhere in Western Europe, I felt shamefully phony. At these times, my biblical education stood me in good stead, because— curiously—telling myself, "ye are like unto whited sepulchers, which indeed appear beautiful outward, but are within full of dead men's bones" always made me feel better.[3]

Although I didn't have to worry about running out of food, a few weeks into my stay I found that I was running out of soap faster than planned because I'd been giving a lot away without bothering to take stock. I should have had one bar more than I did, but I'd had an unhappy accident not long after arriving. Jana had insisted that I take a fat bar of sandalwood soap with me. I was trying to pack as light and be as tough as possible, and I protested that I would be just fine with the manly, unpleasant-smelling soap I would buy in Wewak. But when I went to the stream in Kragur and lathered up with the sandalwood soap, its fragrance set me awash in pleasantly sentimental thoughts of home. Sadly, while bathing one day long before I'd used it up, the sandalwood bar slipped out of my hands and I had to watch it whirl away and slide over the rock dam on the downstream side of the pool, speeding toward the lonely open sea. If I hadn't been so manly, I would have shed a tear. I did, however, write some haiku about the event that evening, the best of which follows:

> Aromatic gift
> Her parting gesture
> Lost in the long waves

But I didn't spend very much time being homesick. When I did feel a little low, I often treated it with a hike up the mountain or along the coastal trail. This was also a good way of practicing anthropological "not doing" because it put me in the way of many interesting chance meetings. Once, when I stopped to catch my breath at Kafow, where there was a fallen tree to sit on, a group of young men on their way up the mountain caught up with me. One of them was Charlie Numbos (Philip's son), president of the Kragur Surf Club. After a brief chat at Kafow, we arranged to get together later, back in the village, so I could meet the rest of the club, they could show me the best Kragur surfing spots, and I could see their homemade boards.

A couple of days later, Charlie came over early in the morning with some other club members, all carrying their boards. The boards were carved from solid logs, and the fins were nailed on. They were heavy and not very aerodynamic looking, but Charlie said that when the waves were good, he could do a 360-degree spin on his. Several club members called their boards *mok*, which they told me is the Kairiru language word for "plank." But a lot of the other terminology they used was right out of the international surfing vocabulary, so—even though I hadn't surfed for years—we had no trouble communicating. Unfortunately, there were no waves on which the club members could demonstrate their skills at that time because, they said, the surf in Kragur's waters is highly seasonal. For really good waves, I'd have to come back in December and January, when there were overhead breaks that provided long rides before you had to pull out short of the very rocky shore.

I had to be content with taking pictures of the club members and their boards on land, overlooking the sea at Maratak Point at the west end of Kragur. Charlie had decorated his board with a roughly engraved mermaid and christened it "Sexy Lady" (fig. 14). Another of the larger boards was carved with the image of a large bird with a fish in its claws, and its owner called it "Sea Eagle." A third bore the image of a bird with its wings spread and the name "Sea King" in carefully carved block letters. I knew that Kilibop was a good wood-carver and suggested that the club recruit him to try his skills at carving a *mok*. They did just that before I left. In less than a day, Kilibop reduced a thick, heavy block of tree trunk to a smooth and relatively thin short board with graceful twin fins, the fins carved out of the same piece of wood rather than fastened on later.[4]

I thought a series of photos of the whole process would be interesting, but I had to sit out the very first step—going to the forest to cut the timber. Charlie stopped by one afternoon with two other surfers to say that they were to cut the timber at dawn the next day because the tree they had their eyes on was some distance away and far from the main trail, at a place called Rumokayo. When I said I wanted to come along, I could see Charlie and the others exchange concerned glances.

"It's pretty far," Charlie said.

"Well," I said, "I'm used to climbing the mountain." Charlie and the others stood silent.

"Okay," I said. "Is the trail harder than, say, the ascent at Komeru?"

"Yes," said Charlie.

"A lot harder?" I asked.

"A lot harder," said Charlie.

"It's just straight up and straight down, isn't it?" I asked. Charlie nodded yes. I hated to admit I wasn't up to it, but I knew trails like that, and I knew that even if I made it up, coming down would be hell, especially on my knees, so I bowed to their wisdom. That evening, this suggested another haiku:

> Rumokayo!
> The road is unforgiving!
> I dare not go

On another hike, I had a fortunate meeting with Wolfy Kalem of Shagur. Wolfy had written me four or five years before asking if I could send him information on tourism operators in PNG he could contact because he was trying to start a tourist guesthouse. I sent him a list of enterprises gleaned from the Internet, but I didn't hear anything from him after that. When we met on the trail, he told me that most of the companies on the list either hadn't replied to his letters or had no interest in working with his small operation. One, however, had replied saying that the company, Ecotourism Melanesia, liked to work with locally run guesthouses engaged in "community-based" tourism. The company, based in Moresby, sent someone to look over Wolfy's facilities in Shagur and soon began occasionally sending small groups of tourists his way.

Figure 14. Charlie Numbos with his homemade surfboard,
Sexy Lady, 2008. Photo by the author.

A few days later I went to Shagur to see Wolfy's guesthouse and hear more
about the local tourist business. The guesthouse stood at the top of a rise looking down on the bay around which Shagur clusters. It was built in village style,
but high enough off the ground to catch some breeze and guard against mosquitoes, and each of its several small rooms was equipped with a mattress,
sheets, and pillows. Wolfy told me that he took his guests to secluded and
picturesque spots on the stream to bathe, and I saw that he'd built a solid out-

house on a platform over the water in a corner of the bay. He served local food in an open-walled dining area with a nice view of the water, just down the hill from the guesthouse itself.

The accommodations were hardly luxurious, but Wolfy's customers (all Yuropians of some stripe in the photos he showed me) apparently were getting just what they wanted, judging from the comments they had written in the guest book he kept, such as these:

"The food was absolutely delicious."

"We have learned so much about village life. Thanks to you all."

"The best day in PNG."

"It was all delightful."

"Best of all, no mosquitoes at night!"

Kragur people didn't seem to mind that I'd been able to give a boost to a business in another village. Some Kragurs themselves were interested in getting into the tourist trade and found Wolfy's modest success intriguing. For his part, Wolfy told me that he'd like to see more islanders getting into the business so that the entire Wewak Islands area could develop a reputation as a tourist destination. But it was going to be hard to push tourism in the islands far beyond a certain point, he said, until it became easier to communicate with Moresby and Wewak.

When people in Kragur asked me for advice on how to get into tourism, I referred them to Wolfy, but I also repeated the advice I'd given every time the topic had come up in years past. The kinds of tourists likely to want to visit Kairiru and stay in a village, I suggested, wanted to stay in breezy and dry village-style houses, not the sturdier but hotter and less aesthetically pleasing cement-floor and metal-roof structures that one or two potential entrepreneurs talked about building. I also emphasized that anyone with a guesthouse had to provide tourists with lots of things to do. Bored tourists are unhappy tourists. Wolfy seemed to have mastered this principle and offered, for additional fees, both walking and boat excursions to several places of beauty and interest on and around Kairiru and neighboring islands.

There are also enough skilled wood-carvers in Kragur, Bou, and Shagur to offer for sale to tourists an impressive array of masks, figures representing mythical beings, and items such as broad wooden bowls or ornate walking sticks. In 1998, Klarok had introduced me to Raphael Wapsi, one of the better-known carvers on Kairiru. I looked him up again in 2008 because he had given me a beautiful walking stick as a gift when we first met. Although I'd sent him a gift in return when I got back to the United States, in 2008 I brought a set of Stanley chisels for him. I also wanted to see what kind of work he was doing now. Many of Wapsi's carvings are versions of long-standing patterns. For instance, in 2008 he gave me a pair of what he called *tangbwal* masks, male and female. They were his take on masks once incorporated in the elaborate full-body costumes worn by dancers in rituals that have a long history in the area and are described in some detail by anthropologist Ian Hogbin as they were performed around 1940 on Wogeo Island.[5] But, Wapsi told me, a lot of tourists preferred masks he'd carved with ghoulish skull-like faces, like nothing from the East Sepik I've ever seen in any of my travels or in any of the many large museum collections I've explored. Other tourists, Wapsi said, wanted things that were *"samting bilong tumbuna"*—that is, "things of the ancestors." Wapsi and his customers, however, had quite different ideas about what it meant to be *samting bilong tumbuna*.

I've met quite a few men in Kragur, Bou, and Shagur who are skilled wood-carvers. Some claim no special pedigree for carving, but others say that their carving skill is like skill in making fruitful gardens or building and sailing swift canoes. That is, it comes down from the ancestors, and it has a magical component. Wapsi has practiced his craft for a long time, but he also inherited a family tradition of carving and esoteric knowledge of magical procedures that inspire his work. To some tourists and commercial art dealers, age pure and simple is the mark of "things of the ancestors." This attitude puzzled and annoyed Wapsi because, he said, "Where do they think I got my skill?" In his eyes, virtually everything he makes is imbued with his ancestral heritage. The *tangbwal* masks he gave me looked brand new because he made them while I was in Kragur in 2008, using the chisels I gave him. They also don't duplicate the style of the early twentieth-century *tangbwal* masks I've seen in photos. But to be faithful to Wapsi's own understanding of his art, I have to recognize them as *samting bilong tumbuna*.[6]

Kairiru people have shown me a lot of objects—such as carved magical figures, the long and heavy steering paddles of famous voyaging canoes, much-used dance decorations, and fire-blackened clay pots obtained in trade from distant places by previous generations—that I wouldn't necessarily call beautiful but that were all fascinating because their owners told me the objects' stories. In 1998, a prominent Shagur man invited me to his house to show me some of the objects he used in performing various kinds of magic. Some looked no different from objects anyone might find on the ground; for example, smooth stones of several sizes. One of his prize possessions, though, was very distinctive. This was his father's lower jawbone, dyed to give it a pink tinge, the open arc of the mandible reinforced with a crosspiece of bamboo tightly wound with narrow bamboo strips, and the reinforcing bamboo structure decorated with three shell rings, each about two inches in diameter. The rings, smooth with age, were of the kind used to decorate dance finery and, in the past, in trade and ceremonial gift exchanges.

I've seen lots of objects equally exotic to the Western eye in museums, sometimes neatly labeled with their place of origin and a note on their use. The Shagur man explained that he used his father's jawbone for divination— that is, for answering difficult questions with the aid of his father's spirit. It would be one thing to see such an object in a museum, labeled "Decorated human mandible, used for divination. Kairiru Island, Papua New Guinea." It was entirely different, however, to hold the object in my hands as its owner explained how he put questions to his father and read his answers in slight vibrations of the bone. Some people suspected him of using his father's bones to practice sorcery. He was well aware of this but dismissed these rumors with a laugh. All of this, though, was part of an ongoing story. The jawbone was part of the life of a family and a community; it was anything but an inert object.

I'd heard about using human bones in sorcery and divination before this. It wasn't until 2008, however, that someone in Kragur showed me his divining bones—his mother's mandible. This, too, was reinforced with carefully wound bamboo strips. The decorative rings, however, were porcelain, not shell, although the patina of age they bore obscured this difference. These rings undoubtedly dated from the German colonial period, when artificial shell ornaments and dog's teeth were manufactured in Germany to use in trade with New Guineans in lieu of the local shell items. Despite the age of its accoutrements, this jawbone was also part of an unfolding contemporary story.

The first Monday after I arrived in Kragur, there was a village meeting about church matters in front of the prayer house. One item on the agenda was whether Kragur should invite someone from the mainland known as Brother Peter to come to Kragur. Brother Peter, I soon understood, was a kind of Christian seer or clairvoyant who claimed he could identify people who practiced sorcery and find hidden sorcery paraphernalia, such as human bones. In one village, Brother Peter had allegedly identified someone who had killed more than twenty people with sorcery. The accused denied any knowledge of sorcery, but—according to the story—Brother Peter told him that if he tried to use sorcery again, God would kill him. The accused man, it was said, went ahead and tried to ensorcel someone else anyway, and sure enough, he died.

Over the years, Kragur villagers have habitually suspected particular men of having knowledge of sorcery (as one of their hereditary *kokwal* or *tiptip*) and of sometimes using it. These men have all been otherwise upstanding citizens, and they all have denied knowledge of the art. I understand, though, that after an unusual spate of deaths in the village a few years before my 2008 visit, many villagers blamed some of the usual suspects. A group of village leaders got together and told the suspected sorcerers to cut it out. I don't know what sanctions they threatened, but I was told that the death rate went back to normal after that confrontation.

When someone suggested that Kragur invite Brother Peter to come root out evildoers, several villagers raised objections. For one thing, they pointed out, Brother Peter charged money for his services. Some opponents of the idea also stood on a kind of Kragur pride: in this case, the sentiment that "we can deal with our own problems; we don't need to bring in outsiders." At one point, however, someone suggested that people opposed to the idea might have something to hide. That remark brought several angry rejoinders. Finally, a conciliator suggested that they write to the bishop for advice or ask the parish priest.

When the issue came up in the following days, I didn't even try to hold my tongue, because I thought inviting Brother Peter to Kragur was an excruciatingly terrible idea. I was not alone in this. Some villagers had heard that Brother Peter was opposed to all magic, not just sorcery, and one man told me that he couldn't see any sense in that at all because God must be the ultimate source of beneficial magic, and supposedly Brother Peter was a man of God. Some simply thought that Brother Peter was probably a charlatan, only in it for the money. To me, whether or not Brother Peter believed in his powers was irrelevant. There was already plenty of fear of sorcery in the village, and it didn't need stoking. And everyone in Kragur already knew who the usual suspects were, and their reputations didn't need embellishing. Worse, Brother Peter might add new names to the list. How could such people then defend themselves? So I encouraged people who thought Brother Peter was a fake and those who appealed to Kragur pride.

This brings us back to my friend's mother's jawbone. My friend was worried that if Brother Peter came, he might somehow learn of the jawbone, assume it was a sorcery tool, and call on him to destroy it or suffer divine punishment. The mandible's owner told me that he used it only for communicating with his mother, but that he was thinking of burying it if Brother Peter did come. He didn't ask for my advice straight out, but he was obviously worried, and it sounded as if he wouldn't object to hearing my views. I suggested that if Brother Peter did turn up and did call on him to destroy the bone, he should tell Brother Peter that he had no power in Kragur; that he should say, "I'm a *ramat wolap* of this place! Who are you to come here, to my ground, and tell me what to do?" I also might have added that destroying her decorated mandible was a heck of a way to treat your mom. Fortunately, Brother Peter didn't come to Kragur during my stay, and as far as I know, he still hasn't been invited.

There were a lot of other items on the agenda for the church meeting at which villagers debated the wisdom of inviting Brother Peter to town. The week after the election, the usual Wednesday charismatic prayer service was cancelled, apparently for fear that some of the younger disappointed voters might take the opportunity to express their discontent, perhaps with the help of Kragur's inexhaustible supply of stones. But villagers were going ahead with plans to celebrate a number of Catholic festivals, and with the exception of the one evening of charismatic worship, church activities went on as usual before and after the election with a richness and variety that deserves attention.

Chapter 11

God the Father, the Son, His Mother, and the Holy Spirit

In my Father's house are many mansions.
—John 14:2, the Bible (King James Version)

I've already been to church once in this book, but that is hardly enough for any visitor to Kragur serious about getting to know its people, for they have always been very religious. Religion also has played a starring role in Kragur people's experience of the modern world. Encounters with Yuropian religion have not been, I think, as disruptive for Kragur people as the encounter with a world in which money is central. They have always had an active relationship with greater- and other-than-human beings and powers, a relationship they consider vital to everyone's welfare and central to clan and village leadership. There was, however, no indigenous precedent for money or relationships based on money in Kragur. In fact, Kragur people have used religion to try to control money, an effort I've seen lose momentum over the years. But the modern melting pot of religious ideas and practices is as dramatically visible as ever in village life.

In the precolonial Kragur world there were, as there are today, many kinds of spirit beings and many kinds of rituals for coping with supernatural entities. And when villagers traveled far afield, some of them undoubtedly came home with knowledge of new kinds of rituals involving new kinds of spirit beings or powers. I don't think, however, that in those days Kragur people thought about all the variety and novelty of this aspect of their world as made up of discrete packages of beliefs and practices fundamentally different from each other—that is, as different religions.

In a way, Christian missionaries created indigenous religion. To the best of my knowledge, there isn't a word in the Kairiru language that translates cleanly as "religion." I know of Kairiru words for different kinds of nonhuman or spirit beings that play important roles in the Kragur world, and I know of terms for different kinds of activities relating to the supernatural. Similarly,

linguist Richard Wivell's Kairiru language lexicon includes words for supernatural beings and activities related to the supernatural, but it has no word for
religion.[1] I've brainstormed with groups of Kragur people in the village and in
Moresby trying to identify a Kairiru word that is a neat counterpart to this
English word, but we've had no success. Since I've known them, when Kragur
people want to talk about distinct religions or religion in general, they have to
use the English word or the Tok Pisin word *lotu*. The latter is a word of non-
PNG origins; Christian missionaries adapted it to their uses from a Polynesian
term related to spiritual matters and brought it with them to the southwestern
Pacific, including what is now PNG.[2]

In Tok Pisin, Catholicism—Kragur's brand of Christianity—is called *lotu
Katolik*. Kragur people are by no means unusual in PNG for being either
Christians or Catholics. The PNG constitution guarantees freedom of religion,
but in its preamble it also gives a nod to the widespread influence of Christianity when it speaks of "our noble traditions and the Christian principles that are
ours." About 96 percent of PNG's people are affiliated with a Christian denomination, and Catholicism leads all others in number of adherents.[3]

When I gave a talk on religion in PNG to an American Museum of Natural
History tour group in 1998, I began by noting that most of PNG's people were
Christians. A few members of the group found this a little disconcerting. One
even wondered aloud if Papua New Guineans were "real" Christians. Arguments over who is a "real" Christian, of course, have sometimes led Western
Christians of slightly differing inclinations to slaughter each other in large
numbers. Not wanting to start another such episode, I replied that I didn't
know who was qualified to make that judgment, but I was pretty sure it wasn't
me. It wasn't surprising, though, that some of these American visitors found
my opening remarks a little confusing. The tour showed them nothing of
PNG's pervasive Christianity. On the contrary, the main events in some of the
villages at which the tour stopped along the Sepik River were displays of song-
and-dance performances and artifacts intimately associated with the indigenous spirit world, including heavily decorated men's cult houses, some built
explicitly as tourist spectacles. Promoters of tourism in PNG undoubtedly
assume correctly that most of their customers will prefer such sights to a
Catholic Mass or a Seventh-Day Adventist worship service.

I once suggested to Brother Herman that if the first Christian missionaries
to arrive on New Guinea's north coast had been Lutherans or Methodists rather
than Catholics, he and thousands of others in the East Sepik would probably
be ardent followers of a different Christian creed. He nodded in agreement
but said that in the end it wouldn't matter much, because the basic Christian
message was the same. I knew Herman well enough by then to assume that
to him the basic Christian message was in large part a message of compassion

and service to others. I have since heard him speak with regret of the way many contemporary Christian evangelists in PNG seem to focus on sowing fear of divine retribution rather than on encouraging compassion and service.

German Catholic missionaries from the Society of the Divine Word, however, did get to Kragur's corner of New Guinea first, and they pressed people hard to abandon old religious practices and convert to Catholicism, sometimes by speaking of the terrors of hell and sometimes by destroying indigenous religious artifacts. These early missionaries also had the power of the secular colonial authorities behind them, not simply the courage of their convictions. I've heard, however, that sometimes religious artifacts themselves took exception. A Shagur man, for example, told me of how a priest on Kairiru once gathered up carvings used in indigenous magical rituals, and when he threw them into a bonfire, one of the carvings jumped back out of the flames and was saved.

Nevertheless, by around 1930 Kragur people had abandoned the men's cult, and in the late 1930s a team of priests came to the seaward side of Kairiru to conduct mass baptisms. Since those days of hellfire preaching, idol burning, and saving souls wholesale, the Catholic Church has taken a turn toward greater concern with the social dimensions of Christianity, a reorientation formalized by the Vatican II Ecumenical Council of 1962–1965. Some Kragur villagers who lived through this transition found it disturbing. In the 1970s, more than one villager complained to me that first the missionaries told people to quit practicing all indigenous ways of dealing with the supernatural and get rid of the men's ceremonial house and all ritual objects; then, a new generation of missionaries came and said that magic that wasn't used to harm people was alright and even began appropriating indigenous art motifs— virtually all of which were originally associated with indigenous religious practices—for decorating churches.

Kragur people sometimes find it curious that I profess no religion, but they are not offended that I am not a believer. Nor does anyone appear to find it unseemly that I, a nonbeliever, like to poke around in their own faith. After the Pentecost Sunday service, I asked if it was okay for me to wander around the church and photograph the decorations, and the leader of the day's events readily invited me to photograph whatever I wanted. At a first-communion service a few weeks later, the leader sought me out beforehand to tell me to feel free to range around and take pictures during the proceedings. The villagers I know best even tolerate my irreverent religious humor. No one in Kragur has ever done anything but laugh when I apologized for a social misstep with the Tok Pisin version of the Latin confessional phrase, "mea culpa, mea culpa, mea maxima culpa" ("through my fault, through my fault, through my most grievous fault"); that is, in Tok Pisin, *rong bilong mi, rong bilong mi, bikpela rong bilong mi*. And Brother Herman readily honored my request to bless my luggage, putting it in God's keeping with mock seriousness, when I found on leaving Port Moresby that I had to check through a rather delicate item—a finely carved wooden drum with a lizard skin head known in Tok Pisin as a *kundu* (this one was Kilibop's work)—that I'd hoped to carry with me on the plane.

In my discussions of religion with Kragur people, of course, it has helped that I am no stranger to Christianity, albeit a nondogmatic variety. My family—including my mother and father and my patrilineal grandparents, aunts, uncles, and cousins—was active in the Presbyterian Church when I was growing up, but my parents were also open-minded and freethinking. My father, an escapee from an oppressively pious upbringing, knew not only his Bible but also something of modern theology, and he enjoyed intellectual sparring about religious questions—perhaps in part because his own father undoubtedly never allowed it. My mother grew up a largely unchurched gentile (that is, a non-Mormon) in Salt Lake City, Utah, where Mormon missionaries had never given up the effort to bring her family into the fold, leaving her with little patience for pushy proselytizers and the shunning of heathens. She was more of a Christian humanist than a seeker of divine salvation. She found the idea of divine retribution silly, but she admitted that on many Sundays she thought the quality of the hymn singing in our church probably merited at least a warning lightning bolt.

Papua New Guineans aren't very dogmatic about their religion either. Early Christian missionaries in the Pacific didn't rely on the free play of ideas to put their message across; Pope John Paul II officially apologized in 2001 for "shameful injustices done to indigenous peoples" by missionaries in the Pacific Islands.[4] But a characteristic openness to new religious ideas, an openness that predates enduring Western contact, probably made the missionary task in PNG easier. Donald Tuzin's writings on the *tambaran* cult among the Ilahita Arapesh provide a striking illustration of such openness. Tuzin's various works show how central this institution was to the lives of Ilahita people when he first encountered them; but he also concluded that the Ilahita *tambaran* cult was only a few generations old in the early 1970s, and that the Ilahita had probably adopted the institution from a neighboring people in the middle of the nineteenth century.[5]

Kragur people in the current era have a lively interest in new religious ideas, whatever their origin. I hadn't been in Kragur long at all in the 1970s when someone asked me about the rumor he'd heard that some Yuropian people said there wasn't any God at all. He was more curious about this than alarmed. Kragur people have also found it very interesting that my wife Jana isn't a Christian or even of Christian heritage. Many of those with whom I've talked about Judaism have heard of Moses, and a few—for example, Lucas Wosau, a former seminary student—are well versed in both Old and New Testaments. It has been easy, then, to explain that when some Jews decided to follow Jesus, others stuck with the *lain bilong* Moses (the followers of Moses), and that my wife was a member of this ancient descent group. In 2008, some villagers also asked me to send them more information on Judaism, which I did after I got home.

At this point, it won't surprise the reader to hear that Kragur Catholicism is not entirely orthodox. Some Kragur villagers in the 1970s found a number of basic Catholic and Christian ideas a little puzzling. A few villagers I knew in those days seemed to find the Christian heaven a plausible promise and described it as a place of eternal good health and material plenty available without physical effort. But more often, villagers told me that they weren't sure what to make of the Christian afterlife and that there was nothing like it in the indigenous world. A few villagers told me they had heard that their ancestors believed that when people died, they went to the place where the sun went down, but they had heard nothing, they said, about what went on there. Belief that the spirits of the dead were often near at hand, however, was virtually universal. Villagers not only credited them with a role in magic and causing and curing illness, they also bumped into them once in a while, sometimes in dreams but also in the bush or near the village at night. As one man said to me, "There isn't any special place where the dead go. They just wander around. Why is it they just wander around the bush or near the streams? If they have a place to go, then why don't they go there?"

Some villagers also thought it odd that no Catholic priests had ever seen the God they always talked about. Some of them added that they found the ancestors, especially the spirits of deceased mothers and fathers, more plausible spiritual powers because they were decidedly less abstract than the Christian deity. As one man put it, "[God] is different, because you can't see God, you can't see his face. Your mother and father, you've seen their faces. This is what makes [God] so hard to understand." Many villagers dealt with such quandaries by giving Catholic teachings a local flavor; for example, by taking references to God as a metaphorical way of speaking of the ancestors or by assuming that God was the missionaries' name for Wankau or other indigenous supernatural beings or forces. Many such ways of reconciling Catholicism with the indigenous spiritual world persist. In 2008, it would have been hard to find anyone in the village comfortable with the idea that there is no God, but many common ideas about God and Christian teachings would not pass muster with the Vatican. The Spanish Inquisition could have a field day in Kragur, but no one in the Wewak Diocese expects the Spanish Inquisition.[6]

If Kragur eclecticism and flexibility in these matters disqualifies them as "real Christians," then perhaps they are not. However, if knowledge of and conformity to the teachings of one's denomination are what it takes to be a real Christian, then many Americans, too, will have to turn in their Bibles. A recent survey found that 45 percent of American Catholics didn't know that the Catholic Church teaches that the bread and wine do not merely symbolize the body and blood of Christ in Holy Communion, they actually become them, and that 53 percent of American Protestants could not correctly identify Martin Luther as a key figure in the Protestant Reformation.[7]

In any event, a lot of Kragur people don't really care what others think of their religious identity, because they believe that they were already on good terms with God before the missionaries arrived. Virtually all Kragur people know at least the broad outlines of the story of how, several years before the first missionaries showed up, God was made known to Kragur people. Masos, Benedict Manwau's grandfather, was sitting by the stream east of the village sharpening a knife on a large stone at the place called Sumolau, not very far upstream from where the men's bathing place is today, while his small granddaughter played nearby. Suddenly, Masos' hand stuck fast to the stone. Thinking that this was the work of a powerful nature spirit (a *masalai*), he sent his granddaughter running to the village to tell people to bring gifts with which to induce the *masalai* to free him. By the time she returned with people bearing coconuts, shell rings, and other items, Masos' hands were free and he had an amazing story to tell.

After the little girl left, he said, a voice had spoken to him, telling him that it was the voice of God, who lived in the sky. The voice also gave him a list of instructions for good behavior for the people of Kragur. The list varies somewhat in different tellings of the story, but many villagers say that it included admonitions not to steal or fight among themselves and not to kill strangers who came to Kragur but to show them generous hospitality. (The voice didn't instruct Masos to get into the hospitality business—that is, tourism—but those were other times.) So when the first Christian missionaries arrived, the people of Kragur were able to tell them that God had already been in touch. Most Kragur people who have told me this story have either implied or stated plainly that God chose to reveal in Kragur rather than elsewhere because Kragur people were already unusually good people, especially generous and harmonious.

Kragur people keep this heritage fresh by celebrating an annual Sumolau Day. The parish priest comes to Kragur to say Mass for the occasion, but it is really Kragur's day. In 2008, Kilibop, his amazingly agile four-year-old grandson Malachai—an absolute demon for storming his small, naked way up treacherously slick inclines and over craggy rocks and jutting roots—and Kilibop's brother-in-law Otto Maki, prominent in village church affairs, took me to see the cement slab at Sumolau where the yearly Mass is held. It stands at the edge of a stretch of tumbling water, framed by boulders cloaked with deep green moss and ferns; it would be a lovely place to converse with God. Sumolau Day comes in August, but as early as May villagers were meeting to plan for it. At one meeting, someone suggested that this year they put on a play dramatizing Masos' experience, and the chair of the meeting promptly assigned him to form a committee to do so. Some people will never learn.

I'm not sure for how long Kragur has been holding this annual celebration of Masos' experience; I hadn't even heard of Sumolau Day until 2008. Establishing this as a formal event complete with Mass could look like an effort to bring this local religious event into the official bureaucratic embrace. Viewed from Kragur, however, it looks more like a local success in getting the Church to honor villagers' indigenous vision. I don't think that Masos can be tamed. In 2008, after telling me once again the story of Masos, one villager elder concluded, "God isn't the God of the Germans or the Australians! It's *our* God!"

The tradition of Masos is an emphatic affirmation of Kragur's independent connection to a sacred power. It also transcends clan and moiety rivalry. Kragur people are very much aware that Masos' daughter was born into Seksiek and married into Lupelap; so, as one man put it, "almost everyone in Kragur has some of the blood of Masos." That includes the two 2007 parliamentary candidates from opposite sides of the moiety line: both Moses Manwau and Ralph Saulep are descended from Masos; Moses is one of his patrilineal great grandchildren, and it was Ralph's grandmother (Masos' granddaughter) who ran to get help when Masos' hands were held fast to the stone.

Despite God's local pedigree, Kragur people have taken perhaps even more readily to the Virgin Mary. It may be important that, in contrast to God, she has a human aspect and a more purely compassionate nature. In any event, she has long been very popular in Kragur. Yuropian Catholic priests brought the Legion of Mary to the East Sepik Province as early as the 1950s. I'm not sure when the legion took root in Kragur, but although villagers didn't erect the statue of the Virgin at Iupulpul until April 1976, devotion to her was firmly entrenched in Kragur when I first arrived in late 1975. It was, I understand, a coincidence that brought the statue—donated by the priests who had first proselytized for the legion—to Kragur so soon after national independence. But some villagers did not take this as a chance event and it looked as if some of their passion for the Virgin at that time grew out of fear of the problems, vague but dark, that many villagers expected independence to thrust on them and the hope that a special relationship with Maria could help them pull through.[8]

In the early 1970s, a good many villagers had turned to the Virgin for much more specific aid. A part of the village had engaged in a prolonged and intense effort to solicit money from the dead. During nighttime rituals at what was then the main village cemetery, numbers of villagers called on their dead kin to send money, but they also petitioned the Virgin to help clear the way for this miracle. This effort eventually petered out when no money appeared and when both participants and critics began to fear that meddling with the dead was causing people to get sick. But in 1975–1976, some villagers still suspected that the key to obtaining Yuropian money on a significant scale—not the small handfuls of bills and coins they could get from backbreaking labor—was religious and that a compassionate Virgin might eventually divulge it.

While some villagers thought religion might offer a relatively direct way of obtaining money, others found in religion reasons for keeping money at arm's length. Christianity provides plenty of support for the idea of poverty and generosity as virtues, and in the indigenous world generosity was highly esteemed. Banning buying and selling with money within the village thus was conveniently both the Christian and the ancestral right thing to do. It made a firmly rooted virtue of villagers' otherwise galling money poverty. I'm quite sure that some also hoped that being virtuous in this way might eventually catch the attention of supernatural powers that would reward them with knowledge of the mystical secret of money.

Neither of these efforts to exercise more control over money—either by getting more of it via the dead or the Virgin or by making a virtue of its absence— has lasted. Every time I've returned to Kragur since the 1970s, villagers have been more at ease with using money within the village; and if people's hopes for a religious route to money riches have not necessarily disappeared altogether, they have at least gone more or less underground. Religious life in Kragur, however, is still vibrant. Villagers still revere the Virgin Mary, but other ways of pursuing Catholicism have come to share center stage. The most obvious development in Kragur Catholicism I've encountered since my first residence there was the advent of charismatic worship, a kind of Catholic Pentecostalism. The Christian Pentecostal movement originated early in the twentieth century in the United States, and it has spread rapidly around the world since then. Pentecostalism was largely a Protestant phenomenon when it began, but some Catholics in the United States began adopting charismatic forms of worship in the late 1960s.[9] Charismatic worship draws its inspiration from passages in the Bible describing the experiences of Christ's disciples when they gathered for the first Feast of the Pentecost, a Jewish celebration, after Christ's resurrection and were filled with the Holy Spirit, accompanied by the sound of rushing wind and the sight of "tongues of flame." They also began to speak in tongues—that is, in unknown languages. The name "charismatic" comes from the theological term "charism," which means a power or talent given by God, such as speaking in tongues or healing the sick.

Charismatic Catholic worship was popular in some parts of the East Sepik as early as the 1970s. Kragur people told me that it got its start in their village in 1993, when a devout follower of the Virgin invited a charismatic "team" from Kerasau Island—local islanders, not foreign missionaries—to come to Kragur to "fast and pray" and teach Kragur villagers about charismatic worship. When I visited Kragur in 1998, only a relatively small number of villagers were regularly involved. They appeared to represent most of the clans in the village, but women and the young were definitely in the majority in the services I attended. Charismatic worship offers a direct, personal experience of God, sometimes in a trance state and sometimes manifested by speaking in tongues. This is pretty much what some Kragur villagers told me about their own experiences during charismatic worship, including a man who told me that he had never believed in God until he had gone into trance during a charismatic service.

You might well wonder why someone who didn't believe in God was at a charismatic worship service at all. It's easy to understand doubters in Kragur joining their neighbors at Sunday services, both for the social life and to keep up a good public image; but the majority of villagers seldom attend the Wednesday charismatic services. Yet it's easy to see that charismatic worship might be fun, even without a direct experience of God. Charismatic services are held outdoors in the comparative cool of the evening and include singing to the accompaniment of guitars. They also offer anyone, including women, the opportunity to spontaneously come to the front of the group and lead everyone in praising God. In fact, it is only at charismatic worship services that I have ever seen Kragur village women speak at length in public—and not only speak at length but engage in lively and passionate oratory, raising their voices, pacing the ground, and deploying their arms, hands, and bodies dramatically. And while the men who lead services on Sunday at Bou talk a lot about God's propensity for punishing sinners, the preaching and testimonials at charismatic services—by both women and men—focus on God's power to help and heal.

In the charismatic services I attended in 1998, the excitement built gradually, the praise, prayers, and testimonies becoming more and more fervent. People clapped in time to the music with raised hands and one by one began swaying and dancing. At the first event I attended, someone eventually appeared to go into a trance and speak in tongues, sweating profusely and jerking spasmodically. I don't know how the charismatic services I attended in 1998 would have ended if left to follow their own courses, because for two weeks in a row young men hidden in the darkness above the meeting ground broke up the services by throwing stones among the worshippers. It looked as if they were careful not to actually hit anyone, but maybe they were just lucky. After the second stoning incident, there were no more charismatic worship gatherings while I was in Kragur. Some said this was because the parish priest had asked his flock to give up charismatic worship for Lent, but almost everyone assumed that this was also a convenient way to give people time to cool down and sort out the accusations and anger the stone throwing left in its wake.

The diocesan leaders in Wewak kept an eye on charismatic worship in their patch from its beginning, and as it became more and more popular, they followed the same course that the Catholic Church has followed in other parts of the world. That is, rather than try to discourage people from joining the charismatic movement, they set about to domesticate it. They assigned a priest to oversee charismatic worship in the diocese, and he brought local charismatic enthusiasts into classes in the proper way to conduct services and interpret their experiences. Kragur people know that charismatic worship had originated in America, and some have been disappointed that, as an American, I don't know more about it. The textbook that Kragur participants brought back from their training was, however, by an American author and published in America, and the priest assigned to oversee the movement in the diocese was an American, Father Eddie Bauer. (I would like to add that he was ably assisted by Father L. L. Bean, but it is—unfortunately—not so.)

I have to admit that I got some enjoyment out of the chaotic scramble to clear the meeting ground when stones rained down on some of my first charismatic gatherings, but if I had been a village leader I would have seriously considered putting a stop to charismatic worship, as some indeed did. Even before these incidents, some aspects of charismatic worship worried a lot of villagers. Some feared that in trying to get the attention of the Holy Spirit, the worshippers might call up some unholy spirits as well; some men didn't like the sight of women being such prominent public actors; some husbands didn't like it when their wives went to meetings of charismatic groups away from the village and left them to fend for themselves; some *ramat wolap* didn't like what they saw as the young charismatic worshippers' lack of respect for their elders; and some villagers thought that the most passionate charismatic worshippers were just showing off.

Nonetheless, charismatic worship was still very much alive and well when I returned to Kragur in 2008, although it had lost some of its outlaw edge. My very first Sunday in Kragur was Pentecost Sunday. When I entered the church and sat down, still perspiring and wobbly from the unaccustomed heat, I would have advised the Holy Spirit to make itself known as a cool breeze, maybe carrying a Hawai'i shave ice, rather than as a rushing wind. As I gathered my senses and began to take better note of what was going on, I saw that the church was full to overflowing with worshippers and handsomely decorated. The church beams and the altar were hung with depictions of teardrop-shaped tongues of fire rendered in red poster paint on white paper. A single

Figure 15. Poster decorating the church at Bou Village on
Pentecost Sunday, 2008. Photo by the author.

large painting hung on the beam across the front of the apse. This displayed
a shower of red flames emanating from the beak of a white bird, meeting in
midair a burst of fire from a volcano (fig. 15). Dozens of hibiscus blooms of an
almost iridescent red were strewn on the cement steps to the apse and combined in bouquets with woven palm fronds and long sprays of white orchids.
Behind the altar, both red and white hibiscus adorned a white figure of Christ
on the cross.

If it hadn't been for the occasional references to saints, fathers, and bishops
at this service, I might have assumed I'd wandered into an evangelical Prot-

estant gathering. "God is good!" shouted the leader, a Kragur man in fresh black pants, white shirt, and shiny black shoes, pacing and gesticulating. "All the time!" the congregation shouted back, and the call and response was repeated and repeated. All the services at Bou I saw in the coming weeks featured a group of young people with guitars to start and accompany the singing. This Sunday, however, the congregation also contributed enthusiastic hand clapping not found at ordinary services. True, not everyone clapped with equal abandon. Someone told me later that a lot of older men didn't go to the weekly charismatic services in part because they didn't like being "pushed" to clap and sing. But on Pentecost Sunday, the enthusiasts more than made up for the tepid hand tapping of those who found it a bit undignified. And neither the leader nor a large portion of the congregation could stop shouting the name of Jesus.

Only three days later I was at Kragur's own weekly charismatic prayer service, and I attended charismatic services every week I could during my stay. For each service, charismatic enthusiasts decorated with palm fronds and flowers a table in front of the prayer house on which stood a statue of the Virgin. Here too there were hibiscus blossoms and long, trailing sprays of luminous white orchids. I've grown accustomed to the abundance of hibiscus blossoms in Kragur life, but coming as I do from far north of the equator, it still amazes me to see people decorate with orchids in such profusion and treat them so expendably. Attendance at charismatic worship rose and fell over the weeks, but there was never anything apathetic about the worshipers who did show up. They sang, clapped, and swayed with raised hands, and those who came forward to testify had style and energy that could have held the stage successfully at any American revival meeting. The proceedings did seem more controlled than what I'd seen ten years before. I noticed fewer spontaneous outbursts of praise or prayer from the congregation, and if people were speaking in tongues they were doing it inconspicuously. A couple of younger men who came forward to testify at some of the services paced, gesticulated, and preached with fervor, but they told me in later conversations that one of the things they really liked about charismatic worship was that the atmosphere gave them a confidence about public speaking that they didn't have in ordinary village affairs. This sounded as much like the Rotary Club as the Gift of Tongues.

Paul Bashu, former army officer and hard-headed analyst of polling strategies, led the charismatic worship services on several occasions. He told me that he became a devout Christian after prayer cured him of a seven-month paralysis and that he had brought one of his children out of a coma through prayer. Combining his military posture and air of authority with genuine enthusiasm, he was a very effective leader, and I felt confident that I could doze in my Egg Layer Folding Lounger without fear of stoning.

Since I first went to Kragur, I've also seen the effects of efforts by the PNG church hierarchy to become active leaders in village Catholic life. Kragur is in St. Martin's Parish, which includes Kairiru and Mushu islands, and in 1996 a parish "Evaluation and Planning" committee, made up of local parishioners but led by the parish priest, a Yuropian, had come up with a new organizational plan that included a host of new bodies and leadership positions for local people at both the parish and the village levels. The written plan included a crowded organizational diagram that would have meant little or nothing to most adult villagers in the 1970s. Members of later generations, however, seemed to feel quite at ease with it, and there were more than enough villagers eager to fill in the various boxes in the chart with their names. The Legion of Mary was included in the new structure, but it was only one box among several. The new organization provided for a single village church leader, but there were also plenty of other functionaries and even a "Community Steering Team" to spread responsibility around, including to a few women.

The written plan and organization chart noted the titles of all the new entities in the kind of instant Tok Pisin that simply gives English words Tok Pisin spelling and pronunciation. So Evaluation and Planning becomes Ivaluesen na Plening, Parish Steering Team becomes Peris Stia Tim, and Community Steering Team becomes Komuniti Stia Tim. I have no idea what such terms mean to villagers with little or no knowledge of English, but plenty of villagers do understand them and almost everyone has adopted the habit of referring to these entities by their initials, so the Peris Stia Tim is the PST and the Komuniti Stia Tim is the KST.

Although by 2008 charismatic worship services were less volatile and the acronymic parish bureaucracy was even more firmly in place, there was still ferment in Kragur religious life. Like many of the elders I met in the 1970s, men concerned about passing on *tumbuna save* to their descendents could still get exercised about how early missionaries had tried to stamp out such indigenous forms of spiritual power. And there were men younger than I who, at least in private, had a lot to say against the Catholic Church. One such man told me quite emphatically one evening, while we sat on the small veranda of his house, listening to the sounds of his wife preparing taro and fish for dinner in the deepening shadows inside, that although the Catholic Church had given Kragur people some good things—some good "services," he said, using the English word—it had done this mainly to "pull" people into the new religion. And simultaneously, it had destroyed his people's original religion, a religion that he said could still bring them health and material plenty if they would follow it. He then insisted that I put in my new book what he was about to tell me, because the younger generations didn't know these things and needed to hear about them. Thinking that his views might be more than a little controversial, I asked him then and again some time later if he was sure he wanted this in print for the entire world to see, and he said that indeed he did.

Here is a much abbreviated version of what he told me. The original religion of Kairiru people, he said, came to them from a spirit being called Bokasar, who taught the ancestors that the sun was God. I had heard hints of this from close kin of my host but only in the shape of vague memories of things they'd once heard from their elders. This was the first time anyone had told me of this with conviction and in any sort of detail. Bokasar, my informant said, also taught the ancestors how they should honor the sun by abiding by numerous taboos and purification rituals—many of which pertain to managing the "mystical impurities left by the residue or odor of sexuality."[10] Adhering to these, he said, would also keep people healthy and prosperous. Bokasar, like many supernatural figures in Kairiru stories, could take the form of a snake; the missionaries, however, told people that a snake represented Satan. The missionaries had also distorted the story of Masos at Sumolau: it was the sun that spoke to Masos, he said, but missionaries convinced Kragur people that it had been the Christian deity. And placing the statue of the Virgin at Iupulpul had "covered up" the real spiritual meaning of the higher reaches of the island. Iupulpul is not far below the place on the mountain called Rokup, and Rokup was once the site of important rituals for the old powers; some villagers, he said, still went there to "pray" to the sun and to Bokasar.[11]

Some villagers I know have heard this man's account of a primal Kairiru religion and are quick to dismiss the notion that it was the sun that spoke to Masos at Sumolau. But some also say that while the sun wasn't involved at Sumolau, it is fair to equate the God the missionaries spoke of with powerful spirit ancestors native to Kairiru. Many villagers recognize Rokup and its environs as a place of indigenous spiritual significance. Their heterodoxy, however, doesn't stop even some of the strongest adherents of the sun god from taking part in village Catholic activities.

Kragur people are hardly the only Catholics in the world who take their religion in this way.[12] Such an attitude is especially easy to understand in a place where the idea of distinct and strictly bounded religions is something of a novelty. It's also possible that some villagers who hold Catholicism suspect may be active in church life in part because it offers opportunities for village leadership. I wouldn't, however, advise anyone to vie for leadership in Kragur without giving it a lot of thought. The village is rife with warm debates not only about who's in charge but also about in what direction, both moral and material, they should be leading.

Chapter 12

No Two Ways about It

I will lift up mine eyes unto the mountains:
From whence shall my help come?
—Psalm 121:1, American Standard Bible

Over the many years I've known Kragur, questions about who is or should be leading the village have only multiplied. In the 1970s, some villagers blamed many of Kragur's problems on lack of strong, centralized leadership, and many argued that the wealthy Yuropian countries of the world owed their strength in part to such leadership. But ironically, the more entangled Kragur gets with the wider world, the more leaders and would-be leaders proliferate and the more complicated become the choices they face about which direction to lead.

The coming of the council system decades ago opened a new arena in which people— including those without multiple *kokwal*—could compete for positions of leadership. The growing importance of the Local Level Government has added yet another sphere in which people can seek authority, and if there is room for only one Wewak Islands LLG president, there are lots of other ways village-level activists can get involved in LLG politics. Within the village there are also committees with chairs, secretaries, and treasurers for local involvement in managing every other kind of relatively new secular institution, such as the school at Bou and the medical clinic.

Catholicism also has made a substantial contribution to complicating the leadership situation by providing opportunities for leadership to people without the credentials of a *kokwal*—women in particular. Opportunities for women to become leaders or even compete for positions of leadership are still extremely rare in Kragur. This may well be one reason women tend to be more active in many church functions than men. Women carried the flowery platform elevating a colorful statue of the Virgin in the Corpus Christi procession I watched in 2008, and women crowd the front rows at charismatic worship. The bigmen may not like clapping their hands and waving their arms, but they like even less the fact that some women say charismatic worship has given them "new life." Theologically, "new life" means a new, personal connection with God. In everyday village life, some men claim, it means that women feel safer in flouting the authority of the bigmen, for example, by not heeding taboos they might impose in aid of garden fertility or other magic.

In 2008, I saw clear public disagreement about the scope of the authority of Catholic institutions in village life. When in 1998 I first learned about the bureaucratic structure introduced in the parish, I thought it might be too complicated and confusing to last long; I know *I* found it complicated and confusing. But in 2008, it was more firmly established than ever. Parish-level bodies such as the Parish Steering Team and the Parish Team of Pastoral Animation sit at the top of this organizational hierarchy, but the entity most important in village life is the KST—that is, the Komuniti Stia Tim (Community Steering Team). Most of the KST membership slots are marked for leaders of different kinds of village church groups, such as the Legion of Mary, the Catholic women's group, a church youth group, the young people who provide the music for worship services, and the leaders of charismatic worship. The KST, however, also has slots for "customary leaders" (that is, the *kokwal, ramat wolap,* or bigmen), one of the ward councilors, and a member of the committee that provides local support for the health clinic.

I'm not sure what the parish priest and village Catholic leaders intended when they first devised this structure in 1996, but in 2008 some Kragur people regarded the KST as a general village governing body, not just the body in charge of village Catholic affairs. The sitting chair of the KST held that it was the principal governing body of the village and he had interjected it into a number of quite secular issues, such as regulating the prices of goods in the Kragur market and levying fees on people from other villages who wanted to offer goods in the market. Some villagers had no quibble with this, but others thought that the KST was overstepping its bounds—and they weren't afraid to say so.

At one community meeting called by the KST, when someone started to talk about problems in collecting market fees, another villager quickly rose to say that this wasn't KST business. One of the newly elected ward councilors backed him up, stating very firmly that the KST was wandering into the councilors' territory; the KST was for "*lotu*" (religion) he said, not "*gavman*" (government). Several villagers told me later that they agreed with the new councilor.

Some bigmen of today are also more than a little sour about being relegated to mere members of the KST. Many villagers, however, still put them ahead of either church leaders or elected village leaders. The bigmen, with Kitok at their head, were the *real* government of the village, one older man told me in 2008, and many others agreed. But the bigmen and other established or would-be leaders all face the same challenge: how to show villagers that their leadership can accomplish things for the village. During the 2008 elections, one of the highest compliments villagers could pay to a candidate for office at any level was that he was an *ekshen man* (action man)—a phrase derived from English but rapidly becoming part of everyone's Tok Pisin vocabulary.

As I understand things, even in the old days a bigman couldn't ignore public opinion. He could easily lose people's respect if he failed to use his power for the general welfare or, worse, if he used it maliciously. If he went too far in abusing his power, other bigmen might even use their power to bring him low. Today I know that some villagers wonder what the bigmen can do to help Kragur cope with the rush of new political and economic challenges that don't respond to magic. Yet at the very least, bigmen still enjoy prestige that they can lend to any endeavor, like royalty in a constitutional monarchy. Also, and crucially, they still have the firmest grip on the "spear of the village"—that is, deep and authoritative knowledge of clan histories with their intimate connection to land and other resource rights. But prestige and knowledge unexercised for valued ends can eventually lose their luster.

Other kinds of leaders also have to show what they can do for people. The Catholic Church led the way in bringing health services and education to Kragur people, as well as in giving people—including young people and women—alternative homes for their considerable religious energies. But simply wearing the Catholic label doesn't automatically give a leader clout. In 2008, it looked as if the KST was able to enforce only the edicts of which villagers readily approved; what villagers disliked, they simply ignored. If the KST and KST chairs want to make themselves and the Stia Tim central to village life (whether in church life alone or in a wider sphere), they will have to show villagers the benefits of granting them authority, not merely assert their authority. Ward councilors and LLG leaders also have to show what they're made of. They can draw to some extent on networks and resources outside the village, but villagers are expecting more from ward councilors these days than they used to, and LLGs are under a lot of pressure to deliver tangible benefits.

Kragur's *susok* people don't fit into the pattern of village leadership in any easy and comfortable way. Educated migrants and their village families generally don't reach the same conclusions when they assess the benefits the migrants have brought to the village. At the poles of opinion, villagers see migrants as tendrils reaching out from Kragur to the wider world to draw in new strength, while migrants regard themselves as seeds carried from the village to take root elsewhere. Villagers and migrants do agree that they live in strikingly different worlds. They struggle, however, with how to communicate between them. In 2008 it would have been amusing, if it hadn't been troubling, to hear villagers complain that visiting urbanites were often haughty and condescending, while some urbanites complained to me that it was hard to talk with villagers when they went home because the villagers treated them with too much deference—"like kings," one of them said. Such distance between the barefoot and the *susok* people of Kragur has grown without anyone's willing it from circumstances new to those on each side of the divide. But it's up to Kragur people on both sides to try to bridge the lengthening distance. Achieving better mutual understanding may be easier now—while the leading *susok* people are still Kragurs who grew up in the village—than it will be for their progeny, who will have had little or no direct experience of village life.[1]

Anyone who could help villagers put more money in their pockets would have a strong claim to leadership in Kragur, but not just any way of accomplishing this would do. For example, villagers generally say that they are virtually united against mining on the island, especially if it were to entail one widely discussed plan that would require relocating the entire island's population to the mainland. Nonetheless, finding more and better ways to make money is high on most villagers' agendas for change, even though many are aware that while money solves some problems, it creates others.

One of the dangers of money is that it can weaken villagers' ability to trust each other. In many small communities, people are highly dependent on each other for the good things in life, but they also can see clearly how easily the actions of others can do them harm; hence, trust is vital but fragile. In PNG villages, belief that someone else's mere uncharitable feelings can harm you— in Kragur, through the medium of ancestral spirits—can make people look askance at their neighbors when misfortune strikes, and misfortune strikes quite often where access to modern medicine is limited and people earn their bread lifting heavy things, using sharp implements, and taking to the sea.[2] While a low background hum of suspicion is an old part of life in Kragur, a relatively new part of village life—money—often amplifies it. I've often heard Kragur villagers accuse each other of unethical dealings with money, such as the money I sent for buying tools after the 2002 earthquake or various funds collected for villagewide projects over the years. And while Kragur people have often told me that I'm lucky to have ended up in their village, where the people are more hospitable and generally ethically superior to those of almost any other village, many also tell me that they don't trust anyone in Kragur in matters of money, and I shouldn't either.

What could account for such rampant suspicion of others in money matters? Chronic bad financial management is one obvious reason. I know that many individuals or committees charged with managing public money in Kragur have made a mess of keeping their books. Bad record keeping in itself isn't evidence of bad intentions, especially among people who generally have had no training in financial record keeping. But without decent records, money can seem to disappear for no reason—as anyone with a checking account or a credit or debit card knows—and there is no way to prove that the responsible people weren't helping themselves to the funds rather than just managing them poorly.

Beyond simple poor accounting, some of money's distinctive qualities make it tinder for mistrust. In contrast to fish or taro, money is easy to hide and hoard, it is chronically scarce in Kragur, and it has an astounding variety of uses. All this helps make it easy to imagine that one's kin aren't sharing their money as they share their tobacco or betel nut (although there is a fair amount of betel nut hiding in Kragur when supplies are low). It may in fact strengthen the temptation not to share. If you can accumulate enough money, you can be more independent of your kin and neighbors. Taken too far, this could seriously fray the network of obligations to share both goods and labor that has long knit the village together, helped maintain a basic level of material security for everyone, and even shaped villagers' identities.[3]

Even in the most affluent settings, there would be virtually no society at all (as British prime minister Margaret Thatcher famously claimed was essentially the human condition, anyway[4]) if there weren't some checks on what money can buy and there weren't public institutions—such as health, education, and social welfare programs—to provide people with important things that are hard to provide universally at a profit.

Perhaps the greatest check on the power of individual desire for money to carry everything before it in Kragur—and much of PNG—is that fact that people can't buy or sell land. PNG's Land Act states that a Papua New Guinean has "no power to sell, lease or dispose of customary land otherwise than to natives in accordance with custom, and a contract or agreement by him to do so is void."[5] Papua New Guineans can make deals with mining companies or other organizations that want to use land held under customary title—that is, any part of some 97 percent of the land in the country—but they must do so as groups formed along customary lines under the Land Group Incorporation Act. Dozens and perhaps even hundreds of commentators on PNG's economy have opined that the country would "develop" faster if individuals could get undisputed title to land and so be able to use it with greater market efficiency by making permanent changes in it (including making it unfit for agriculture or habitation through denuding it of resources), accumulating more of it, or selling it off to finance other investments.

Keeping land under customary title does inhibit completely free play with land in business; that, of course, is the point. It is a big mistake, however, to assume that Papua New Guineans face a stark choice between preserving traditional ways of managing land at the cost of economic stagnation and making a radical break with the past that sets people adrift in a world of unfettered greed and competition. Papua New Guineans have often proved that they are too innovative to get trapped in such a dilemma. Famously—at least among anthropologists—the growth of the money economy in many parts of Papua New Guinea has led people to expand what anthropologists call the "gift economy" by distributing greater quantities of goods through ceremonial giving, rather than abandoning such practices to invest more money in their businesses.[6]

In the face of the need to organize themselves to deal with huge multinational mining companies, many Papua New Guineans have improvised ways of defining and asserting land rights that no one could have predicted.[7] Looking to the people of Lihir Island again for an example, anthropologists Martha Macintyre and Simon Foale have reported not only that Lihirians created a Council of Chiefs where no such thing existed before, but also that they now assert individual rights over land in some contexts but insist that all land is clan property in others.[8] Anthropologist Laura Zimmer-Tamakoshi found that the Gende people mightily confused outsiders by the way in which they sorted out claims to land in order to allocate compensation from nickel mining. As in Kragur, Gende establish original rights to land by clearing it for planting. These rights, however, don't necessarily pass to their children. Instead, subsequent generations establish rights by sponsoring mortuary feasts for the deceased proprietors, leaving room for a lot of variation in paths of inheritance. To outsiders, Zimmer-Tamakoshi observed, it looked as if the Gende were casting the rules of social organization to the wind as they scrambled for land rights, but only because outsiders assumed that Gende "tradition" entailed rigid rules prescribing land rights unequivocally across generations.[9]

It isn't only in land matters that Papua New Guineans often surprise those hoping to identify unbendable social rules that will let them predict people's behavior. Most anthropologists working in PNG agree with C. A. Gregory: "The essence of the PNG economy today is ambiguity."[10] And anthropologists have described Papua New Guineans' general approach to organizing themselves as "ad hoc," "loose," "more Lamarkian than Darwinian," and characterized by a "willingness to innovate on the basis of custom."[11] Alex Golub goes so far as to describe this dynamic characteristic of PNG "tradition" as "simply modern."[12]

I wouldn't even try to predict the ways in which Kragur people might improvise if necessary on the basis of the *straksa* I've helped them put down on paper. I could only discover this by watching closely what actually happens. To keep things simple in this book, I've left aside some important aspects and rough edges of Kragur villagers' own descriptions of their social order, but who knows when some of these might become important? The men I worked with on the *straksa* project, for instance, acknowledged that how people were related through women was important—some of them discoursed at length about the complex histories of marriages between clans—but they couldn't take on everything at once and stuck to identifying relations of descent through men.

Another rough edge I've ignored is ambiguity about the meaning of the term *koyeng*. I've been more than happy here to follow villagers' lead and use the terms *klen* (Tok Pisin) or "clan" as though they were always interchangeable with *koyeng*. But when I first arrived in Kragur, the ways people used the term *koyeng* confused me a little. While houses in Kragur are not arranged in neat rows or blocks like those in a suburban housing development, villagers see Kragur as made up of several irregularly shaped, individually named geographic areas. Among these are geographic areas that bear the names of each of what Kragur people today call *klen,* and men of these *klen* head most but not necessarily all the households in each of these areas. But several areas bear names that do not appear in the *klen* roster, and in casual conversation villagers sometimes use the term *koyeng* as though it meant simply a named geographic area, whether it bears the name of a *klen* or not.

Most villagers will explain that the primary meaning of *koyeng* is a named patrilineal descent group. But when I was new on the scene, the slippage between *koyeng* as a group based on descent and *koyeng* as an area of residence often caught me off guard. And it still can. In 2008, one of my collaborators on the *straksa* work spoke of one geographic area populated by households headed by members of more than one group defined by common patrilineal descent as a *koyeng*. He acknowledged that there was no dominant *klen* in that area, but the area's residents had, he said, "made a *koyeng*" there. Other Kragur people might tell me that this collaborator simply has it wrong; but maybe, in some circumstances, where people live—versus from whom they're descended—counts more than I realize.[13]

The problem here—if I insist on finding a problem—isn't that some Kragur people don't understand their own system or that their system isn't properly systematic. The problem is that as an outsider I sometimes wish Kragur people's conceptions of things were simpler and neater, imagining perhaps that if they were I could predict how Kragur people will behave as their circumstances alter. Well, I can wish myself good luck with that. I wouldn't trust anyone who claimed to be able to make more than very broad and qualified predictions about much of anything in Papua New Guinea that wasn't sitting right on the surface, and I would expect a lot of apparently sound predictions to fall apart when examined closely.

Not only are Papua New Guineans prone to "innovate on the basis of custom," they also sometimes "change their minds about the things that are important to them," as Martha Macintyre points out.[14] This is a very human thing to do, but when we are trying to figure out what other people are likely to do in the future, it is often convenient to ignore it. Ambivalence about the pull of individual autonomy and both the obligations and satisfactions of enveloping social ties has probably been an integral part of the Kragur world since long before the first Yuropian showed up. But in the modern era, the ambivalence is undoubtedly sharper and more out in the open.

Will Kragur people someday change their minds about this and tip the precarious balance? Things such as the growing importance of money, an ideology of individual autonomy in voting, and the possibility of highly personal experiences of God in charismatic Catholic worship probably put weight on the individual or immediate family side of the scales. There is also at least one force in PNG that is promoting a focus on individuals and immediate families (as opposed to extended families, clans, or other larger kinship-based groups) through what can only be called direct propaganda. This is something called the Entrepreneurial Development Training Centre Personal Viability Program, most often known as the Personal Viability Program or just PV. PV has taken off in PNG since its founding in the late 1990s and has even gained the endorsement of the national government, which has sponsored PV training courses for civil servants. You wouldn't think that it would get much notice in a place as rural as Kragur, but it has made a deep footprint on Kairiru Island.

I first got to Kairiru in 1975 by hitching a ride on a boat going to St. John's Seminary, a small boarding school for young PNG men considering going into the Catholic Church, located less than a mile along the coast from St. Xavier's. Viewed from the sea, the scatter of tin-roofed buildings among the palms and the small white church looked like someplace where you might bump into Somerset Maugham or some of his fictional characters. The seminary has now been closed for many years, but the Catholic Church still owns the facility and operates both a chicken farm and a small commercial conference center there. The PV organization has made it a favorite meeting place, and several Kragur men have taken advantage of its proximity to attend PV training courses.[15]

What does PV teach? Judging from the PV Web site, the program is a lot like any other half-baked self-help promotion, touting—for example—"a 'New Science' which works with the invariability of physical science in the field of the human mind," and "owning yourself and being yourself."[16] More concretely, it promotes, among other things, business success through a kind of self-reliance that entails learning to say no to the requests of relatives for financial aid and to "control" one's time—for instance, through limiting "sitting idle around the village" and visiting relatives.[17] Simplistic advice of this kind doesn't take into account what village life is really like. "Sitting idle around the village," for example, doesn't sound like a good thing, but people apparently sitting idle are often having conversations in which they make important decisions about things such as agricultural work, the conduct of religious activities, the government of the village, and other matters that in the so-called developed world we delegate to full-time specialists with narrowly defined responsibilities. Critics of PV also find larger problems with its teachings. In the words of anthropologist Nick Bainton, the overall thrust of the PV message is "learning to favor personal ambition over collective stability."[18] That agenda is a very heavy stone to throw into the middle of the life of any PNG village.

How has the PV stone landed in Kragur? With a muffled plunk, not a resounding thud, and even the plunk has had a different timbre than PV trainers probably intended. The Tok Pisin PV manual a Kragur man loaned me doesn't push individual ambition quite as hard as I'd expected. It is full of talk of doing things for *mi yet*—that is, for myself alone. But the manual also advises that no one can succeed alone; to succeed, you have to work together (in Tok Pisin, *wok bung*) with like-minded people. Your kin and fellow villagers, of course, might not be like-minded people, so this can be taken as advice to cut loose from village ties if they drag you down, and that is indeed the tenor of much of the manual. But the most vigorous advocate of PV in Kragur took from his training a different message. He's fiercely in favor of people managing their money with long-term business goals in mind and keeping track of how they use their time. But he tells Kragur people that they have to do this together in what he calls (in English) a "communal" spirit, and he doesn't see this as contradicting his PV training. It looks as if it would take a much stronger dose of training to get Kragur people to consume the PV message without local seasoning.[19]

In any case, advocates of PV in Kragur are bumping shoulders with many other aspiring leaders with diverse ideals. This will continue to confuse everyone, but it is probably just as well, because no one can really be sure exactly where Kragur should strive to go or by what route. Obviously, political and economic decisions made by national and international authorities that take little or no account of the welfare of villagers limit what Kragur people can accomplish on their own initiative, but many choices still remain in their own hands.[20]

These choices are considerably more complex than selecting between such artificial alternatives as tradition and modernity, inertia and progress, or underdevelopment and development. This means that Kragur will need all the leadership it can get in years to come—leadership in seeking innovative ways to manage village lands, exploring new ways of earning money, pursuing ways of using money that don't poison people's vital social relationships, trying to manage the tensions between individual autonomy in electoral politics and villagers' deep interdependence in other spheres, forging wider roles for women, and finding in religion both solace and an impetus to keep pondering difficult moral issues. (It wouldn't hurt, either, if someone embarked on a serious antismoking campaign. As much as it would spoil my fun in Kragur, it's probably the single most important thing villagers could do to improve their health.) It's impossible to say how many or how few people it will take to provide this leadership or whether they will be familiar kinds of leaders or leaders of kinds no one has even thought of yet.

As much as invocations of Kragur pride move me—and they do—Kragur leaders will have to go considerably beyond this: they will have to step up to address the perplexing details and conundrums of what Kragur wants to take pride in. I may get to see the general direction things take in the next two or three decades, but I probably won't see things come to rest, because it's in the nature of the modern world that things don't come to rest.

Chapter 13

The Long Good-bye

Me that 'ave been what I've been—
Me that 'ave gone where I've gone—
Me that 'ave seen what I've seen—
'Ow can I ever take on
With awful old England again . . . ?
—Rudyard Kipling, "Chant-Pagan"

A couple of weeks before my departure from Kragur, villagers started inviting me for farewell meals, and a few started talking about putting on some kind of villagewide farewell event. The event would be modest, in view of the post-election tensions in the village. Also, no one knew when they'd get news from Moses Manwau about the progress of his legal battle for a parliamentary seat, and no one could guess whether the news would call for public rejoicing (and perhaps some private grumbling) or would leave Kragur people dejected (with perhaps a few pockets of private rejoicing). Perhaps, someone suggested, some of the younger men could put on a short traditional song-and-dance presentation at the end of a village meeting, followed by a few brief speeches. I said that whatever anyone wanted to do or not do was fine with me. Not knowing what to expect, I composed in my mind a much better speech than the one I'd given extemporaneously early in my stay.

My speech aside, plans for a farewell event did not get far, but I knew enough of all that was going on in Kragur not to take it personally. As the days prior to my departure ticked away, it looked more and more likely that to mount even a modest villagewide observance would require people who had been at odds with each other politically for months to quit reflexively getting in each other's way, and even my closest friends were wary of stirring up additional animosity. Everyone in the village was perfectly nice to one another in public, and many villagers went out of their way to tell me they were sorry I had to go so soon. It was nevertheless a rather tense time. Even after skipping a week to let the village mood mellow, attendance at charismatic worship suffered. At the first postelection charismatic service, Paul Bashu commented rather acidly on the singularly small number of adults present. "I think your parents all must have died!" he said to the usual crowd of children ready and eager to sing and shout, before shaking his head sadly and muttering, "Politics is breaking up the village."

My departure, though, didn't go entirely without public spectacle. Patrick Beka, with whom I'd had some long conversations about local politics, organized an event for me in Bou the day before I left for Wewak. There were songs with gestures from a group of schoolchildren, speeches from a couple of local leaders, a tribute to the retiring school headmaster (Beka knew how to get mileage out of a public event), and an impressive buffet of local food laid out on tables in Bou's small thatched church near the beach. Beka presented me with a colorful *bilum* (a bag woven of handmade string) adorned with seashells, and I presented him with a copy of *Village on the Edge*. The speech I'd prepared for Kragur wasn't quite right for Bou, but I mentally cribbed from it to make better thank-you remarks than I usually manage.

By the last week of my stay, I had more than enough to keep me busy. I needed a few more short sessions to get as close as I could to making a clean sweep of all the clan histories. I also had to think about what parts of my gear to take home with me, what to leave behind, and—very important—what to leave with whom. I took the water purification equipment I'd brought with me and a few items from my medical kit down to Vincent at the clinic. Jack Mari had commented admiringly on my white New Balance trainers a number of times, so when he invited me for a farewell meal with his family, I took him the shoes. It was also no problem finding people happy to have things such as my collapsible water jugs, the numerous rolls of toilet paper still left in my stores (toilet paper is not a common household item in Kragur, but it is appreciated when available), and even the loyal trekking poles I had named Harry and George, which were quite unnecessary in Wewak.

Also, as my departure approached, a number of people had special requests to make. Teresia Salol, who had taken Sarah under her wing during her brief and disastrous stay in Kragur decades before, still worried about her and asked me if I would ask Sarah to write to her. When I contacted Sarah—for the first time in many years—shortly after getting home, I told her to be sure to send Teresia a picture of her children so she would be completely certain that Sarah was well and happy. Someone asked me to send her a book by an American evangelical Christian on spiritual healing, several younger people asked me to try to find them pen pals in America, and the members of the surf club asked me to try to publicize the good waves at Kragur so foreign surfers would come visit. To do the latter, after I got home I located a Web site where surfers around the world share information about their favorite spots and new discoveries and entered some words about the Kragur Surf Club, their homemade boards, and the waves off Maratak Point.[1]

A group of older men asked me to investigate what definitely sounded like a scam. Someone had been going around the province telling people that the Japanese government was still paying war damages to Papua New Guineans and that he would, for a fee, apply on their behalf. He had even circulated a very official-looking notice of the service he was offering. When I got home, I wrote to the Japanese Embassy about this and received a reply saying that payment of war damages had ended a long time ago. I sent a copy of the embassy letter to the men in Kragur with advice that they tell everyone they knew to watch out for this con game.

A number of people also found private moments to ask me for help paying their children's school fees. By this time I could honestly say that I simply didn't have enough cash left to give any away. I could, of course, have arranged to wire money to a bank account for them when I got home. I have done this for quite a few villagers, but the number of requests for such help has grown mightily over the years, and I have had to set a limit. Although I didn't mention the flurry of such requests to anyone, one village leader intuited that this was going on. He told me that he was advising people not to ask me for money unless they had done something substantial to help me. That sounds like a good standard, but it isn't easy to apply. Just what is hospitality, conversation, careful explanation, a large bunch of delicious bananas and several pineapples, or guiding me along an unfamiliar trail worth in money? Also, the general pattern of giving and receiving gifts in PNG doesn't require that they balance immediately. I knew, for example, that people I helped with school fees now would not forget it when I came back again. Even so, I appreciated the leader's effort to help me manage this issue. He also, however, thought it would be nice if I would think about financing in Kragur some kind of what he called in English a "permanent monument" of my work there. To tell the truth, I wouldn't mind a nice plaque somewhere: "Michael French Smith once sat on this rock and whined pathetically about the heat." I told him, however, that it was nice thought but that my books would have to serve as my monument.

There were a few more things I wanted to photograph before I left, and a few friends wanted their pictures taken with me. Kilibop usually did the camera work for these. He had a steady hand, but lighting could be tricky. In some circumstances, no matter how we arranged ourselves, the camera's light meter seemed to read only the glare from the vast expanse of balding white forehead revealed when I took off my cap. Even when we got the lighting straight on my head, I wasn't always pleased with the results. Against a dark background and with a dark companion, my body sometimes looked like a long drink of milk—and skim milk at that.

A number of people gave me going-away gifts, all fine examples of local crafts. I did have to turn down the offer of a softly tanned tree-possum skin,

which would never have made it through customs—and would have reminded
me too much of Tricks, anyway. Several days before I left, Rokerai and some
of his friends gave me something valuable, imperishable, and easy to carry—a
Kairiru name. There had been talk in Kragur of giving me a local name for
some years, and I may long have had one or several nicknames, but none that
anyone felt free to use in my hearing. Rokerai, however, suggested one evening that since I'd been coming to Kragur for so long, I should be called
"Michael Tau." As the aboriginal Kairiru language name of Kairiru Island,
Tau is not associated with a particular clan as most Kairiru personal names
are, so it wouldn't be contentious in that respect. By the time I left, a number
of villagers had started calling me Tau or Michael Tau, which pleased me very
much. In addition to the considerable honor I felt, it also pleased be because
although Michael Tau is not a nickname as such, it has the swagger of classic
place-linked nicknames like Chicago Slim, Nevada Smith, Indiana Jones, and
that of a somewhat shady friend of my father-in-law whom my wife always
knew only as Uncle Brooklyn.[2]

I declined Rokerai's offer to tattoo "Tau" on my arm using soot from a kerosene lantern mixed with juice squeezed from coleus leaves, inserted under the
skin with a sewing needle. Rokerai had tattooed his own nickname, "Reef," on
his left arm, framed with a simple but dramatic pattern of short radiating
lines. I was envious, but I feared getting a fly-borne infection while healing,
and I wanted to save my antibiotics for any more unanticipated messages on
my left leg (such as the infections I'd suffered) about Jana's state of mind.

I spent most of my last day in Kragur packing and sitting on the veranda
with visitors. Although there was to be no public event, many people came to
sit with me, some for hours at a time, not necessarily expecting conversation
but simply to show me local courtesy. (For anyone interested, several clans and
both moieties were represented.) And as the sun went down, this gathering
evolved into a going-away party with which no planned public ceremony could
have compared.

It had already been established that I liked to sing. A few days earlier, Rokerai and I had sat up late on the veranda; I was lying with my head on the flour-
sack pillow and he was sitting cross-legged smoking and intoning in a low voice
a Kairiru language song that I thought I recognized. He told me that it was the
song called "Kalpiu," a traditional lament for a loved one who has died or is
simply far away that I had heard before on several occasions. Sparely melodious
laments seem to make up a lot of the Kragur songbook. Sung by a group, they
can sound strident to a Western ear, but sung quietly solo they are very beautiful and sad. They are meant to be sung to the accompaniment of the thumping
of a *kundu,* but if drums aren't available men will knock out the rhythm on
anything handy. That night on the veranda, as Rokerai sang to himself he softly

knocked out the rhythm on the bamboo floor with the fingernails of one hand. I encouraged him to sing out more so I could hear him better, and he went on to sing laments composed by several men of his *koyeng* when they were far from home working on plantations or in gold mines. I couldn't offer any songs composed by members of my family, but I do know a lot of sad folk and country songs, and I offered a few of these quietly a cappella in exchange.

At some point during the evening before my departure, a very well-used guitar appeared among the men and boys on my veranda, and it didn't take much encouragement to get someone to start the tunes. Rokerai, Kitok, and Wapsi could all play more than a little, and Wapsi, although rusty, was skilled in a kind of fingerpicking I'd never seen before. Someone brought a *kundu* out of the main room of the house, and I got the *kundu* Kilibop had given me out of my room. Several traditional laments were performed, with me trying to follow the stop-and-go pattern of the drumming, but the Kragur songbook also includes lots of Tok Pisin numbers composed for guitar or ukulele accompaniment, several of which I knew. Some of these are also songs of journeying and homesickness, and we started out with some of these. One of the best was composed by Kragur's own Michael Washol. To a memorable melody, it tells of a young man leaving Kairiru for Wewak and other more distant places where the white men live. Standing on the prow of the *Tau-K* (the old St. Xavier's boat) playing his guitar, he is filled with the excitement of this new adventure; but, rounding Kairiru Island's Urur Point, rough seas toss and tumble the boat.

Eventually I got a turn with the guitar and, using my full repertoire of twelve chords, I offered "Cielito Lindo," "Ramblin' Boy," "Blue Eyes Crying in the Rain," and a couple of other tearjerkers. Then I brought us back to Tok Pisin with a song that everyone knew: a ditty about a young girl bathing in a lagoon who manages to escape unharmed after a saltwater crocodile catches her by the leg. Despite the gruesome subject, the song is a bit naughty; the principal sign of the girl's good health after the attack is the continued buoyancy of her youthful breasts. I'd learned this one in the Admiralty Islands in 1973, but apparently it's a widespread and perennial favorite. Almost everyone there knew it, and we performed it two or three times to make sure we got the harmonies just right.

Another song that we repeated—because everyone knew it, everyone liked it, and we harmonized better each time we sang it—was one Rokerai had taught me a few days before. I'd heard snatches of it on previous visits, but I'd never caught all the words and committed them to memory. This one was all in English, and Rokerai thought students at St. Xavier's had written it. It is a nostalgic song about the beauties of Kairiru Island, a place the St. Xavier students, who might have come from anywhere in the province, would leave behind them when they graduated. The English is not the kind spoken in England or America, but it is highly effective. Here are the lyrics:

Slowly the sun is rising
Over the sparkling sea
Soft, soft white clouds floating
In the sky of blue

In my heart is resting
Kairiru home of mine
Kairiru breeze is floating
Always come and see

You will always thinking
Thinking back your home
The memories of an island
Surrounded by the sea

Looking back and forward
Kairiru reaching high
Kairiru always lonely
The world is always round

The guitar changed hands many times as the evening progressed and—
with the exception of Washol's song, the story of the crocodile attack, and
"Slowly the Sun is Rising"—we kept going for several hours without repeating
ourselves. When I didn't know the words, I just drummed, whatever the style
of song. When I took the guitar and sang songs no one else knew, the drum-
mers improvised and the others listened politely. Despite being badly debili-
tated by *sotwin*, Kitok performed with energy and animation, sitting cross-
legged but dancing with his eyes and his upper body as he played and sang
(fig. 16). It was all men on the veranda, but the main room of the house was
full of children and women who occasionally called encouragement or laughed
loudly at other songs with risqué lyrics.

I often heard Munbos' voice among the others, talking and laughing. At
one point I looked up to see her coming out on the veranda, where she stepped
through the small crowd to my side—I too was sitting cross-legged on the
floor—to bend over, clasp my head to hers, and wail in mourning, ending each
wail with a chant of "ai ai ai ai ai ai ai ai ai," diminishing in volume with each
syllable, like those that punctuate "Kalpiu" and other Kairiru laments. She
wailed in Tok Pisin, however, and I could understand her clearly:

Oh, tomorrow you'll go!
We won't see you again!
We don't know when you'll come back!
I won't hear you in your room in the morning!

Figure 16. Chief Alois Kitok playing and singing at my going-away party, 2008.
Photo by the author.

> I won't cook for you!
> Oh, now you're going!
> Oh, who will help me now!

Rhythmic, punctuated by sobs, this was something I'd seen, but I'd never before been the object of such mourning. She kept my head clasped tightly to hers, and I could feel her tears running down my face. I was not embarrassed, and I don't think anyone else was either. When she stopped she did so suddenly, breaking off without winding down. She stood straight again, wiped her face with the back of her hand, and stepped quietly back into the house. A few men murmured that, yes, a lot of people would be sorry to see me go; then whoever held the guitar started another song, and we kept singing for a while longer. During a pause in the singing for rolling smokes and grinding betel nut, someone leaned toward me, and gesturing with his head toward the room where Munbos sat, said, "That's what we're like. When someone leaves, it's as though they're dead." A few days before, Munbos had told me that she had dreamed that this was the last time I would come to Kragur. I told her that her dream was mistaken: I'd be back. I didn't know this for certain, but there is nothing else one can say. In fact, a few days earlier I, too, had had a dream—a dream within a dream, really: I dreamt that I was at home in Silver Spring,

Maryland, and that I had just awakened from a deeply nostalgic dream about the pleasures of being in Kragur.

The singing continued, and I felt like I might be able to make it until dawn, but I remembered that I was supposed to be on the beach waiting for the boat at eight in the morning and that tomorrow was going to be a long day, so I excused myself a little after 1:00 a.m. and went back into my room to try to sleep. The party on the veranda wound down quickly after that, although when I got up at 5:30 a.m. to the smell of wood smoke and something cooking over the fire, I could hear Kitok in the main room talking in a low voice with a few others who had apparently stayed all night.

After a filling breakfast, including a good strong cup of coffee, we still had plenty of time to get down to Minamisil to meet Patrick Beka, who was bringing his boat around from Bou to take Kilibop, Munbos, and me all to Wewak. Munbos would go back to Kairiru the same day, but Kilibop was going to stay on until I left to keep me company, give me a hand with my baggage, and see me safe through the streets on some final errands. These included changing some of the US dollars I had left into kina to have on hand in Moresby, and Kilibop cautioned me that the thieving element in Wewak considered people leaving the bank, especially foreigners, likely prospects for quick profits.

Before we left for the beach, there was one more parting gesture. The Umari family had a sprouting coconut ready to plant in front of Rokerai's house as a memorial of my stay there and a marker of the time elapsed until I came back again. The ground in Kragur is rocky below the surface as well as above. Kragur people, however, generally don't have pickaxes. Instead, someone produced the local tool for such work, a four- or five-foot length of heavy metal pipe with a short horizontal handle welded to one end. To dig the planting hole, I loosened the ground by ramming the pipe down again and again, each time making a satisfying crunching sound, while Kilibop, squatting beside me, scraped out the loose dirt and stones with his hands between crunches. If I had been considering making this my last visit, this simple ceremony would have tipped the scale against that idea. I know there are people who think me unsentimental, but my occasional crustiness is more often than not a defense against the thick stream of sticky sentiment that flows in my veins.

The digging and planting took only a few minutes, and then we were off to the beach. Numbers of people came down from their houses to shake my hand as we walked through the village, and a small gathering waited with me for Beka to pull into the small earthquake-formed inlet. The wait was mercifully short. As a couple of my companions hustled my bags down to the water and into the boat, there was a final round of handshakes and—something relatively new to me in Kragur—several two-arm hugs. Until then, exactly one Kragur villager had ever hugged me, shortly before my departure from Kragur in 1998. Not only that, I had rarely ever seen any Papua New Guineans hug one another. But on this morning I received several unreserved bone-crushers: Kragur people, even the slightest elderly women, are strong. I was a little slow in returning the first hug, but I was ready for those that followed and did my best to inflict equal affectionate damage.

The weather was perfect, and we made good time over only slightly rolling seas. In a small boat with a loud engine, the water racing along the sides and a stiff breeze around your head, you can't have a conversation unless you're inches from someone, so on a calm day such a trip can be a very peaceful time. It stayed peaceful until we were quite close to Wewak, and Beka, alert at the tiller, noticed a small boat off to our left, drifting, one of its occupants waving at us with the boat's red gas tank. The ease with which he waved the rectangular tank above his head strongly suggested that it was innocent of gas. Beka slowed down and steered toward the drifters, a middle-aged man and a young boy. They were, indeed, out of gas. "So why aren't you paddling?" Beka asked. The man replied that they had set out not only without enough gas but also without even a single paddle. At this admission, Beka launched into a blistering lecture on the consummate foolishness of this and his utter incredulity that such foolishness could possibly exist in an adult. He then pulled our boat close enough so that he could hand over one of his own two wooden paddles and told the drifters that they still had time to make their way to Wewak by dark if they paddled hard. As we pulled away, still gathering speed, Beka apologized to us for his fiery outburst. He hated to see people do such dumb things, he said, and—he allowed—he was probably still more than a little upset about losing the close election.

We came ashore in Wewak not at the post office beach, under the casuarina trees, but on the opposite side of the neck of the point, at the western end of the market. There is no beach here, but the shore is sheltered from wind and waves, and boats can tie up at the jumbled coral and cement waterfront. This approach to Wewak is picturesque from a distance, but on slowing down and pulling in to shore you can see how much trash lies on the bottom of the aquamarine shallows, and the aroma from the backside of the market is not appealing. This landing, however, put us only a short walk from Martarina Wai's guesthouse, where Kilibop and I were booked again. We set off then to take my gear to Martarina's. Beka had business in town, including picking up medications for the village clinic, and we promised to meet him and Munbos later under the casuarinas to see them off back to Kairiru.

My business in town included confirming my flight reservations, buying a few final presents to send back to Kragur (including sets of wood-carving tools, available at Garamut Hardware, for Kilibop and Wapsi), and getting some souvenirs, including a red, yellow, and black PNG baseball cap for my brother (which I later decided to keep for myself). Back at the post office beach, nothing was happening. Munbos and some other Kragur people already in Wewak were sitting under the trees, some of them waiting for a boat, some of them just passing the time. Munbos had brought a few items of garden produce to try to sell in the informal market that often coalesced at the beach landing place, and she had spread these out on a cloth in front of her. Farther along the beach, other vendors were selling soft drinks, betel, local tobacco, and commercial cigarettes, the latter not by the pack but individually. Beka wasn't back yet from his errands, so Kilibop and I joined the waiters. I hate waiting for planes and boats to leave, especially when the impending parting threatens to be emotional. I purchased and smoked a couple of filter cigarettes and was reminded that smoking *brus* kills the time better: it takes a while to make one, they're longer, and inch-for-inch only the experienced can smoke one down with the speed that you can inhale your way through the weak fillings of a clean, white, filtered tobacco tube out of a pack.

When Beka did arrive, he was in a truck with friends and supplied with beer. He invited Kilibop and me to jump in the truck and ride the short distance around the base of the point to the parking lot in front of the yacht club, once a bastion of the white governing and commercial population of Wewak but now a gathering place for any Papua New Guineans with money in their pockets. There, we sat in and leaned on the truck and drank our beers. I declined a second. I am no longer the man who can hear a can or bottle of beer open hundreds of yards away, and—if I do happen to hear it—I'm no longer one of the first to track it down. Kilibop accepted a second but put it in his shoulder bag for later.

When the group decided to send someone to the yacht club for more beer, I decided we should take our leave, both from the drinking party and from the beach. My delicate intuitions suggested that this second round of beers might not be the last and that Beka's boat would not be leaving right away. When I told Munbos that I was going to say good-bye now and walk back to the guesthouse before dark, she looked upset. I don't know if it was simply because of the parting or because I was being discourteous by not waiting until I could stand on the beach waving as the boat pulled out to sea. But I don't think it would have been much easier if I had waited until the last drop of lager had been sipped.

I'd given myself too much time in Wewak before my flight out to Moresby on July 1, but we managed to fill it. I went to the market again and bought more bead necklaces, we repacked the drum and other breakable items using cardboard scavenged from one of the general stores, and we walked to almost everywhere I'd ever been in and around the town to see how things had changed since 1998. After schlepping up and down Kairiru's slippery slopes for a couple of months, walking around Wewak, even on its steep but comparatively short hills, was like being carried on a palanquin. Since the water and electricity in Martarina's neighborhood were going on and off unpredictably, we also could have amused ourselves by betting on whether we'd be able to shower or cook when we got back from one of our excursions, but we didn't.

I ran into a slight problem changing money at the bank. My last hundred-dollar bills had been in my wallet for several hot and sticky weeks now, and they hadn't been new to start with. The bank clerk told me that they couldn't be exchanged for kina because the bank's customers for US dollars preferred clean, new notes. I was taken aback. I hadn't realized how much I apparently believed in the universal popularity of the American dollar, even when not looking its best. I also needed the cash and didn't give a toss about their other customers' aesthetic preferences. Was I, too, not a customer, I asked, indignantly? The clerk quickly referred me to a manager, who listened politely as I queried her haughtily about whether or not the bank wanted foreign visitors to spend money in Wewak, visit Wewak at all, or even visit Papua New Guinea. I was weary and irritable, I guess; but, one more manager later and despite my haughtiness, the exchange was approved.

We were four nights at the guesthouse. Kragur people in town stopped to visit on a couple of evenings, and on the others Kilibop and I settled for our own conversation. The guesthouse veranda as the sun went down was conducive to conversation or simply to sitting in silent contemplation of the sound of the sea, the chirping of geckos, the small cries of the night's flying foxes (that is, less mellifluously, the fruit bats), and—in my case—the curious but enjoyable feeling that I get in Wewak or on Kairiru of comfortable familiarity fused with vivid novelty.

The morning of my departure we got to the airport in plenty of time to check in early for my 8:30 a.m. flight. I have lost interest in the long story of why I did not actually leave Wewak until 5:30 that afternoon. And the story of how we filled our time after the airport snack bar closed, the ceiling fans slowed to a halt when the power went off, and the airport shut down until the late afternoon flights began arriving and leaving is also lacking in excitement. After Kilibop nearly injured me permanently with a departing hug and as the boarding line finally started shuffling toward the door out onto the airfield, a line of passengers just arriving from Moresby began coming through the adjacent door. Among them were a couple of Kragur village men who had gone to Moresby with Moses Manwau. We greeted and said good-bye to each other as we passed in opposite directions, and Joe Boko called over his shoulder that there was still no movement in Moses' efforts to get the courts to review the parliamentary election results.

In spite of the delay, Ralph Saulep, Jacob Yabai (a clansman of Ralph's, also with a career in Port Moresby), and Lazarus Shorai, until recently councilor for Kragur's Ward 12, met me at the airport in Moresby. I was in Moresby only one day and two nights. This gave me time to get some clothes washed so I wouldn't trigger any smoke alarms on the rest of the trip (everything in a Kragur house eventually smells like it's been hanging over a wood fire) and for a long conversation with Brother Herman, who was passing through Moresby on his way to Wewak, returning from a long stint of teaching in the Philippine Islands.

My last evening in Moresby, I dined with Ralph, Jacob, several other Kragur people, and two friends of Ralph's I'd not met before. One was a Papua New Guinean chemist who had lived and worked in the United States for several years. The other was a young woman from the Trobriand Islands. Anyone who has been surfing the Web for information on tours to the Trobriands, originally made famous in the West by the books of early twentieth-century Polish anthropologist Bronislaw Malinowski (including *Argonauts of the Western Pacific, Coral Gardens and their Magic,* and *The Sexual Life of Savages in North-Western Melanesia*) might have expected her to show up in a grass skirt and little else. Since this was actual and not tourist-fantasy Papua New Guinea, she showed up driving a new black SUV and wearing a stylish, straight dark skirt, white blouse, and high heels.

The restaurant Ralph had chosen—the Point—seemed to be located in a light-industrial part of town, and patrons were admitted by sliding open a heavy metal gate across the front of the otherwise welcoming lobby. Such is Port Moresby. But once inside, our round table was quickly covered with attractively arranged platters of several types of delicious seafood, wine glasses, and a frosty march of what are called in PNG "white cans"—that is, cans of South Pacific Lager that display the colorful SP bird-of-paradise logo against a white background. I woke early the next morning to go to the airport with a sharp reminder of these plentiful white cans in my head and a dry one in my mouth.

All went well at the airport, except for a delay in paying my excess baggage charge because the power went off and the necessary computers went down. But when the power came back on, I was able to check in on time, and Herman blessed the drum, which was also protected—I hoped—by the layers of cardboard Kilibop and I had taped around it, as it slid onto the conveyer behind my overstuffed duffle bags. There were quick handshakes all around, and then I was alone in the international waiting area, plunged back into an anonymous crowd. In the Brisbane airport I had the expensive brewed coffee with cream I'd been daydreaming about, but it wasn't the thrill I'd been imagining. At the very outset of the long journey home, I was already becoming emotionally flat, and in such a condition I made the rest of the trip.

Back in the Washington area, it was an unusually steamy July, so climate shock didn't aggravate my jet lag. The whole family was well, the house still solid, and the garden only a little overgrown, so no crises greeted me. Jana was accustomed to the jungle aroma that poured out of my bags when I opened them in the living room and eager to hear more about the trip than I had been able to put in the few letters there had been time to send home. But she also respected my inability to organize my thoughts so soon after the fact and let me dribble out bits of the story as they came to mind. Our dog didn't care where I'd been as long as I was home now, still interested in efforts to overcome barriers to interspecies communication, and still fit enough to play Tennis Ball Challenge in the backyard until both our tongues hung out.

I made one significant mistake in managing my reentry into metropolitan Washington normality. Concerned about starting to put money into my bank account and our retirement coffers again, I returned to work at the office only five days after landing at Dulles International Airport. I don't really know, however, if putting it off a few more days would have helped. The offices of my employer enjoyed exceptional natural light, but like other modern offices (in the narrow technological sense) they were sealed against the considerable outdoor heat and traffic noise. They were cool and quiet—a little too quiet. There was, of course, the white noise of the ventilation system, the hum of printers, the ringing of phones, murmurs from the closed conference room, and the bubble and squeak of colleagues with summer allergies. But this struck me at the time more like the silence of the tomb than the peace and order of civilization, and I did not adapt quickly or smoothly. Among other things, I couldn't take breaks at my desk to stimulate my brain by playing the ukulele or stretch out on the floor during a long meeting and say, "Go ahead, I'm listening." I could see a career transition on the horizon, and it did in fact sail into port several months later.

Those of my colleagues who had themselves done long-term anthropological field research understood what I was going through. They also appreciated my excitement about secret ancestral names and the evolution of liberal democracy in PNG, and they empathized with my restlessness with days bound by project identification codes. Others sometimes asked me if I'd had "fun" on my trip. This was not a thoughtless or unreasonable question, but it didn't really apply to the kind of venture from which I had just returned. I enjoyed telling stories about things like the going-away songfest and the dead python in the water supply, just as I have always enjoyed telling of how I shared cigarettes with lepers on previous travels. Such things, however, are whitecaps on a substantial deep, one which I still struggle to understand and to articulate adequately. But I would not trade this struggle for anything.

Chapter 14

One More Look

Only the other day the Prime Minister himself said, "Talbot,
you're becoming a deuced bore about that voyage of yours."
—William Golding, *To the Ends of the Earth: A Sea Trilogy*

Early in 2011, I found myself with no pressing commitments, due to my career transition, yet with a little money in the bank. I took this rare opportunity to go back to Kragur again for a few weeks, from the beginning of February through early March. I wasn't suffering from the scourge of the staff meeting or the knout of the time sheet, but this was a chance to finish a couple of missions in person.

I had finished organizing the clan history information and—with the help of Tina Zarpour, an anthropologist with better computer skills than mine—putting it in neat digital charts. Then I'd mailed copies of each clan's chart to its *straksa* project participants, asking them to examine the charts for errors or omissions. Letters and packages I send to Kragur frequently disappear before they get there, so I sent the charts via Brother Herman—now teaching at St. Benedict's Teacher's College, just outside Wewak—whose mail tends to be relatively immune to whatever mishaps befall things I try to send directly to the village. I could have called my work done when Herman confirmed by e-mail that he'd received and distributed the charts. But there was no realistic way to get the clan leaders' comments on the adequacy of the work at a distance. If I could sit down face-to-face with them one more time, I'd feel that I had truly done all I could.

I had another mission, too. Linguist Richard Wivell had sent me copies of both his lexicon of the Kairiru language and his thick tome describing its grammar not long after he finished them in the 1980s.[1] He told me that he had also mailed copies of both works to his principal linguistic informants in Kragur, Kitok and Washol, but when I next saw Kitok and Washol they told me that they had never received the books. In years to come, I found that while Kragur people remembered Wivell's stay in the village in the 1970s, almost no one knew that the result had been such records of their language. Although it had been at John Samar's instigation that a linguist had come to Kragur in the first place, he and other urban Kragurs I knew hadn't seen Wivell's final products either.[2] Both the grammar and the lexicon are technical works, not intended for nonlinguists. (For example, the grammar points out that "there are a number of instances where verb stems are subject to vowel syncope when indexed by certain object person marking suffixes.") But I thought that Kitok and Washol should have copies just the same, and I was pretty sure that many villagers would find the lexicon, a more easily understood document, interesting. I wanted to hand this task back to Wivell, but for some time we lost track of each other. I tried making photocopies of the lexicon, but the original manuscript yielded only a faint and scarcely legible reproduction.

The subject came up again in Kragur in 2008. Kitok in particular had been annoyed for years that he'd never seen the results of his work. So when I got home, I set out to find Wivell again, and we finally renewed contact. He sent me scanned electronic copies of the original typescripts of both the lexicon and the grammar, and I sent the electronic files to Ralph Saulep and asked Wivell to send paper copies to Herman, whose e-mail service at St. Benedict's is pretty unreliable. By this time I was already planning to go to Kragur again, so I would deliver paper copies to Kitok and Washol myself.

Some incidental missions also accumulated once I decided to make another trip. Browsing through the latest edition of the Lonely Planet guide, *Papua New Guinea & Solomon Islands,* in a bookstore, I noticed that it mentioned both Kairiru Island and Wolfy Kalem's guesthouse in Shagur as points of tourist interest.[3] I knew Wolfy would like to see this, and I figured that Kragur people interested in hosting tourists could use the guidebook to learn more about the tourist business in PNG, including what other village-level entrepreneurs were offering.[4] When Ralph learned I was coming back again, he asked me to bring copies of all the journal articles I'd published about my research in Kragur. I also had several outstanding requests from villagers for copies of both *Hard Times* and *Village on the Edge* to fill, so I threw some copies of these in my luggage as well.

To be on the safe side, I also packed two large bars of sandalwood soap for emotional support, and I brought another set of trekking poles. I considered doing without the poles this time. But Jana wisely counseled that the insurance against injury was worth the expense. She was, of course, right. I made several short and long treks on the mountain on this trip, and several times the poles helped me stay upright or avoid wrenching a knee. Twice, however, I became so overconfident while descending—attempting what were intended as nimble leaps from foothold to foothold—that even the poles couldn't save me. Both times (I'm a slow learner), I lost my footing, went horizontal, and slid a few steep yards in mud and gravel. I covered a lot of vertical distance quickly in this way, but at the expense of long scrapes on my bare legs. I also suffered abrasions on my ego, because word spread quickly through the village that "Smith fell down!" and—after the second incident—"Smith fell down again!"

I didn't worry that my bloody scrapes would become infected, because on this trip I was taking low daily doses of the antibiotic Doxycycline, rather than Malarone, to prevent malaria. I'm not sure if changing my malaria medication was what did it, but I didn't feel the heat as poignantly as I had in 2008, and I neither rejected nor ejected a single meal. The temperatures were in the low nineties Fahrenheit in Moresby when I arrived. It felt about the same in Kragur, where it was easing into the season of northwest winds and heavier rain. But the wind was dithering, and it was actually raining less than it had during the so-called dry season of 2008. When the weather did shift to the northwest, I sometimes woke up at night expecting storms that didn't come, because Kragur's coastline is more exposed to that quarter, and the waves churning the rocky shore sound literally like rolling thunder.

It rained enough, though, to cool things off occasionally and to keep the water deep in the bathing pools. And between dealing with the heat better, sturdier knees, and Doxycycline-supported resistance to infection, I felt pretty good. But I guess I didn't look as good as I felt. Entering the village twirling my poles and feeling pleased with myself after one hike to Iupulpul, I met a couple of twenty-something villagers who asked where I'd been. When I replied that I'd walked to Iupulpul, one of them looked at me with genuine surprise and said, "I didn't think you were up to it!" I wasn't quite sure how to take that. Two or three other villagers made themselves clearer, saying flat out that I looked older. A young man at the bathing pool put it all too clearly, looking at me and saying, "Before your body was tight, but now you're sagging." This puzzled me a little because he wasn't remotely old enough to remember the era when my body actually was "tight." I suppose the lesson in this is that it's best to concentrate on keeping your knees in good condition, because vanity about your appearance is doomed to disappointment.

A couple of Kragur men I knew well actually looked more robust than they had in 2008, the result of taking regular medication for their *sotwin* and stopping smoking. The latter is a heroic measure in Kragur, where giving gifts of tobacco leaves and lighting one's in-laws' cigarettes are even parts of the traditional marriage ceremony (so I'm told; I've never seen it). I congratulated them sincerely, even though I was again taking advantage of being in Kragur to enjoy a little tobacco. Kitok had stopped smoking, too, but he had waited too long. He was suffering from emphysema and rarely left the old rattan chair on his veranda. I visited him there regularly, and sometimes he sent a youth with a note telling me to come at a certain hour bringing navy biscuits to eat with the coffee he supplied.

My first full day in the village, I brought Kitok two copies of the Kairiru lexicon, and at his instigation we went through most of the document page by page. Despite his scant formal education, Kitok could make out most of Wivell's spellings of Kairiru words and phrases, but the lexicon provides only English definitions and translations. More accustomed to moving between Kairiru and Tok Pisin than between Kairiru and English, Kitok often found it hard to judge the lexicon's adequacy. My job then was to translate the lexicon's English translations of Kairiru into Tok Pisin for Kitok's consideration. We had several sessions with the lexicon, and Kitok proved a tough critic. He often noted translations he thought not quite on the mark, definitions he found inadequate, or spellings of Kairiru words that suggested to him incorrect pronunciations. But he was very pleased with the lexicon on the whole and thought it should be expanded and improved before people forgot some of the subtleties of the language and it became more shot through with Tok Pisin. When I passed though Wewak on the way home, I found that Herman had also been studying the lexicon and was eager to push work on the Kairiru language further, perhaps creating a user-friendly dictionary and school texts in Kairiru. He'd already been in touch with Moses about getting support for a conference on the Kairiru language, and he had contacted Wivell, who was also interested in getting involved.

I was glad to find Munbos still very active. She was taking medication for *sotwin* and nursing the deepening aches and pains of a lifetime of hard work, but she was still going up and down the trails to work in her gardens or collect firewood, and she was still smoking her pipe. Her children and grandchildren were in good health and increasing in number. Rokerai had married since 2008, and he and his wife Claudia were parents of a boy named Sepram only a few months old (fig. 17).

I already knew of several deaths in the village since 2008. I'll mention only one here, both because it was particularly unexpected and because it may not have put an end to my relationship with the deceased. Jack Mari was a middle-aged man in robust health, but to everyone's surprise he succumbed to a severe case of malaria. I kept a lookout for Jack, though, because he'd been seen around the village postmortem. Munbos for one had seen him, sitting in the same broken-down chair on the veranda where he had often stationed himself, usually bearing some drinking coconuts, when he used to visit me. She didn't seem to find this disturbing. In fact, she laughed when she told of Jack coming to see me after death and said I shouldn't be surprised if he showed up in Silver Spring one day.

Jack had been deeply involved in the *straksa* work in his clan and probably

Figure 17. Agnes Munbos with her new grandchild Sepram, 2011. Photo by the author.

would have been eager to talk about the charts I'd sent back. I'd half expected that the men I'd worked with would find these records of our discussions riddled with serious problems, but most of the problems they did find were minor and uncontroversial. One middle-aged man, however, took the absence of his children on his clan's chart very much amiss, saying that it looked like his children had been pushed out of the clan. The main challenge in 2008, of course, had been to get a grip on knowledge of the past, not to census living generations. But putting things down on paper tends to magnify the importance of both what's included and what's left out. Several times in 2011, I explained to men disgruntled by an omission or an error that the charts were never meant to be the final word on anything; they were just the beginning of something that the clans could carry on themselves without my help. Many of the participants in the project did see it this way. As one man put it, they could carry on recording their *straksa* and adding details to their written history even after Smith was dead (a pleasant thought for me). But I did remind the *straksa* groups repeatedly that as soon as they had clan members with computers and electronic mail, I could send them electronic versions of the charts to curate.

There were disagreements within a couple of clans about the ancestral successions they'd instructed me to record in 2008. Some of these differences we sorted out, but others remained unresolved when I left. "Never mind," clan members told me. "It's not your problem," and they were right. I ended up bringing home notes for significant revisions on the charts of two clans, and when I finished these I sent paper copies back to the village and electronic files to trusted urban clan members. I hope, however, that Kragur people remember that the authority of these records rests solely on the authority of the people who provided the information and not on the fact that they are now not only written down but computerized, and that they feel as free to challenge them as they would to challenge spoken testimony.

I didn't need the full three-and-a-half weeks I spent in Kragur to deliver the lexicon, to go another round with the *straksa* project, or even to get in shape to hike to Iupulpul, but there were plenty of other things to keep me busy. The rifts in and between families left after the 2008 election had been formally closed, I was told, but the young man who had caused a ruckus on Rokerai's veranda hadn't had a chance to include me in his fence mending. One evening he brought a large plate of pounded taro and fresh fish to Rokerai's house and made a short speech of apology for having disturbed my peace there. I gladly accepted his apology, of course, because politics—I acknowledged—can make people a little crazy.

As far as I know, my name wasn't coming up in connection with any new village political scandals. I did venture once onto the public stage, but I tried to stay as apolitical as possible. One of the councilors, a strong opponent of gold mining, asked me if I would say a few words about—that is, against—mining at an upcoming public assembly of both council wards. I told him that while I thought that mining on Kairiru was a bad idea, I didn't think I should take a public stand on it.[5] I suggested, however, that I could say a few words about Kragur's water. If and how the water supply could be protected would be a key issue in any decision about mining, and I felt comfortable talking about what people stood to lose if the water supply was damaged. Kragur people are quite aware that their village has a much better water supply than most other villages and many urban areas, but I wasn't sure that they appreciated just how rare their water situation was.

So it came to pass that one Monday morning I stepped out into the sunny center of the outdoor meeting ground and held forth on water. I said that I had no place telling people what to do about mining, but that I thought they should always ask what effect mining might have on their water, and that they should remember three things about Kragur's water: it was clean, it was plentiful, and it was free. Everyone knew this, I said, but maybe they didn't know that even in some of the world's richest countries, including America, many people didn't have clean, plentiful, and free water. I told them that American cities spent large amounts of money cleaning their public water supplies, and some big cities had to bring water from hundreds of miles away. Americans, I emphasized, paid for this through taxes, which got a few villagers shaking their heads in disapproval. But I think I really got people's attention when I described the water meter on our house that measures how much water Jana and I use so the local government can charge us for it. Americans, I said, would love to have water that was clean, plentiful, and free, so keep a close watch on your own.

I didn't speak of the extreme pleasure of lying in the stream, letting the water flow over me and scratching my back on a rock. I thought that "Clean, Plentiful, and Free" probably sounded weightier that "Clean, Plentiful, Free, and Fun." But rich Americans do spend a lot of money at spas and resorts to enjoy ersatz versions of Kragur's burbling jungle pools. I'm convinced that soaking in the stream has helped me cure or ward off a host of sore muscles and joints, and when I once mentioned this to a group of Kragur men, they heartily agreed that it was just the thing after a day of work on the mountain or a night in a fishing canoe.

The Sunday following my talk on the Three Great Truths about Kragur water, the parish priest came to Bou to hear confessions and celebrate Mass. Although someone rang the village bell at about 8:00 a.m., word on the street was that confessions would last for quite a while, so I didn't leave for Bou until about 9:30. Father Paul Kotecki—a very tall, very fair Polish priest, clad in a lightweight white cassock over shorts, T-shirt, and sandals—heard confessions sitting in a chair at the front of the church, in full view of the assembled worshippers but distant enough that no one could hear his whispered exchanges with those coming forward to kneel on the stool beside him. Those waiting to confess formed a line down the central aisle. When I arrived the line was short, but whenever it nearly reached its end someone already seated would get up to join the queue. I thought I saw a few repeaters, but I couldn't be sure.

Eventually confession concluded and the service began. Father Paul took his text from Matthew 6:25–29, which—in the King James Bible—is as follows:

> Therefore I say unto you, Take no thought for your life, what ye shall eat, or
> what ye shall drink; nor yet for your body, what ye shall put on. Is not the life

more than meat, and the body than raiment? Behold the fowls of the air: for they sow not neither do they reap, nor gather into barns; yet your heavenly Father feedeth them. Are ye not much better than they? Which of you by taking thought can add one cubit to his stature? And why take ye thought for raiment? Consider the lilies of the field, how they grow; they toil not, neither do they spin: And yet I say unto you, that even Solomon in all his glory was not arrayed like one of these.

He read, of course, from a Tok Pisin version of the New Testament, and I admit that the passage lost something in grandeur for me in translation. Even so, the verses moved me, but as Father Paul discoursed on them I began to feel that perhaps they weren't the best choice when addressing people conspicuously lacking in meat and raiment. My attention wandered, but I became alert again when he began to recount what he said was a newspaper story about a woman, either Australian or American, who had been found dead from starvation in her home although she had over $70,000 in the bank. Kairiru people, he said, should avoid the fate of grasping after money at the expense of their lives. Their island was rich in ways to make a modest living, and—he emphasized this—it was rich in water, and they should take care not to sacrifice its secure benefits for money that would be spent all too fast. He'd seen, he continued, what mining had done to the land in other parts of PNG and feared what it might do to Kairiru.[6]

This woke me up completely. I'd had no idea that Father Paul was heading in this controversial direction on this quiet Sunday morning. Let me explain why I say "controversial." Although almost all the Kragur people I know, both in Moresby and the village, tell me that most Kragurs squarely oppose mining, they also say that many people in other villages—including other villages whose people attend the church at Bou—are eager for the money. The fact that I'd been asked to make a public statement about mining also suggested that Kragur mining opponents weren't completely sure of their overwhelming majority at home, either. One of the Moresby Kragurs has told me that gold exploration on Kairiru so far has been very sporadic, and it isn't likely that islanders will have to make any decisions in the near future. Yet even at a considerable distance, a possible shower of kina or the irremediable destruction of streams and garden land can rivet villagers' attention. Father Paul wasn't just preaching the ultimate vanity of worldly concerns; he was weighing in on what may become a very warm debate about worldly things.

That I was asked to speak to the village about mining and water just a few days before Father Paul did so at Bou struck me as quite a coincidence. Many Papua New Guineans are quick to ascribe mystical significance to an unusual concurrence of events. I wouldn't go that far, but it did look like the pros and cons of mining were very much on people's minds, even though movement on mining may hang fire for years to come.[7]

One local political issue that was ready for decision in 2011 was very familiar: health care financing. If I'd had any lurking delusions that in Kragur I was distant from all the problems of home, this dealt them the death blow. At least Kragur had not yet split into factions, each accusing its opponents of trying to kill the elderly or the unborn or trying to destroy the fundamental basis of society. For some time, each family in Kragur had been asked to pay an annual fee of one kina per head per year for use of the medical clinic. To help meet increasing expenses, the village clinic support committee, after consulting with the ward councilors and Vincent Kasian, was asking that the fee be raised to two kina per person. At a characteristically lively village meeting, several people objected that this was too high, especially for people with many children. Someone suggested that there be a flat rate per family, no matter how large. Others, naturally, objected that this wasn't fair to people with small families. Both ward councilors pointed out that at the only other clinic on Kairiru, on the other side of the island, people had to pay for each service, whereas in Kragur your annual fee covered everything, no matter how many visits you made to the clinic. Compared to that system, they said, even two kina per head should look like a pretty good deal.

Provincial government funds, of course, heavily subsidize the cost of care at the clinic. Villagers couldn't come close to affording either fees for service or per capita fees high enough to support the clinic independently. As it was, the clinic was chronically underfunded. A serious recurring problem was how to pay for emergency transportation to the hospital in Wewak. Even if the clinic had a boat and engine in good repair, there was no money to cover the cost of fuel. Vincent sometimes paid one of the few Kragur boat owners out of his own pocket to take patients to the hospital, but the issue came up again each time there was an emergency. Because he owned a boat and a forty-horsepower outboard motor, ideal for a fast emergency trip, Ward Councilor Lucas Saulep often had to cope with this problem, and he had created his own system of medical transportation insurance. He periodically bought cacao beans from other villagers to resell in Wewak. Those who sold to him could agree to accept a slightly lower price and put the difference into a fund from which Saulep would cover the cost of medical transportation in his boat if they needed it. Those who took the full price for their cocoa would have to bear the costs of a medical trip in his boat themselves.

Some villagers took part in his plan, and others preferred to take their chances. Predictably, among the latter were some who suspected that there was a swindle in it somewhere. Administration of the annual medical clinic fee had also run up against predictable suspicions that the money wasn't being

Figure 18. Nick Kung Urim with three of his children and the
catch of an evening's fishing, 2008. In 2011, Nick was serving
as chair of the Kragur Medical Clinic Executive Board. Photo
by the author.

managed honestly. When I got to Kragur in 2011, collection of the annual fee
had been suspended because of suspicions that the committee was misusing
the funds. A new committee—called an Executive Board—had only recently
been selected and was just starting its work. Nick Kung had been chosen as
chair of the Executive Board, and he was determined to avoid the problems of
the previous board (fig. 18).

Nick came to see me soon after I arrived, asking for help in setting up a
system to keep track of the funds raised from annual fees and the occasional
fundraising event. Nick had a mixture of qualifications for leading the clinic
board that would be hard to duplicate. He had great prestige in the traditional

system of leadership, and he'd also learned a lot from his travels as a merchant sailor to seaports in Asia and the Pacific. After my talk about Kragur's water, for example, he backed me up with an account of how dangerous it had been to drink the water in the Indian ports he'd visited. Nick didn't have any bureaucratic experience or training, but neither—it appeared—had the members of the previous board. When I asked Nick if I could look at the financial records the previous board had kept, he said that there weren't any, or if there were they hadn't been passed on to him.

The clinic board didn't need anything more complicated than a checkbook system for logging credits, debits, descriptions of transactions, and running balances, and I drew one out for him in one of my spare bound notebooks. We went through a few hypothetical examples, and then I set up the columns to begin a new record-keeping regime. Later on I also helped him tend to some paperwork regarding the clinic board's bank account and other administrative matters. As I did this, I realized how many bureaucratic skills I'd absorbed in my lifetime in the *susok* world without even thinking about it, much the same way Nick probably learned to handle a canoe expertly or argue his clan's case in a dispute about land rights. A few villagers joked that Nick had made me his secretary, but I told them that I was glad to help and that Nick was smart to seek advice.

When I visited Wolfy Kalem in Shagur to give him a copy of the Lonely Planet guidebook, he'd assembled a group of Shagur wood-carvers who were looking for ways to sell more of their work beyond the very small market provided by Wolfy's guests. (Wolfy had hosted about twenty-five guests in 2010.) After a little speech making to mark what Wolfy called my "second coming"— that is, the second time I'd visited him at his guesthouse—Wolfy showed the guidebook around. I'd already seen that the guide's entry on the island and the village was very spare, and I promised to send fuller details to the Lonely Planet publisher and to post it on the Lonely Planet Web site, including information on surfing opportunities and the skillfully made works that Shagur and Kragur craftspeople offered to visitors.

The carvers showed me two or three rooms in nearby houses filled with finished artifacts: masks, mythical figures large and small, taro pounders, betel nut mortars, and ornate walking sticks. They had finally convinced a wholesale buyer to come to Shagur to make a quantity purchase. This was better for them than taking their work to Wewak, where wholesale buyers might or might not purchase enough of it even to cover the cost of the trip, let alone provide a decent return on their skills and labor. But they were still depending on middlemen to connect them with wider markets, and they suspected—rightly so, I'm quite sure—that they were unlikely to get ahead this way.

My second coming, however, was small potatoes compared with the really big news on Kairiru since 2008. Toward the end of 2009 the courts had finally granted Moses Manwau a review of an earlier decision throwing out his claim that ballot box tampering had cost him the 2007 parliamentary election. A review was granted, his charges finally were heard, there was a ballot recount, and—more than two years after the election—Moses was awarded the seat for the Wewak Open Electorate. By 2011 he was serving as deputy chair of the Public Accounts Committee and getting his name in the national news: "Manwau Requests Leaders to Help Him Fight Corruption" read the headline of a newspaper article being passed around in Kragur.[8] I wanted to hear about all this from Moses himself, but two appointments for dinner in Moresby fell through when he got stuck in parliamentary committee meetings stretching into the night.

One thing I knew without hearing it directly from Moses was that the 2012 campaign was already staring him in the face. His supporters in Kragur were talking strategy for the coming campaign, wondering if Ralph would challenge Moses again and discussing other candidates already crisscrossing the Wewak Open Electorate building campaign organizations. Moses' successful battle for a recount probably burnished his image as a foe of corruption. However, I was told that the ejected member for the electorate had used up most of the discretionary funds that Moses might have given out for local development projects, denying him this usual incumbent's advantage. How much money he could dish out to constituents really shouldn't be so important, one Kragur man said, but—he lamented—Papua New Guineans didn't understand politics; members of parliament had to address national issues as well as local problems. Your parliamentary member, added another man, shouldn't be like a brother who has a high-paying job in town to whom you go with your hand out when your family is in need. But he knew that Moses was up against a very different reality.

As significant as Moses' election was, another change had taken place since 2008 that in the long run may do even more to change Kragur than having one of its own people in parliament: there had been an enormous increase in PNG in access to mobile phone service. The government-owned telecommunications company, Telikom PNG, began offering mobile phone service in 1997, eventually spinning off the public-private mobile service company Be-Mobile. The cost to individuals and limited national infrastructure, however, restricted access severely. After the private firm Digicel entered the market in 2008, the cost of mobile service began to fall, while the percentage of the country in which service was available began a dramatic expansion. In 2011, observers estimated that mobile access had increased from five to eight times or more since the opening of the market, and it was likely to continue to expand with the help of a large, interest-free World Bank loan to PNG for improving telecommunications infrastructure and services in rural areas.[9]

Kragur's side of Kairiru Island is still off the grid, but from 2008 through early 2011 the number of phones in the village had increased from fewer than a dozen to, according to villagers, at least two hundred. You still couldn't make or receive a call from the village, but the lower cost of calling was encouraging more and more Kragur and other north coast Kairiru villagers to buy phones and hike to the top of the mountain to use them. The favored place for this is about a ten-minute walk through thick rain forest from Iupulpul to a spot just over the crest of the island, from where you can see St. Xavier's High School far, far below, the full expanse of Mushu Island just to your left, tiny Yuo and Kerasau islands to your right, and Wewak, which from this distance is not much more than a light-colored smudge at the edge of the mountainous, thickly forested mainland. A Boy Scout troop at St. Xavier's used to camp here, and it has been known ever since as the Skaut Kem (Scout Camp). The forest here has been cleared and people keep the brush and grasses cut back, but no one has built any shelters.

In 2011, I'd still never been to the Scout Camp. I think I'd imagined that it was another hard trek up even steeper grades from Iupulpul, where I was usually very happy to stop and rest. I had made the additional trip to Kairiru Lake, which is an additional steep and difficult trek. When I finally visited the Scout Camp—with Kilibop and Malachai, the latter still intrepid but now habitually clothed—it turned out to be just what Kilibop had said it was: a short and easy walk through patches of sunlight and cool forest shadows, with just enough negotiation of slick roots and mossy fallen trees to keep me busy with my poles.

Malachai led the way, but when we came to a daunting mud escarpment he stepped aside and motioned for me to go first. This seemed unwise, unless he wanted to be sure not to miss the spectacle of me falling down, of which he'd undoubtedly heard so much. But I asked no questions, and after pausing to study the terrain I chose the best of a narrow selection of shallow, widely spaced footholds and heaved myself up and over the top. Emerging into the Scout Camp clearing, which extends partway down the landward slope of the mountain, I met a fresh breeze, a spectacular view, and an enhanced appreciation of a phrase from the song Rokerai had taught me: "Kairiru reaching high." Joining me, Kilibop indicated the many points of interest in the hazy distance, while Malachai attempted to find the most dangerous possible places to perch on the extended limbs of a large fallen tree at the edge of the clearing. In spite of the sweeping vista, I think I was most affected by the sight of a very, very small object almost imperceptibly easing across the ocean toward Mushu

Island from the direction of Kerasau Island: a sailing canoe, Kilibop said, insisting that if I looked closely I could see its single mast.

The other man-made features of the view—a glimpse of thatched roofs on Mushu, the smudge of Wewak at the edge of the mountainous mainland—did not excite my imagination much, except for the grounds of St. Xavier's far below. Although its roofs, walkways, and lawns were toy sized from this height, the mountain fell away toward it so sharply that it looked as if a running start and a strong leap might land you right in the middle of the campus—although in no condition to boast about your feat.

Several villagers had told me that the Scout Camp would be an ideal place for a tourist guesthouse if you could just get the tourists up there, and now I understood why. It would also be a good place to set up a snack stand—or better yet, a coffee bar—because Kilibop said that he'd seen as many as thirty north coast islanders here at one time using their phones. Kilibop had his phone with him and a few calling minutes left. After quickly calculating what time it was in Silver Spring, he suggested I call Jana. I was so unaccustomed to being able to do this that at first I declined. Perhaps I also feared it would burst my bubble. But I quickly relented; for Jana, I would acknowledge that I was not actually at the raw edge of the world, where only the bravest and strongest dare go. But I'd already told Jana of the rigors of making a call from Kairiru, so I was proud to say when she answered the phone, "We just walked up to the top of the mountain; I'm drenched in sweat. How are you?"

In places the ground at the Scout Camp was littered with torn-off code numbers from Digicel phone cards and a few of the small paper cards themselves. Islanders buy these from any of several general stores in Wewak and punch the numbers into their phones to obtain their calling minutes. Each red and blue Digicel Flex Kad (Flex Card) bears a photo of six smiling young Papua New Guineans, some in Western clothing and some in shells, pigs' tusks, feathers, and face paint. The latter models look too fleshy and soft to be real villagers, but all the young people are decidedly ecstatic about their phones.

Studies of attitudes regarding mobile phone use in PNG actually have found mixed feelings. The rapid spread of phone use is clear evidence that Papua New Guineans find them a plus overall. For example, rural entrepreneurs can deal directly with urban buyers of goods as diverse as cacao beans and carvings, avoiding the high cost of selling their products through middlemen or at least staying informed of urban prices. Telephones are also extremely useful in medical emergencies and for keeping in touch with family members; for example, when organizing such traditional events as marriage festivities and funerals when large, widespread families have to coordinate scheduling and travel to and from towns and villages. (Remember that land lines in PNG never extended far beyond urban enclaves; and I've already commented on the uncertainties of the postal system.)

Some Papua New Guineans, however, say that if they aren't careful, they find themselves wasting large sums of money on calling. Prank calls are already common, as is harassment of women via mobile phones; criminals are known to use their phones to coordinate highway robberies; and many believe that mobile phones facilitate sexual infidelity. Anthropologist Nancy Sullivan has observed that the "privacy [mobile phones] afford is perfectly suited to anti-social behavior." But what some consider antisocial behavior is liberation to others. Sullivan notes that increasing access to telephones "will inevitably play a part in the gradual independence of both male and female youth from their parents," something welcome to youth if not to their parents—especially the parents of young women.[10]

I had a taste of the effects on life in Kragur of multiplying mobile phones the day I arrived in Wewak from Moresby. Herman met me at the airport in a St. Benedict's vehicle and dropped me at his house before going back to his office for awhile. He told me that whoever was coming in from Kragur to pick me up was to phone him when they arrived to make further arrangements. Kilibop and his daughter Ani arrived in Wewak that evening, but Herman's phone wasn't working, so they walked the several miles from the beach to the teacher's college in the rain and stayed the night, sleeping on the floor. The next morning, Kilibop got a call from the boat captain saying that the boat was back on Kairiru, in the south coast village of Yuwun, but he was about to leave for Wewak again and we'd see him there soon. While this was not quite pinpoint coordination, it was a far cry from schlepping back and forth to town on speculation and sitting on the beach under the casuarinas waiting to see what happened.

There was a funeral in Kragur while I was there, which Kragurs from several PNG towns attended. Although it took several trips to the Scout Camp—which, unlike me, many villagers make quite casually and at astounding speeds—villagers organized their visitors' transportation to and from Wewak with efficiency impossible without telephones. When in March I left Kragur for Wewak, in a twenty-three-foot boat packed with sixteen people and their cargo, passengers started getting out their phones to make calls as soon as we rounded the eastern end of Mushu and came in sight of the mainland. There was no one waiting for us at the beach, but calm prevailed as several men sat down on the ground at the edge of the road, took out their phones, and started calling friends and family for rides to our various destinations.

How much telephones may contribute to other changes in Kragur life is impossible to predict. Sullivan opines regarding PNG in general that "it is entirely in the hands of the [users] whether [telephones] reinforce traditional values or undermine them."[11] Whatever the case, Kragur people are adapting to telephone use adroitly. At home in Silver Spring, I now get calls from the Scout Camp or from Wewak almost routinely, and my callers are getting better and better at calculating the time difference and catching me early in the morning or late in the evening instead of in the middle of the night, which I appreciate.

Kragur village phone owners and would-be phone owners are fluent in the vocabulary of phone technology and service-provider comparison. They also have ways of keeping their phones charged. Kilibop periodically walks over the mountain to St. John's, where his brother Frank Boreo works, with a rucksack full of phones that he charges there. There are only one or two gasoline-powered generators in Kragur. One is just up the slope from Rokerai's house and belongs to a migrant who keeps a house in the village built of manufactured materials and wired for electric lights. Members of his family run the generator once a month, to test it I was told, but also to charge mobile phones. I was there on one testing and charging day in 2011, and for the very first time in Kragur found myself disturbed by incessant loud noise—the insistent roar of the generator.

Telephones and roaring generators, however, are bringing Kragur in closer touch with the larger world, and most villagers are very interested in what is going on in other parts of the globe. They are also greatly interested in just where other parts of the globe are. Rokerai had told me in a letter that world maps I had sent him at his request after I left in 2008 were very popular. So I brought about a dozen with me in 2011, as well as an inflatable globe. I gave away the maps, along with push pins for hanging them, more or less first-come-first-served, but we hung the globe on the veranda where anyone could see it. Several people told me that even at the Bou school, which comprises several classrooms and has a satellite dish, there was no globe and only one world map, kept in the headmaster's office. That helped account for the number of people who came to Rokerai's to look at the map posted on the wall of the veranda and the globe, asking me to point out not only where I lived in America but, just as often, the places they frequently heard about in the news.

In the 1970s, many older villagers were not at home with the idea of the world as round and still tended to imagine it as an immense expanse of ocean with unknown boundaries: "After America," one older woman asked me, "are there more islands or is that all?" By the 2000s, everyone with whom I was acquainted took for granted that the world was round. A lot of villagers, however, had never seen a globe, and they knew a lot more about world events than they did about world geography. The biggest newshounds took a lot of satisfaction in finally seeing where events were taking place that they had followed through newspapers, the radio, or conversations with urban friends and family, poring over the globe to locate other Pacific Island countries, the countries of Europe and Africa, Russia, China, Japan, Indonesia, East Timor, Iraq, Afghanistan, and others. After satisfying an initial curiosity, many lingered to examine the map and the globe to discover places they'd never heard of before and sometimes ask me what they were like.

In 2011, both the Kragurs I spent time with in Moresby and villagers again helped me repay the information debt by quizzing me about America, as they had in 2008. Barack Obama was still a popular topic and apparently had become a popular figure. Frances Wosau demonstrated his mobile phone ring tone one afternoon as we sat under the trees in Ralph's Moresby backyard: the digitally cut-and-pasted voice of Barack Obama announcing, "This is Barack Obama. The time for change has come. Answer the call." But how was Obama doing? Wosau was especially interested in Obama's health care plan, what it called for, why the House of Representatives had just voted to repeal it—an event with which Wosau was familiar—and what that vote meant. This brought us to a discussion of the differences between PNG's Westminster-style parliamentary system and the US system of government, a discussion numbers of villagers had also initiated and that had even required me to explain the electoral college. Above all, however, people were concerned about news of American's shaky economic condition—its national debt, its growing budget deficit, its heavy borrowing from China, its high unemployment rate, and its multiplying business failures and mortgage foreclosures. America, several said, was important because what happened in America affected the whole world, and they clearly wished my country would get its act together.

Decades ago, Papua New Guineans commonly spoke of America as a place of near-mythical power, wealth, and even virtue. Many now found the sight of its clay feet disturbing. Even in the village, people asked me, their expressions concerned, "Is America alright?" I am a habitual critic of each successive government in America, and I am strongly averse to American-style capitalism. When I travel abroad and have to talk about America, I don't hide my opinions. But I also discourage people from either demonizing or romanticizing my home, and I try to give them some of the more complicated facts behind the headlines. But in 2011, I couldn't deny that at the moment America was not alright and many Americans were suffering. PNG villagers have no trouble seeing that losing your home because you lost your job is something very bad. Both urban Kragurs and villagers were deeply sympathetic, but it also made them nervous that America the Great could fall so low. And perhaps it was unsettling to find that even in the most "developed" countries, there was still no relief from change that turned people's lives upside down.

How was PNG faring in 2011? The most dramatic event on the national scene since 2008, other than expanding mobile phone access, was initiation of massive liquefied natural gas (LNG) projects, which the PNG government estimates could generate up to US $50 billion dollars of public revenue over some three decades. There's potential here for sorely needed increases in public expenditures on infrastructure, health, education, and diversifying the national economy into sectors other than natural resource extraction—provided the public revenues and the effects of rising private wealth in a small segment of the population are managed well. Many observers doubt that PNG's public sector has the organizational and policy capacity to spend the revenues wisely and prevent accelerating inflation and an increase in the value of the currency from damaging other sectors of the economy. It looks likely, however, that the government will take some of the pressure off by creating a sovereign wealth fund, putting a large portion of the LNG revenue in long-term overseas investments, the gradual returns of which can be managed at a more considered pace.[12]

But LNG development, which was still in an early phase, was already unsettling the lives of many Papua New Guineans. During my short stay in Moresby on the way home, Ralph Saulep and Jacob Yabai took me for a driving tour of the town so I could see the plethora of new residential, commercial, and highway construction projects going on in anticipation of an influx of foreign workers and foreign money. It was making several parts of town look much brighter, cleaner, and taller than I'd ever seen them, but—said Ralph and Jacob—the boom was already driving up housing prices, and average Papua New Guineans could forget about finding reasonable rents, let alone buying homes.

A lot of Papua New Guineans join outside observers in concern about how the government will use LNG revenues. Transparency International ranks countries in terms of their citizens' perceptions of corruption among public officials and politicians. In 2010, PNG shared the rank of 154 with Laos and Russia, with Somalia bringing up the rear with a rank of 178 (the United States had a rank of 22).[13] Papua New Guineans may trust their government with money even less than Kragur people trust each other. To the extent that Kragur villagers are right to mistrust each other, village corruption is—of course—infinitesimal compared with the millions of dollars in public investment of which corrupt PNG public officials have deprived the country in recent years.[14] Unfortunately, the ethical climate and material uncertainty created by ineffective and untrustworthy national government help weaken the bases of local trust. A bright spot is that some institutions within PNG—not just international organizations that might be accused of mistaking for corruption the workings of a different kind of political culture—are also striving to hold the national leaders' and public servants' feet to the fire.[15]

My last evening in Kragur was a quiet one with a few friends on Rokerai's veranda. On arriving, I'd received a fine ceremonial greeting. The Kragur *sing-sing* group had met me on the west side of the village, where I'd climbed up from the beach, and led me to Rokerai's house, near the east end, drumming and singing. But when I left, a funeral observance several days long was just drawing to a close, and there could be no such marking of my departure. We didn't even mark the coconut palm planted on my last departure, because a very strong and hungry pig had uprooted it while it was still small, leaving no trace. My morning leave-taking was emotional but simple. On the beach, things moved fast. The boat was soon loaded and finessed between the coral heads into deep water, where a burst of speed brought us safe beyond the breakers.

Pulling out to sea from Kragur, what seems an expansive place of vibrant lives when one is in its midst rapidly comes to look meager and insignificant. Then it disappears. Travelers returning to the world's metropolitan centers from places like Kragur or Wewak can easily come to think of them as not even quite real. But no matter where you live, there are people elsewhere who consider it insignificant and less solidly real than their own homes. Breaking that habit would be good for all of us.

My house in Silver Spring is full of souvenirs of Kragur. Even after their perfume of damp and wood smoke has faded, they bring back vivid memories; but letters and now telephone calls from the Scout Camp and e-mail from Moresby or Wewak do a better job of reminding me that life and change in Kragur go on even when I'm not there. A souvenir I picked up in 2011, how-ever, is more potent than others: in 2011 I gave in to suggestions that I get a tattoo of my Kairiru name, "Tau." Thanks to the skills of Rokerai, Kilibop, and Andrew Mukiu, it looks good, stretching in blue-black block letters—formed by hundreds of sewing-needle pricks—from my left shoulder almost to my elbow, accented by two chevrons at each end. I look forward to showing it to Jack Mari if he ever shows up on my front porch.

Appendix

Tok Pisin and Tok Pisin Pronunciation

Written Tok Pisin is usually spelled as phonetically as people can manage. Not everyone in PNG, however, pronounces Tok Pisin exactly the same way, nor are people's ideas of phonetic spelling necessarily the same. The closest thing to standard spelling is that used in Reverend Francis Mihalic's dictionary and grammar, originally published in 1957 and published in a revised edition in 1971 as *The Jacaranda Dictionary and Grammar of Melanesian Pidgin*. Despite its vintage, it remains the standard dictionary of the language. The term "Melanesia" refers to a geographic and cultural area comprising the entire island of New Guinea (including independent PNG and the Indonesian province of Papua), the independent countries of Solomon Islands and Vanuatu, and the French territory of New Caledonia. The lingua francas of Solomon Islands and Vanuatu, known respectively as Solomons Pijin and Bislama, are very similar to PNG Tok Pisin, and some linguists regard Tok Pisin, Solomons Pijin, and Bislama as different varieties of a single "Melanesian Pidgin."[1] Mihalic's volume, however, deals only with the PNG language that today is called Tok Pisin.

Linguist Geoff P. Smith's 2002 book, *Growing up with Tok Pisin: Contact, Creolization and Change in Papua New Guinea's National Language*, is written primarily for linguists, but the first chapter in particular ("Pidgins, Creoles, and Tok Pisin") would interest anyone who wants to know more about the past and possible future of Tok Pisin. Smith also provides many examples of vocabulary and idioms that were not part of the language when Mihalic compiled his dictionary. These include what Smith calls "catch phrases."[2] Knowledge of these could spare one considerable embarrassment in some situations. Unfortunately, the very nature of "catch phrases" is that they come into and go out of fashion rapidly, although some that Smith notes seem to be enjoying sustained popularity.

To pronounce written Tok Pisin, pronounce consonants just as you would in English. Vowels are pronounced as follows:

a as in "arm" or "papa"

e as in "bed"; or as the *a* in "plate"

i as in "hit" or "little"; or as in "machine"

o as in "hot"; or as in "old" or "no"

u as in "put"; or as in "tulip"

Notes

Epigraphs

Book epigraphs. Elizabeth Bishop (2011), "Questions of Travel," in *Poems* (New York: Farrar, Straus, and Giroux), p. 91; and *Harper's Magazine* (December 2010), "Findings," p. 84.

Chapter 1: An Eccentric Longing

Epigraph. W. H. Auden (1989), "Journey to Iceland," July 1936, in *W. H. Auden: Selected Poems,* New Edition, ed. Edward Mendelson (New York: Vintage Books), p. 46.

1. This is according to a report on the 2002 earthquake on Kairiru prepared by Hugh Davies of the University of Papua New Guinea (2002).

2. Prior to Christian missionization, Kragur people were generally known by a single name associated with their clan. They now have Christian names, like Stephen and Agnes, and many also use their fathers' names as surnames, giving them a string of three names. The three-name option wasn't common in Umari's generation, but if it had been he would have called himself Stephen Umari Porshem. Villagers usually address each other or speak of each other in the third person using either Christian names or indigenous names (but not the surnames derived from their fathers). In this book I use Christian names for some people and indigenous names for others, but I don't switch between them as people do in the village.

3. Lipset and Stritecky (1994), p. 6. See also Strathern (1988), pp. 105–106.

4. Women's social status is generally lower than men's throughout PNG. This generalization, however, masks considerable variety and nuance that I don't address in this book. A 1998 World Bank report (Brouwer et al.) provides a summary of the social and political situation of women in PNG that remains an unusually concise and valuable source in 2012. Unfortunately, male violence against women is common in contemporary PNG. I have heard of—but not seen—Kragur men physically abusing their wives, but I have never heard any villager, male or female, speak of this with ap-

proval. And I know that a Kragur man known to treat his wife and children badly can lose the esteem of fellow villagers and even votes in local elections on that account.

5. I use the standard spelling of the explorer's name here, although the particular volume I was reading (Mikloucho-Maclay 1975) uses an unorthodox spelling.

6. On Roosevelt's trip on the River of Doubt, see Millard (2005).

7. According to legend, Kairiru came from Wogeo Island, about six kilometers or sixteen miles away, in the distant past after an argument with his brother Trogup. In other publications, I have described Kairiru Lake as an extinct volcanic crater. According to Borrell (1989, p. xi), that is incorrect. Rather, the lake "is the result of a depression, not a crater." Further, "The water seems to maintain its level by internal springs." At the time of Borrell's study of the lake, "no fish were found except eels, and no macrowater plants," although tilapia were introduced in 1976.

8. Among the most famous of these competitive exchange systems is that described by Andrew Strathern in *The Rope of Moka* (1971).

9. Kragur villagers' understanding of and relationship with money was very complex in the 1970s. I explore this in detail in *Hard Times on Kairiru Island* (Smith 1994).

Chapter 2: Thoroughly Modern Kragur

Epigraph. Marshall Berman (1988 [1982]), *All That Is Solid Melts into Air: The Experience of Modernity* (New York: Penguin Books), p. 15.

1. Alois Kitok permitted me to study his copy of this report, prepared by consulting engineer Ian C. Brooks (1997).

2. For deeper analyses of Kragur attitudes toward time, see Smith (1982) and Smith (1994), pp. 190–224.

3. *Time* (December 17, 1973).

4. Moore (2003) discusses the naming of New Guinea, trade, and habitation on pages 1, 48, and 21, respectively.

5. Tuzin (1997).

6. Moore (2003), p. 181.

7. See Griffin, Nelson, and Firth (1979) for a thorough account of the political history of Papua New Guinea up through independence.

8. Frazier (2010).

9. On the challenges inherent in "the experience of modernity," see Berman (1988).

10. Moore (2003), pp. 27–29.

11. On change as an end in itself in the modern world, see Berman (1988), especially pages 49–50.

12. *The Blithedale Romance* was first published in 1852. I take this quotation from my own notes, in which I did not indicate the precise location of this passage in the work.

13. From the lyrics of "Thoroughly Modern Millie," by Jimmy van Heusen and Sammy Cahn.

14. McGregor (2005), pp. 15–16.

15. Ibid., p. 19.

16. Ibid., pp. 19–21.

17. Ibid., pp. 16, 19, and 26.

18. British anthropologist Marilyn Strathern makes what is probably the best-known argument along these lines regarding the people of PNG (1988) and the peoples of the larger Melanesian region of the Pacific Islands (comprising, in addition to the island of New Guinea, the Solomon Islands, Vanuatu, New Caledonia, and Fiji).

19. Novotny (2009), p. 42.

20. Ibid., p. 43.

21. Leavitt (2004), pp. 183–184.

22. Deborah Gewertz and Frederick Errington (1999) provide a unique view of such dilemmas in the lives of middle-class Papua New Guineans living in Wewak in the 1990s.

23. Amit and Rapport (2002), pp. 92–96.

Chapter 3: Hot Times on Kairiru Island

Epigraph. Frank Clune (1943), *Prowling through Papua with Frank Clune* (Sydney and London: Angus and Robertson, Ltd.), p. 2.

1. Borrell (1989), p. xi.

2. Davies (2002).

3. Gibson and Rozelle (1998).

4. Fleetwood (1984), pp. 33–44, gives a more detailed account of Wewak in World War II.

5. Ibid., pp. 11–12.

6. I am indebted to Kathy Creely of the Melanesian Archive at the University of California–San Diego for assistance in locating PNG population information. In a 1999 study of "middle-class" Papua New Guineans in Wewak, Deborah Gewertz and Frederick Errington give a population for Wewak of "by some estimates, 50,000."

7. Hanson et al. (2001), pp. 12–13. See also Connell (1997).

8. The history of ethnic Chinese immigrants in PNG, most of whom are engaged in business, dates back to the colonial period. See Chin (2008) for an overview of the contemporary ethnic Chinese community in PNG.

9. Tobacco is not native to PNG, but it traveled there from the West via Indonesia more than four hundred years ago (Haddon 1947, cited in Marshall 1982), p. 7.

10. US Department of State (2010).

11. I don't think the Anglo-American cultural references in this book will mean much to many Papua New Guinean readers, but that's hard to judge; to explain his views on one topic to me in 1998, a thirty-something villager used a quotation from a Cyndi Lauper song.

Chapter 4: *Wu Wei Wu*

Epigraph. Lao-tzu (1989), *Tao Te Ching: A New English Translation*, trans. Stephen Mitchell (New York: Harper & Row), p. 5.

1. Schwartz (1962), pp. 292–301.

2. Among anthropologists, there is no single universally accepted explanation or

interpretation of cargo cult phenomena in what is now PNG. Those interested in this topic, however, can find a good, up-to-date summary of anthropological thinking and argument in Ton Otto's 2010 discussion, "What Happened to Cargo Cults? Material Religions in Melanesia and the West."

Chapter 5: Is Kragur Poor?

Epigraph. Herman Melville (1992 [1851]), *Moby Dick; or, The Whale* (Penguin Edition), p. 144.

1. *New York Times Magazine,* March 18, 2007.

2. Bourke (2001).

3. United Nations Development Program (2010).

4. Hanson et al. (2001), p. 11.

5. Golub (2007), pp. 38–48, gives a good summary and analysis of issues regarding land rights in Papua New Guinea.

6. Gibson (2001), p. 408.

7. Other factors contributing to generally better urban childhood health, including better access to medical care and better educated mothers, are described in Gibson (2001), p. 409.

8. Hanson et al. (2001), p. 296.

9. Kantha (2009), pp. 365–372.

10. On increasing income inequality in the United States, see Reich (2010), Hacker and Pierson (2011), and Whoriskey (2011).

11. Hanson et al. (2001), p. 209.

12. The consumer price index (CPI) in PNG has risen greatly—by a factor of nine—since independence. A drop in the value of the kina when it was "floated" against international currencies in 1994 made a major contribution midway through this period. The PNG CPI, however, focuses on the cost of living in urban areas. There is no comparable measure of the cost of living in rural areas (Bourke and Harwood 2009, pp. 272–277). Rural people, of course, are affected by the prices of the many manufactured and imported goods that have become rural staples or rural luxuries.

13. US Energy Information Administration (2011).

14. My own book, *Hard Times on Kairiru Island* (Smith 1994), illustrates this in detail.

15. Tiesler (1969–1970) describes this trading system in detail. I'm indebted to my father, Victor Earle Smith, for translating relevant passages of Tiesler's study from German to English. See also Hogbin (1935).

16. For example, see Lipset (1997, p. 28) on the coastal Murik, and see Lutkehaus (1995, p. 58) on the people of Manam Island.

17. Hogbin (1970), pp. 27–28.

18. Schwartz (n.d.).

19. Brooks (1997). Borrell (1989, p. xi) suggests that Kairiru's "rivers and creeks" are fed by an artesian system linked to the Prince Alexander Mountains on the mainland, but I find Brooks' assessment more plausible.

20. Bromby (2009).

21. WHO/UNICEF (2010).

22. A good source of more information on this topic is the Web site of Water Advocates, http://wateradvocates.org/, which noted in 2010 that "Diseases caused by unsafe drinking water and inadequate sanitation remain humanity's most serious public health problem, causing 80 percent of sickness in developing countries."

23. The spread of HIV is a serious problem in PNG, but there are virtually no data on the extent to which this is affecting Kairiru Island people. Leslie Butt and Richard Eves (2008) provide invaluable insights into the complexities of the HIV epidemic in PNG as a whole and the surrounding region.

24. Bourke (2001), pp. 8–10.

25. Hanson et al. (2001), p. 10.

26. Ward (2004).

Chapter 6: Ancestors on Paper

Epigraph. Bernard Cornwell (1995), *The Winter King: A Novel of Arthur* (New York and London: Penguin Books), pp. 291–292.

1. Smith (2002), p. 147.

2. *The National* (2007a).

3. *The National* (2007b).

4. Macintyre and Foale (2007).

5. Filer (1997), pp. 176–177.

Chapter 7: Meetings and Magic

Epigraph. Herman Melville (1992 [1851]), *Moby Dick; or, The Whale* (Penguin Edition), p. 166.

1. The full verse reads (in the Cambridge Edition of the King James Bible): "For where two or three are gathered together in My name, there I am among them."

2. I describe this case in chapter 6 of *Hard Times on Kairiru Island* (Smith 1994).

Chapter 8: Preferential Ballots and Primeval Brothers

Epigraph. Walt Whitman, editorial in the Brooklyn *Eagle,* excerpted in Douglas Crase (1996) *AMERIFL.TXT: A Commonplace Book* (Ann Arbor: University of Michigan Press), pp. 79–80.

1. See Griffin, Nelson, and Firth (1979) for a detailed account of this period of PNG's history.

2. Griffin, Nelson and Firth (1979), p. 133. See also Chin (2003), pp. 458–459, on lack of interest in issues of more recent "ordinary voters."

3. Standish (2002), p. 11.

4. Commonwealth Pacific-Islands Forum (2009), p. 2; Standish (2002), p. 12.

5. Chin (2003), p. 457.

6. Commonwealth Pacific-Islands Forum (2009), p. 2.

7. Ibid., especially pp. 5–6 and 10.

8. Bowles (2010). See also Lopez (2010).

9. I described the moiety system as "now nearly defunct" in *Village on the Edge* (p. 120). It is certainly not as important as it used to be, but declaring an institution dead or nearly so is dangerous business, and I would avoid words as strong as "defunct" if I were to write that paragraph again. I believe I was led astray partly by the opportunity to use the word "defunct," which is almost as much fun to say or write as, say, "plethora" or even "prelapsarian."

Chapter 9: A Clean Election and Its Messy Aftermath

Epigraph. Barbara Pym (1990 [1955]), *Less than Angels* (New York: Obelisk/Dutton), p. 186.

1. *The National* (2003).

2. For a discussion of the relationship of electoral democracy and individuality in other spheres of life, see Amit and Rapport (2002), pp. 92–96.

Chapter 10: Life Goes On

Epigraph. John Lennon and Paul McCartney, "Ob-La-Di, Ob-La-Da," first released in 1968 on the album *The Beatles,* also known as *The White Album.*

1. I describe the work of Kragur villagers in the 1970s in *Hard Times on Kairiru Island* (Smith 1994), pp. 190–224 and 237–240.

2. As early as 1847, Charlotte Brontë noted the aversion of some Europeans to sago in *Jane Eyre*: "'And the sago?' [asked the cook]. 'Never mind it, at present . . .' [replied Mrs. Poole]." I draw from vol. 1, p. 198, of the Everyman's Library edition.

3. The full passage, from Matthew 23:27 (King James Version), is as follows: "Woe unto you, scribes and Pharisees, hypocrites! For ye are like unto whited sepulchres, which indeed appear beautiful outward, but are within full of dead men's bones, and of all uncleanness."

4. For more on surfboard making in Kragur, see Smith (2012a).

5. Hogbin (1970).

6. For more on tourism and wood carving in Kragur and Shagur, see Smith (2011).

Chapter 11: God the Father, the Son, His Mother, and the Holy Spirit

1. Wivell (1981b).

2. This is a rough summary of information gleaned from a discussion on the Listserv of the Association for Social Anthropology in Oceania in the summer (Western Hemisphere) of 2010.

3. US Department of State (2003).

4. D'Emilio (2001).

5. Tuzin's basic work on the Ilahita people and their religion is *The Ilahita Arapesh: Dimensions of Unity* (1976).

6. Regarding expectations of the Spanish Inquisition and the related issue of the Inquisition's chief weapons, see Graham Chapman et al. (1989), pp. 192–204.

7. The Pew Forum on Religion and Public Life reported these survey findings in September 2010.

8. For further detail on the popularity of the Virgin Mary in Kragur, see Smith (1994), pp. 88–90 and 101–129.

9. For more detail on charismatic Catholicism, see *Village on the Edge* (Smith 2002), p. 127.

10. Lipset and Stritecky (1994), p. 6.

11. A notion of the sun as sacred or as a creative "culture hero" occurs in other parts of PNG. See, for example, Biersack (1991) and Brumbaugh (1990). I have never, however, heard of a religion centered on the sun in either the island or mainland vicinity of Kairiru or even in the East Sepik Province. Aufenanger (1972) wrote about what he called a "Sun Cult" in parts of what is now the East Sepik Province, but other anthropologists have questioned the accuracy of his observations and his reading of the evidence (Scaglion 1977).

12. For just one Yuropian example, pulled out of the online hat of scholarly publications, see Watling (2001).

Chapter 12: No Two Ways about It

1. One of Kragur's own *susok* people, John Samar (2009), comments on the failure of PNG politicians to be careful to use language that the "average person" in PNG can understand. It may sound presumptuous, but I've met numbers of second- or third-generation urban Papua New Guineans who have excelled in formal education and are highly articulate but whose understanding of village life isn't much more sophisticated than that of a lot of westerners. And it doesn't look as if rural-urban mutual understanding in PNG as a whole is likely to improve soon. Colin Filer (2011), 28n, notes that "Most of the members of PNG's political and business elite who were born between 1945 and 1965 were born in rural villages, and most still retain some social connections to their communities of origin. However, . . . the younger generation of national leaders consists largely of individuals who were born in town."

2. See Smith (1994), pp. 44–69, for a discussion of problems of trust in Kragur.

3. I would be remiss here not to cite the famous remark of Groucho Marx to Madame Swempski (in *Monkey Business*): "Love flies out the door when money comes innuendo."

4. In an interview published in October 1987, Thatcher told *Woman's Own* magazine regarding "society," that "There is no such thing! There are individual men and women and there are families."

5. Cited in Golub (2007), p. 39.

6. C. A. Gregory analyzes this phenomenon in depth in his 1982 volume, *Gifts and Commodities*.

7. However, anthropologist Colin Filer warned in 2011 that since about 2003, in what Filer called a "land grab," the use of a legal mechanism called a "lease-leaseback" agreement had effectively taken a large amount of land—about 11 percent of PNG's land area—out of customary control and put it "into the hands of national and foreign corporate entities." That takes the usual 97 percent figure down to 86 percent. This is very worrying, but customary title is still the norm in rural areas.

8. Macintyre and Foale (2007), pp. 57–58.

9. I've heard Zimmer-Tamakoshi speak on this topic, but I'm also working here from the description of her findings in Golub (2007), p. 44.

10. Gregory (1982), pp. 115–116.

11. I rely here on Alex Golub's references to Wagner (1974), Pouwer (1960), and Watson (1990), and his own summation in his 2007 discussion of this topic.

12. Golub (2007), p. 46.

13. The village in which people live certainly counts a great deal. Some villagers broaden the definition of *koyeng* beyond Kragur, pointing out that there are descendants of the deep male ancestors of Kragur people in many other villages and asserting that these widely extended groups of descendants are the real *koyeng*. The branches of a common male ancestral tree that reside in different villages, however, go by different *klen* names.

14. Macintyre (2005), p. 125.

15. St. John's was the site of a major negotiation regarding the terms of gold mining on Lihir Island in which PV's founder, Samuel Tam, played a major role. The resulting agreement is often known as the Kairiru Accord; see Bainton (2010), p. 165.

16. See the Personal Viability Web site: http://www.edtc.ac.pg/PVPhilosophy.htm, accessed October 10, 2010.

17. I'm relying here on Nick Bainton's research on PV (2009), pp. 9–17.

18. Ibid., p. 12.

19. According to Bainton (2010), p. 147, even in parts of PNG where the PV message has had the backing of powerful economic and political elites, local people have resisted efforts to get them to put all else aside to become "self-sufficient entrepreneurial capitalists."

20. PV training emphasizes personal responsibility but takes it too far. Parts of the course teach that "personal failure, poverty and inequality" are in large part the result of a lack of "Personal Viability," ignoring the harsher realities of village life and the injustices of the world economic system (ibid., p. 151). Kragur people already tend to blame not just lack of good leadership but the mass of villagers' lack of moral fiber for their poverty in comparison with America, Australia, Japan, and so on; but they do so in part because they misunderstand aspects of the moral basis of such wealthy societies. I discuss this in several publications: see Smith (1984, 1990, and 1994, pp. 147–154).

Chapter 13: The Long Good-bye

Epigraph. Rudyard Kipling (1940), "Chant-Pagan," in *Rudyard Kipling's Verse: Definitive Edition* (Garden City, NY: Doubleday and Company), p. 459.

1. See also Smith (2011 and 2012a).

2. It's not, however, quite as flashy as Rokerai's own nickname, "Reef," and those of some other Kragur men, such as "Four Xs," "Colonel Three Mistake" (sometimes simply "the Colonel"), "Willy Tinpis" (for a man once judged unusually fond of tinned fish), and "Hap Saksak" (meaning "piece of sago"). These are all Tok Pisin/English names, and there's a story behind each of them, but I don't know them all. Nor do I

know what kinds of Kairiru language nicknames people may use for each other on which I've been missing out.

Chapter 14: One More Look

Epigraph. William Golding (2006), *To the Ends of the Earth: A Sea Trilogy* (New York: Farrar, Straus, Giroux), p. 744.

1. Wivell (1981a, 1981b)

2. Wivell's research on Kairiru provided the basis for his master's thesis in linguistics at the University of Auckland. In PNG he was affiliated with the Summer Institute of Linguistics International (SIL), a worldwide language research and training organization. Once focused in large part on Bible translation, it now describes itself as "a faith-based nonprofit organization committed to serving language communities worldwide as they build capacity for sustainable language development" (http://www .sil.org/sil/, accessed June 13, 2011). I believe Samar sought a linguist to work in Kragur through the SIL, which is very active in PNG.

3. McKinnon, Carillet, and Starnes (2008).

4. Tourism in general is not big business in PNG: according to one source there were only 114,000 "tourist arrivals" in the country in 2008 (Financial Standards Forum 2010), p. 6. I think there are at least that many tourists riding the Metro train every summer day in Washington, DC; at least there are whenever I want to go anywhere.

5. Banks (2005) points out how the pros and cons of mining in PNG depend on whether you look at it from a national or a local viewpoint, on your status in a local mining community, and on how far ahead you look. Mining provides a critical part of PNG's national income and raises average money incomes for people in communities where mines are located. But money pouring into PNG communities in unprecedented amounts tends to aggravate social inequality, not just by putting more money in some pockets than in others but by helping traditional political leaders to increase their power and men to increase their traditional ascendancy over women. Mines also have limited lives. When they play out, if local people haven't used their income to develop new ways of making a living, they may find themselves in trouble. They may have lost arable and forest lands, and a generation raised on mining income may not know how to make a living with traditional skills using the resources remaining.

6. Hyndman (1994) provides a vivid description of some of the most dramatic of the ecological damage wrought by mining in parts of Papua New Guinea.

7. For more on water and mining in Kragur, see Smith (2012b).

8. *The National,* February 11, 2011.

9. I rely here on information obtained from the Telikom PNG Web site (Telikom PNG 2010), a World Bank press release (World Bank 2010), and a Radio Australia news report (Radio Australia News 2010).

10. Radio Australia News (2010); Sullivan (2010), p. 15 on antisocial behavior and p. 28 on control over youth.

11. Sullivan (2010), p. 13.

12. Radio Australia (2009); Joku (2011); Financial Standards Forum (2010), p. 13.
13. Transparency International (2010).
14. Financial Standards Forum (2010), p. 11.
15. Nelson (2011), pp. 9–10.

Appendix

1. G. Smith (2002), p. 14.
2. Ibid., p. 112.

References

Al Jazeera English
2009   "101 East: Chinese Migrants Face PNG Wrath." September 16. http://www
        .youtube.com/watch?v=35LH2CzxMas, accessed April 6, 2010.
Amit, Vered, and Nigel Rapport
2002   *The Trouble with Community: Anthropological Reflections on Movement,
        Identity and Collectivity.* London and Sterling, VA: Pluto Press.
Aufenanger, Heinrich
1972   *The Passing Scene in North-East New-Guinea (A Documentation).* Collec-
        tanea Instituti Anthropos 2. Sankt Augustin, Germany: Anthropos
        Institute.
Bainton, Nick
2009   "Personally Viable Melanesians." In "Parallel States, Parallel Economies:
        Legitimacy and Prosperity in Papua New Guinea," State, Society and
        Governance in Melanesia Discussion Paper 2009/5. Research School of
        Pacific and Asian Studies, Australian National University, pp. 9–20.
2010   *The Lihir Destiny: Cultural Responses to Mining in Melanesia.* Asia-Pacific
        Environment Monograph 5. Canberra: Australian National University E
        Press.
Banks, Glenn
2005   "Globalization, Poverty, and Hyperdevelopment in Papua New Guinea's
        Mining Sector." *Focaal: European Journal of Anthropology* 46, pp. 128–143.
Berman, Marshall
1988   *All That Is Solid Melts into Air: The Experience of Modernity.* New York:
        Penguin Books.
Biersack, Aletta
1991   "Prisoners of Time: Millenarian Praxis in a Melanesian Valley." In *Clio in
        Oceania: Toward a Historical Anthropology,* Aletta Biersack, ed. Washing-
        ton, DC, and London: Smithsonian Institution Press, pp. 231–295.

Borrell, O. William, F.M.S.

1989   *An Annotated Checklist of the Flora of Kairiru Island, New Guinea.* Published by the author, Marcelin College, 160 Bulleen, Victoria, Australia.

Bourke, R. Michael

2001   "An Overview of Food Security in PNG." In *Food Security for Papua New Guinea: Proceedings of the Papua New Guinea Food and Nutrition 2000 Conference, PNG University of Technology, Lae, 20–30 June, 2000,* R. M. Bourke, M. G. Allen, and J. G. Salisbury, eds. Canberra: Australian Centre for International Agricultural Research, pp. 5–14.

Bourke, R. Michael, and Tracy Harwood (eds.)

2009   *Food and Agriculture in Papua New Guinea.* Canberra: Australian National University.

Bowles, Scott

2010   "Oscar's New Voting System Is a Real Puzzler." *USA Today,* March 5. http://www.usatoday.com/life/movies/movieawards/oscars/2010-03-05-1Aoscar05_VA_N/htm.

Bromby, Robin

2009   "Buyer Straits: Cashed-Up Miner Gets the Gold Bug." *The Australian,* June 22.

Brooks, Ian C.

1997   "Turubu and Kairiru Hydro Electrical Potential Feasibility Reports." Deakin West, Australia: AESOP.

Brouwer, Elizabeth C., Bruce M. Harris, and Sonomi Tanaka (eds.)

1998   *Gender Analysis in Papua New Guinea.* Washington, DC: World Bank.

Brumbaugh, Robert

1990   "'Afek Sang': The Old Woman's Legacy to the Mountain-Ok." In *Children of Afek: Tradition and Change among the Mountain-Ok of Central New Guinea,* Barry Craig and David Hyndman, eds. Oceania Monograph 40. Sydney: University of Sydney, pp. 54–87.

Butt, Leslie, and Richard Eves

2008   *Making Sense of AIDS: Culture, Sexuality, and Power in Melanesia.* Honolulu: University of Hawai'i Press.

Chapman, Graham, John Cleese, Terry Gilliam, Eric Idle, Terry Jones, and Michael Palin

1989   *The Complete Monty Python's Flying Circus: All the Words.* Vol. 1. New York: Pantheon Books.

Chin, James

2003   "Melanesia in Review: Issues and Events, 2002, Papua New Guinea." *Contemporary Pacific: A Journal of Island Affairs* 15:2, pp. 457–463.

2008   "Contemporary Chinese Community in Papua-New Guinea: Old Money versus New Migrants." *Chinese Southern Diaspora Studies* 2, pp. 117–126.

Commonwealth-Pacific Islands Forum Election Assessment Team

n.d.   "Papua New Guinea National Election, June–August 2007: Report of the Commonwealth-Pacific Islands Forum Election Assessment Team."

http://www.forumsec.or.fj/pages.cfm/documents/election-observation-reports/, accessed June 3, 2010.

Connell, John
  1997   *Papua New Guinea: The Struggle for Development.* London and New York: Routledge.

Davies, Hugh
  2002   "Second Report on Post-Earthquake Investigation, Wewak." University of Papua New Guinea, September 20.

D'Emilio, Frances
  2001   "Pope Goes Online to Apologize for Abuses: John Paul Asks Pardon for Actions against People of South Pacific." *Lansing State Journal,* November 23, p. 6A.

Filer, Colin
  1997   "Resource Rents." In *Papua New Guinea: A 20/20 Vision?* Ila Temu, ed. Brisbane: National Center for Development Studies, Research School of Pacific and Asian Studies, Australian National University, pp. 156–189.
  2011   "The New Land Grab in Papua New Guinea." Paper presented at the International Conference on Global Land Grabbing, April 6–8, organized by the Land Deal Politics Initiative in collaboration with the *Journal of Peasant Studies* and hosted by the Future Agricultures Consortium at the Institute of Development Studies, University of Sussex, UK.

Financial Standards Forum
  2010   "Country Brief: Papua New Guinea." March 3, 2010. http://www.estandards forum.org, accessed June 17, 2011.

Fleetwood, Lorna
  1984   *A Short History of Wewak.* Wewak: Wirui Press.

Frazier, Kendrick
  2010   "Three-Country Evolution Poll: Stark Contrast in U.S. vs. Canadian and British Beliefs." *Skeptical Inquirer,* November/December, pp. 5–6.

Gewertz, Deborah B., and Frederick K. Errington
  1999   *Emerging Class in Papua New Guinea: The Telling of Difference.* Cambridge: Cambridge University Press.

Gibson, John
  2001   "The Nutritional Status of PNG's Population." In *Food Security for Papua New Guinea: Proceedings of the Papua New Guinea Food and Nutrition 2000 Conference, PNG University of Technology, Lae, 20–30 June, 2000,* R. M. Bourke, M. G. Allen, and J. G. Salisbury, eds. Canberra: Australian Centre for International Agricultural Research, pp. 407–413.

Gibson, John, and Scott Rozelle
  1998   "Results of the Household Survey Component of the 1996 Poverty Assessment for Papua New Guinea." Washington, DC: World Bank.

Golub, Alex
  2007   "Ironies of Organization: Landowners, Land Registration, and Papua New Guinea's Mining and Petroleum Industry." In "Customs, Commons, Prop-

erty, and Ecology," John Wagner and Mike Evans, guest eds. Special issue, *Human Organization* 66:1, pp. 38–48.

Gregory, C. A.

1982   *Gifts and Commodities*. London and New York: Academic Press.

Griffin, James, Hank Nelson, and Stewart Firth

1979   *Papua New Guinea: A Political History*. Richmond, Victoria, Australia: Heinemann Educational Australia.

Hacker, Jacob S., and Paul Pierson

2011   *Winner-Take-All Politics: How Washington Made the Rich Richer—and Turned Its Back on the Middle Class*. New York: Simon and Schuster.

Haddon, A. C.

1947   "Smoking and Tobacco Pipes in New Guinea." *Royal Society of London Philosophical Transactions*, Series B, Biological Sciences, 232:586, pp. 1–278.

Hanson, L. W., B. J. Allen, R. M. Bourke, and T. J. McCarthy

2001   *Papua New Guinea Rural Development Handbook*. Canberra: Australian National University, Research School of Pacific Studies.

Hogbin, Ian

1935   "Trading Expeditions in Northern New Guinea." *Oceania* 5:4, pp. 375–407.

1970   *The Island of Menstruating Men: Religion in Wogeo, New Guinea*. Melbourne: Melbourne University Press.

Hyndman, David

1994   *Ancestral Rain Forests and the Mountain of Gold: Indigenous Peoples and Mining in Papua New Guinea*. Boulder, CO: Westview Press.

Joku, Haralyne

2011   "Huge Influx of Foreign Capital Poses Risk for PNG: 'Dutch Disease' Could Backfire on Agriculture." *Papua New Guinea Post Courier*, April 1. Accessed at East-West Center Pacific Islands Report, June 17, 2011, http://pidp.eastwestcenter.org/pireport/2011/April/04-04-06.htm.

Kantha, Solomon

2009   "Melanesia in Review: Issues and Events, 2008 [Papua New Guinea]." *Contemporary Pacific* 21:2, pp. 364–373.

Leavitt, Stephen C.

2004   "From 'Cult' to Religious Conversion: The Case for Making Cargo Personal." In *Cargo, Cult, and Culture Critique*, Holger Jebens, ed. Honolulu: University of Hawai'i Press, pp. 170–186.

Lieber, Michael D., and Michael A. Rynkiewich

2007   "Conclusion: Oceanic Conceptions of the Relationship between People and Property." In "Customs, Commons, Property, and Ecology," John Wagner and Mike Evans, guest eds. Special issue, *Human Organization* 66:1, pp. 90–97.

Lipset, David M.

1997   *Mangrove Man: Dialogics of Culture in the Sepik Estuary*. Cambridge: Cambridge University Press.

Lipset, David M., and Jolene Marie Stritecky
1994   "The Problem of Mute Metaphor: Gender and Kinship in Seaboard Mela-
        nesia." *Ethnology* 33:1, pp. 1–20.
Lopez, Scott
2010   "Preferential Voting: Good for the Oscars, Good for Democracy." *Vanity
        Fair,* February 10. http//www.vanityfair.com/online/Oscars/2010/02/
        preferential-voting, accessed July 14, 2011.
Lutkehaus, Nancy C.
1995   *Zaria's Fire: Engendered Moments in Manam Ethnography.* Durham, NC:
        Carolina Academic Press.
Macintyre, Martha
2005   "Taking Care of Culture: Consultancy, Anthropology, and Gender Issues."
        In *Anthropology and Consultancy: Issues and Debates,* Pamela J. Stewart and
        Andrew Strathern, eds. New York and Oxford: Bergan Books, pp. 124–138.
Macintyre, Martha, and Simon Foale
2007   "Land and Marine Tenure, Ownership, and New Forms of Entitlement on
        Lihir: Changing Notions of Property in the Context of a Goldmining Proj-
        ect." In "Customs, Commons, Property, and Ecology," John Wagner and
        Mike Evans, guest eds. Special issue, *Human Organization* 66:1, pp. 49–59.
Marshall, Mac
1982   "Introduction: Twenty Years after Prohibition." In *Through a Glass Darkly:
        Beer and Modernization in Papua New Guinea.* IASER Monograph 18, Mac
        Marshall, ed. Boroko, PNG: Institute of Applied and Social and Economic
        Research, pp. 3–13.
McGregor, Andrew
2005   "Diversification into High-Value Export Products: Case Study of the
        Papua New Guinea Vanilla Industry." Food and Agriculture Organization
        of the United Nations, Agricultural Management, Marketing and Finance
        Service, AGSF Working Document 2. Rome: FAO.
McKinnon, Rowan, Jean-Bernard Carillet, and Dean Starnes
2008   *Papua New Guinea & Solomon Islands.* 8th ed. Footscray, Victoria, Austra-
        lia: Lonely Planet.
Mihalic, Francis
1971   *The Jacaranda Dictionary and Grammar of Melanesian Pidgin.* Milton,
        Queensland, Australia: Jacaranda Press.
Mikloucho-Maclay, Nikolai Nikolaevich
1975   *New Guinea Diaries: 1871–1883.* Edited and translated by C. L. Sentinella.
        Madang, PNG: Kristen Press.
Millard, Candice
2005   *The River of Doubt: Theodore Roosevelt's Darkest Journey.* New York: Broad-
        way Books.
Moore, Clive
2003   *New Guinea: Crossing Boundaries and History.* Honolulu: University of
        Hawai'i Press.

National, The

2003   "Waiting for Election Promises." *The National,* January 20. http://www
        .thenational.com.pg/0123/letter4.htm, accessed February 7, 2004.

2007a   "Islanders Install Saulep as Chief." *The National,* May 29. http://www
        .thenational.com.pg/052907/nation22.htm, accessed May 12, 2008.

2007b   "Stumped by Chief's Appointment." *The National,* July 17. http://www
        .thenational.com.pg/071707/nation22.htm, accessed May 12, 2008.

2011   "Manwau Requests Leaders to Help Him Fight Corruption." *The National,*
        February 11.

Nelson, Hank

2011   "Cranks Emerging." *Inside Story,* January 28. http://inside.org.au/cranks-
        emerging, accessed March 17, 2011.

New York Times Magazine

2007   "Papua New Guinea: Stability Lays the Foundations for Growth." Spe-
        cial advertising supplement, *New York Times Magazine,* March 18, pp.
        73–80.

Novotny, Vojtech

2009   *Notebooks from New Guinea: Fieldnotes of a Tropical Biologist.* Oxford and
        New York: Oxford University Press.

Otto, Ton

2010   "What Happened to Cargo Cults? Material Religions in Melanesia and
        the West." In *Contemporary Religiosities: Emergent Socialities and the Post-
        Nation-State,* Bruce Kapferer, Kari Telle, and Annelin Eriksen, eds. New
        York and Oxford: Berghahn Books, pp. 82–102.

Pew Forum on Religion and Public Life

2010   "U.S. Religious Knowledge Survey." http://pewform.org/Other-Beliefs-
        and-Practices/U-S-Religious-Knowledge-Survey.aspx, accessed October 7,
        2010.

Pouwer, Jan

1960   "Loosely Structured Society in Netherlands New Guinea." *Bijdragen tot de
        Taaal-, Land- en Volkenkunde* 116, pp. 109–118.

Radio Australia

2009   "PNG Considers Sovereign Fund for LNG Revenues." November 11. http://
        radioaustralia.net.au/pacbeat/stories/200911/s2740099.htm, accessed
        June 17, 2011.

Radio Australia News

2010   "Dramatic Increase in Mobile Phone Use in PNG." July 26. http://www
        .radioaustralianews.net.au/story.htm?id=31351, accessed July 27, 2010.

Reich, Robert B.

2010   *Aftershock: The Next Economy and America's Future.* New York: Knopf.

Samar, John M.

2009   *A Public Relations Guide for Managers in Papua New Guinea.* Boroko and
        Port Moresby, PNG: Wexl Public Relations and Marketing Consultants.

Scaglion, Richard
  1977   "A Critique of Aufenanger's: *The Passing Scene in North-East New-Guinea (A Documentation)." American Anthropologist* New Series, 79:1, pp. 134–135.
Schwartz, Theodore
  1962   *The Paliau Movement in the Admiralty Islands, 1946–1954.* Vol. 49, Part 2, Anthropological Papers of the American Museum of Natural History. New York: American Museum of Natural History.
  n.d.   "Spatial and Temporal Orientation in the Admiralty Islands." Unpublished manuscript.
Smith, Geoff P.
  2002   *Growing up with Tok Pisin: Contact, Creolization, and Change in Papua New Guinea's National Language.* London: Battlebridge Publications.
Smith, Michael French
  1982   "Bloody Time and Bloody Scarcity: Capitalism, Authority and the Transformation of Temporal Experience in a Papua New Guinea Village." *American Ethnologist* 9 (August), pp. 503–518.
  1984   "'Wild' Villagers and Capitalist Virtues: Perceptions of Western Work Habits in a Preindustrial Community." *Anthropological Quarterly* 57:4, pp. 125–138.
  1990   "Business and the Romance of Community Cooperation on Kairiru Island." In *Sepik Heritage: Tradition and Change in Papua New Guinea,* Nancy Lutkehaus, Christian Kaufman, William E. Mitchell, Douglas Newton, Lita Osmundsen, and Meinhard Schuster, eds. Durham, NC: Carolina Academic Press, pp. 212–220.
  1994   *Hard Times on Kairiru Island: Poverty, Development, and Morality in a Papua New Guinea Village.* Honolulu: University of Hawai'i Press.
  2002   *Village on the Edge: Changing Times in Papua New Guinea.* Honolulu: University of Hawai'i Press.
  2011   "Kairuru [sic] Island: Pristine Waters, Little-Known Art, and Undiscovered Waves." *Paradise: Inflight with Air Niugini,* December.
  2012a   "Making a *Mok." Niugini Blue: Papua New Guinea's Premier Water Sports Magazine,* January.
  2012b   "Proposed Gold Mine Threatens Fresh Water in Papua New Guinea." *Earth Island Journal,* September 6, 2012. http://www.earthisland.org/journal/index.php/elist/eListRead/proposed_gold_mine_threatens_fresh_water_in_papua_new_guinea/.
Standish, Bill
  2002   "Electoral Governance in Papua New Guinea: Chimbu Poll Diary, June 2002." http://exkiap.net/articles/miscellaneous/bill_standish_20020628.htm, accessed June 3, 2010.
Strathern, Andrew
  1971   *The Rope of Moka.* Cambridge and New York: Cambridge University Press.

Strathern, Marilyn
1988   *The Gender of the Gift: Problems with Women and Problems with Society in Melanesia.* Berkeley: University of California Press.

Sullivan, Nancy
2010   "Revised Social Assessment for PNG Rural Communications Project." World Bank. http://www-wds.worldbank.org/external/default/WDSContent Server/WDSP/IB/2010/, accessed June 14, 2011.

Telikom PNG
2010   "Introduction." http://www.telikompng.com.pg/AboutUs/CorporateInfor mation.aspx, accessed June 14, 2011.

Thatcher, Margaret
1987   "AIDS, Education and the Year 2000." *Women's Own* 3 (October), pp. 8–10.

Tiesler, Frank
1969–1970   *Die intertibalen Beziehungen an der Nordkuste Neuguineas in Gebiet der Kleinen Schouten-Inseln.* Abhandlungen und Berichte des Staatlichen Museums für Völkerkunde Dresden. Vols. 30, 31. Berlin: Akaemie-Verlag.

Time
1973   "Papua New Guinea: Out of the Stone Age." *Time,* December 17. http://www .time.com/time/printout/0,8816,908333,00.html, accessed August 30, 2010.

Transparency International
2010   "Corruption Perception Index 2010 Results." http://www.transparency. org/policy_research/surveys_indices/cpi/2010/results, accessed June 17, 2011.

Tuzin, Donald
1976   *The Ilahita Arapesh: Dimensions of Unity.* Berkeley: University of California Press.

1997   *The Cassowary's Revenge: The Life and Death of Masculinity in a New Guinea Society.* Chicago and London: University of Chicago Press.

United Nations Development Program
2010   "Overcoming Barriers: Human Mobility and Development." Human Development Report 2009. http://hdr.undp.or/en/humandev, accessed in 2010.

US Department of State
2003   "International Religious Freedom Report." http://www.state.gov/g/drl/rls/ irf/2003/24317.htm, accessed October 20, 2010.

2010   "Background Note: Papua New Guinea." http://www.state.gov/r/pa/ei/ bgn/2797.htm, accessed April 8, 2010.

US Energy Information Administration
2011   "Weekly All Countries Spot Price FOB Weighted by Estimated Export Volume (Dollars per Barrel)." http://www.eia.gov/dnav/pet/hist/LeafHan dler.ashx?n=PET&s=WTOTWORLD&f=w, accessed June 21, 2011.

Wagner, Roy
1974   "Are There Groups in the New Guinea Highlands?" In *Frontiers of Anthropology,* Murray Wax, ed. New York: Van Nostrand Press, pp. 95–122.

Ward, Martha
   2004   *Nest in the Wind*. Prospect Heights, IL: Waveland Press. Cited in Lieber
         and Rynkiewich (2007), p. 92.

Watling, Tony
   2001   "'Official' Doctrine and 'Unofficial' Practices: The Negotiation of Catholi-
         cism in a Netherlands Community." *Journal for the Scientific Study of
         Religion* 40:4, pp. 573–590.

Watson, James
   1990   "Lamarkian Identities in Kainantu." In *Cultural Identity and Ethnicity in
         the Pacific*, Lyn Poyer and Jocylin Linnekin, eds. Honolulu: University of
         Hawai'i Press, pp. 17–42.

Whoriskey, Peter
   2011   "Income Gap Widens as Executives Prosper: Rising Compensation at the
         Top Is at Root of Increasing Inequality." *Washington Post*, p. A1, June 19.

Wivell, Richard
   1981a   *Kairiru Grammar*. A thesis presented to the University of Auckland in
         partial fulfillment of the requirements for the degree of Master of Arts
         in Linguistics. Auckland, NZ: University of Auckland.
   1981b   *Kairiru Lexicon*. University of Auckland Working Papers in Anthropology,
         No. 59. Auckland, NZ: Department of Anthropology, University of
         Auckland.

World Bank
   2010   "Remote Rural Communities in Papua New Guinea to Benefit from Im-
         proved Access to Telecommunications." http://go.worldbank.org/
         DHJ6XJ0200, accessed June 14, 2011.

World Health Organization (WHO)/UNICEF Joint Monitoring Programme for Water
Supply and Sanitation
   2010   "Estimates for the Use of Improved Drinking Water Sources: Papua New
         Guinea." Updated March 2010. http://www.childinfo.org/files/SAN_
         PNG.pdf, accessed April 8, 2010.

Index

With minor exceptions, the names of individuals, including my own, appear in the index only if I have cited their research or they are the sources of literary quotations. Page numbers in **boldface** refer to illustrations.

About the Author

Michael French Smith grew up in a deceptively quiet small town in the American Midwest, attended Michigan State University, and earned his PhD in cultural anthropology at the University of California-San Diego. He began his association with Papua New Guinea in 1973 and has written two books about the country—*Hard Times on Kairiru Island* (1994) and *Village on the* Edge (2002)—as well as many articles in anthropological journals and popular periodicals on topics ranging from the history of time scarcity to surfboard making. He owes much of his knowledge of mushroom growing, HIV/AIDS education, evaluating aid and development projects, regulating street vendors, poultry processing, and diverse other matters to his work with such organizations as the World Bank, the World Health Organization, the US Agency for International Development, the W. K. Kellogg Foundation, Conservation International, and the US Department of Health and Human Services. He is the founder of Michael French Smith Consulting, a company devoted to helping organizations promote health, prosperity, and social justice in the United States and internationally. He lives in Silver Spring, Maryland, with his wife, Jana Goldman, and Zoë the Wonder Dog. His hobbies are landscaping, collage, salvaging useful and interesting things from people's trash, and playing the ukulele.

Production Notes for Smith | *A Faraway, Familiar Place*

Jacket design by Julie Matsuo-Chun

Text Design by Integrated Composition Systems, Spokane, Washington, with text and display type in Minion Pro

Composition by Integrated Composition Systems

Printing and binding by Sheridan Books, Inc.

Printed on 60 lb. House White, 444 ppi.